THERE ARE NO FACTS

THERE ARE NO FACTS

ATTENTIVE ALGORITHMS, EXTRACTIVE DATA
PRACTICES, AND THE QUANTIFICATION
OF EVERYDAY LIFE

MARK SHEPARD

THE MIT PRESS   CAMBRIDGE, MASSACHUSETTS   LONDON, ENGLAND

This book was produced with the support of the Graham Foundation for Advanced Studies in the Fine Arts.

Graham Foundation

The MIT Press would like to thank the anonymous peer reviewers who provided comments on drafts of this book. The generous work of academic experts is essential for establishing the authority and quality of our publications. We acknowledge with gratitude the contributions of these otherwise uncredited readers.

The cover image, *The Complex System of Interactions underlying the Epigenetic Landscape*, originally appeared in Conrad Waddington's *The Strategy of the Genes* (London: Allen & Unwin, 1957). Waddington proposed the concept of an epigenetic landscape to illustrate the process of cellular differentiation, or how genotypes give rise to phenotypes during embryonic development. At various points in this visual metaphor, the cell (represented in an accompanying illustration by a ball rolling down valleys in the surface above) can take specific possible trajectories in response to various environmental conditions, leading to different outcomes or cell fates. The morphology of this landscape of possibilities is influenced by "pegs" in the ground that represent genes, and "strings" leading from them representing the chemical tendencies the genes produce. Image courtesy Taylor and Francis (Books) Limited UK.

This book was set in Stone Serif by Westchester Publishing Services. Printed and bound in the United States of America.

Library of Congress Cataloging-in-Publication Data

Names: Shepard, Mark, author.
Title: There are no facts : attentive algorithms, extractive data practices, and the quantification of everyday life / Mark Shepard, The MIT Press.
Description: Cambridge, Massachusetts : The MIT Press, [2022] | Includes bibliographical references and index.
Identifiers: LCCN 2021058947 | ISBN 9780262047470
Subjects: LCSH: Facts (Philosophy) | Truth—Social aspects. | Knowledge, Theory of.
Classification: LCC B105.F3 S54 2022 | DDC 111—dc23/eng/20220207
LC record available at https://lccn.loc.gov/2021058947

10 9 8 7 6 5 4 3 2 1

For Rosaria Susan

CONTENTS

INTRODUCTION

In 2016, Oxford Dictionaries declared *post-truth* its word of the year, defining the adjective as "relating to or denoting circumstances in which objective facts are less influential in shaping public opinion than appeals to emotion and personal belief."[1] This was, after all, the year that brought us political campaigns for the US presidential election and the UK Brexit referendum. Whether it be the claim by then presidential candidate Donald Trump that climate change was a Chinese "hoax" intended to make US manufacturers less competitive,[2] or the British foreign secretary Boris Johnson's claim in the run-up to the referendum that "the UK sends £350 million to the EU each week" in membership fees,[3] lying to the public as part of a concerted campaign strategy had become commonplace on both sides of the Atlantic. Yet as the *Economist* pointed out in an editorial published in September of that year, it was not so much lying itself that was the problem. Politicians have done this for centuries.[4] Rather, we simply didn't seem to care that much for the truth anymore. Playwright Steve Tesich coined the term *post-truth* in a 1992 article for the *Nation*, writing about the cognitive fallout from the Iran-contra affair: "In a very fundamental way we, as a free people, have freely decided that we want to live in some post-truth world."[5] Years later comedian Stephen Colbert coined the term *truthiness* to describe people who "think with their head, but know with their heart."[6] "Truth is not falsified, or contested," wrote the *Economist's* editors in 2016, "but of secondary importance." In campaigns like the 2016 US presidential election and the UK Brexit referendum, feelings were what mattered, not facts.

From the weaponization of social media through psychometric microtargeting and its radically divisive outcomes, to the proliferation of online fact-checking services and media filtering algorithms intended to counter them, we have witnessed the dissolution of much of the common ground on which truth claims were once negotiated, individual agency enacted, and public spheres shaped. At the same time, the extraction of behavioral data from all walks of life, both online and off, and their subsequent processing and sale for profit, has led to the emergence of micropublics of ever-finer granularity. This statistical world of big data and machine learning—one where "correlation supersedes causation"[7]—is driven by probable futures ranked by degrees of confidence. It presents an epistemology that eschews expressing facts, representing spaces, and developing representative models in favor of evolving models that are in and of themselves territories.[8] Within this context, the notion of ground truth is replaced by that of ground fiction, whereby inference supplants direct observation.

This book explores the uncommon ground we share in a post-truth world. It maps undercharted territory emerging in the wake of these recent epistemic transformations and the spatial milieu within which they have transpired. It attempts to unpack and explicate how these post-truth territories are propagated through machine learning systems and social networks, which shape the public and private spaces of everyday life, govern the social relations that transpire within them, and delineate a politics of possible subject positions we are able to enact individually and collectively. It probes how these spatial conditions bracket what we know about the world, how they construe our agency to act within it, and how they shape these spaces that in turn shape us.

MISINFORMATION MACHINES, DISINFORMATION PLATFORMS

This post-truth world is fueled by the affordances of social media. The balkanization and proliferation of online news sources and the targeted distribution of carefully crafted missives via Facebook, Twitter, and Instagram have contributed to the spread of this terrain of misinformation. At the same time, the rapid migration of the QAnon conspiracy from the fringes of the Internet to mainstream media reports courtesy of online messaging boards such as 4chan, then 8chan, and finally 8kun (after serial deplatforming events) serves as an indicator of its extensivity and tenacity.[9] Yet according to a report by the Center for Countering Digital Hate titled, "The Disinformation Dozen," 65 percent of antivaccine misinformation that proliferates on Facebook, Twitter, and Instagram emanates from just twelve people.[10] This proliferation of falsehoods throughout social media is commonly understood as being related to both the types of news sources the Internet makes available and the inability of consumers of this information to differentiate between valid and invalid statements. And these platforms are designed to capitalize on this. Algorithms driving social media news feeds are designed to filter content based on its ability to maximize user engagement through shares and likes, thereby promoting the proliferation of post-truth terrain across the network.

Research has shown that tweets containing false statements spread six times faster on Twitter than those containing truthful ones, and contrary to conventional wisdom, it is primarily humans, not bots, who are responsible. (Bots are as adept at spreading true statements as they are falsehoods.)[11] Lies shared widely among online communities like 8kun are swiftly believed to be true as their members often trust each other more than they do the proverbial mainstream media. Information that supports previously held beliefs is readily adopted, a tendency known as confirmation bias. Conversely, when confronted with evidence that challenges strongly held beliefs, many have a tendency to dig in and double down. The social psychologists behind the psychometric profiling and targeting practiced by Cambridge Analytica, the political consulting firm involved with both the Trump and Brexit campaigns, knew as much. By identifying segments within populations that were psychologically vulnerable and therefore prone to manipulation, and subsequently *microtargeting* these segments with media content that was designed to provoke and infuriate (regardless of whether they were true), Cambridge Analytica claimed to be able to effectively radicalize these segments of the population, mobilize their vote, and shift public opinion in their clients' favor.[12]

In 2016, the public outcry was deafening. Both the British Parliament and the US Congress conducted public hearings with Cambridge Analytica whistle-blower Christopher Wylie and Facebook founder and CEO Mark Zuckerberg, leading to "alarming" revelations of what had transpired that resulted in predictably "impassioned" calls for reform. One outcome was that social media platforms and online news sources began to introduce fact-checking services. Fact checkers at the *Washington Post* had counted 492 false statements made by President Trump in his first one hundred days in office alone, and no fewer than 30,573 throughout the course of his term.[13] Facebook rolled out its Third Party Fact-Checking project that involved independent organizations debunking false news stories and Facebook pledging to make its users aware of the findings, while lowering the rank of the post in users' news feeds. Yet as evidenced by Zuckerberg's testimony in Congress as late as fall 2019, Facebook continued to struggle in its attempts to combat the spread of fake news using a combination of algorithms and human review.[14] And despite the best intentions of the *Washington Post*'s fact checkers, some people still believe that China invented the concept of global warming in order to make US manufacturing less competitive, despite the fact that Trump himself has walked back that statement.

But is *controlling* truth through sociotechnical gatekeeping systems the best way to address this epistemic conundrum? In discussing "why we can't have our facts back," sociologist and science and technology studies (STS) scholar Noortje Marres asks, "In making the case that public discourse should respect factual truth, what ideal of public knowledge should we invoke? What role for facts in the public sphere should we strive towards?"[15] Addressing the role of online fact-checking services, she questions whether these technologies actually help or hinder the reinvigoration of a public sphere based on publicly verified facts. Modeled on what is commonly known as the correspondence model of truth, a philosophical model that distinguishes between legitimate and illegitimate knowledge claims via logical, empiricist procedures, these fact-checking technologies revive long-standing concerns regarding how (and by whom) knowledge claims are validated. We are reminded that not too long ago, we were concerned that evidence-based political debate can lead to placing authority outside the public sphere and exclusively within the domain of experts.[16] Seeing this as a return to a kind of knowledge demarcation, between those deemed capable of knowing and those who are not, she views this approach as a step backward in the drive toward social inclusion in public debate and the creation of a knowledge democracy—one that further divides existing partisan factions polarized around the notion of an elite class with a privileged claim to knowledge of the world.

THERE ARE NO FACTS, ONLY INTERPRETATIONS

Maybe people will now begin to realize that philosophers aren't quite so innocuous after all. Sometimes, views can have terrifying consequences that might actually come true. I think what the postmodernists did was truly evil. They are responsible for the intellectual fad that made it respectable to be cynical about truth and facts.
—Daniel Dennett

Philosopher Jean Lyotard defined *postmodernism* as an "incredulity toward metanarratives,"[17] whereby the totality of science's grand narratives is supplanted by a plurality of small narratives that compete with each other. Truth in science as a goal is elided by measures of performativity and efficiency. Some, like philosopher Daniel Dennett, have credited the triumph of relativism and the legacy of postmodernism with laying the groundwork for our post-truth era.[18] Against empirical claims that "there are only facts," philosopher Friedrich Nietzsche famously countered, "No, it is precisely facts that do not exist, only interpretations."[19] This statement, which he makes in a posthumously published fragment, can be found in various alternate expressions throughout his work, receiving extended consideration in his 1873 essay, "Truth and Lie in an Extramoral Sense." Such a claim not only marks the birth of postmodernism, his critics argue, but also highlights his shortcomings as a philosopher. The statement "there are no facts, only interpretations," they say, as with any other relativist statement, must also include itself. The "fact" that there are only interpretations is itself subject to interpretation and therefore can't be confirmed.

Others suggest that this critique grossly oversimplifies the matter. Reminding us that Nietzsche's statement was aimed at undermining positivist notions of an *absolute truth*, philosopher Helmut Heit suggests that Nietzsche was arguing in favor of "self-reflexive, pluralistic, and modest epistemic attitudes" associated with relativism. Yet "unlike certain cliché-versions of relativism," writes Heit, "Nietzsche denies that every 'perspective' is equally valid, and develops and employs a variety of interpretational and argumentative standards [that] are not absolute, but allow human evaluations of knowledge-claims."[20] Here, the suggestion that *truth* is the only alternative to *post-truth* is itself a false opposition, one that obscures the role that informed value judgments play in politics and culture.

Philosopher, sociologist, and anthropologist Bruno Latour upended the traditional philosophical distinction between facts (scientific knowledge), on the one hand, and values (human judgments), on the other. To Latour, scientific facts are the product of scientific inquiry. His 1979 book, *Laboratory Life: The Construction of Scientific Facts*, written with Steve Woolgar, shows how facts are produced through the daily practices of scientists working in a lab.[21] For Latour and Woolgar, the validity of a fact is not based on an inherent veracity, but rather on the strength of the assemblage of people and things, institutions and practices that brought that fact into being. Facts that are more "networked" socially, ones involving more people and things in their production, are more valid than those that are less so. Validity here is a function of a broader social apparatus.

Critics argue that by showing that facts are the product of often messy human procedures, Latour and Woolgar have enabled a particularly noxious form of relativism, one that cynical conservatives were quick to appropriate: witness the rise of the climate denier and other antiscience positions, for example. Latour has pushed back on this critique, arguing that "facts remain robust only when they are supported by a common culture, by institutions that can be trusted, by a more or less decent public life, by more or less reliable media."[22] The problem is that there are now those who no longer believe that there is such a thing as a common world, which, for Latour at least, changes everything. "It is not a matter of learning how to repair cognitive deficiencies," he writes, "but rather of how to live in the same world, share the same culture, face up to the same stakes, perceive a landscape that can be explored in concert."[23]

EVACUATED PUBLIC SPACES, DISAGGREGATED PUBLIC SPHERES

This book engages with the questions that inevitably follow what Latour identifies as an inability to "perceive a landscape that can be explored in concert." These questions assemble not just the material realities of an evacuated public space but also the immaterial conditions by which a disaggregated public sphere is perceived. If public space is no longer the geography of the public sphere, what constitutes the ground on which truth claims are based, argued, and validated (or invalidated) today? What may we consider "common ground" when publics are strategically segmented by the deployment of machine learning and artificial intelligence as instruments of political and epistemic design? What may we consider a "public sphere" when the traditional sites of representation and deliberation are disaggregated into a plurality of digitally mediated environments that elide the now vestigial physical infrastructures that helped to shape the very notion of public in the first place?

While these are by no means new questions,[24] they do take on a different character in light of certain recent events and the sociotechnical systems by which they are enabled, engendered, shared, and distributed. As I address in the chapters that follow, the technologies, tools, techniques, and methods by which we perceive this landscape that Latour would have us explore in concert are by no means neutral and are themselves propagating forms of bias, discrimination, and divisiveness for which we must account. Computer scientists Joy Buolamwini and Timnit Gebru have shown how commercial facial recognition systems are less effective for women of color, for instance, and a growing body of research shows how predictive policing systems perpetuate systemic racism.[25] Further, researchers such as sociologist Ruha Benjamin and media theorist Wendy Hui Kyong Chun recount how for certain populations, these forms of social control have long been implemented through specific planning practices, design paradigms, and other technological forms.[26] Indeed, the public realm today is constituted less by what philosopher Hannah Arendt once called a "space of appearance"—a public space within which we appear before each other in all of our resplendent differences to deliberate—but, moreover, by what we might today describe as "spaces of surveillance," incorporating not only the disciplinary and control apparatus that philosophers Michel Foucault and Gilles Deleuze concerned themselves with, but also the more recent techniques for the extraction of behavioral data by surveillance capitalists that social psychologist and former Harvard Business School professor Shoshana Zuboff has described.[27] The challenge we face, then, resides in articulating new forms of appearance within the various shared spaces of contemporary publics through which we come together, ones that extend horizontally across and against the divisive vertical segmentation of spaces of surveillance and support an ongoing struggle to formulate more empowering and enduring collective identities.

WAYS OF KNOWING SPACE

Approaching this challenge involves adopting a spatial framework by which the various sites and situations that this book maps are examined. In focusing on the spatiality of these contexts, I consider them not just through a socioeconomic lens—as the by-product of instruments of control or resource reallocation—but also through a political and environmental one where the *governmentality* (governing rationality) at work and in play across these sites is understood through an examination of the spatial practices mediated by instruments of design and spatial management that operate within them. Foucault defined the notion of governmentality in terms of the strategies and tactics by which society is rendered governable and emphasized the close link between forms of power and processes of subjectification.[28] As sociologist Thomas Lemke notes in tracing the genealogy of Foucault's development of the concept, "In addition to the management by the state or the administration, 'government' also signified problems of self-control, guidance for the family and for children, management of the household, directing the soul, etc."[29] In articulating the disciplinary mechanisms of power, whether those deployed in the management of an eighteenth-century French town during an outbreak of the Plague or those residing in Gregory Bentham's prototypical design for a prison, the Panopticon, Foucault describes these governing principles in terms of the (re)configuration of space.[30] Space, power, and subjectivity are for Foucault inextricably intertwined within the notion of governmentality. Understanding how we come to know space, how we locate and orient ourselves within it, and how we navigate through it are thus critical to understanding the epistemic fragmentation of these post-truth territories and their corresponding implications for subject positioning that this book examines.

Historically, Western epistemological traditions have divided spatial knowledge into that which is understood in purely rational terms and that which is known through experience. From the idealized geometric forms of Plato and Pythagoras, to René Descartes' theory of absolute space and Immanuel Kant's description of space as a pure form of intuition, various (often conflicting) arguments have been made for the differentiation between a priori spatial knowledge and spatial knowledge derived from experience.[31] Others, such as philosopher and critic of Cartesian dualism Gilbert Ryle, have argued for a developmental approach, claiming it is counterproductive (if not impossible) to segregate these different ways of knowing space as experiential knowledge informs the construction of cognitive structures that subsequently inform experience.[32] From this perspective, spatial cognition evolves over time in dialogue with embodied experience.

These ways of knowing space are of course also ways of knowing *our relationship to space*. "With the advent of Cartesian logic," writes philosopher Henri Lefebvre in his influential work, *The Production of Space*, "space had entered the realm of the absolute. As Object opposed to Subject, as *res extensa* opposed to, and present to, *res cogitans*, space came to dominate, by containing them, all senses and all bodies."[33] Kantian space, by contrast, belonged in all its relativity to the a priori realm of the "subject," the seat of consciousness, and as such embodied its idealized, internalized, and transcendental nature. Spatial epistemologies thus define a subject's relation to a world, the preconditions for being in that world, and the limits for movement and action within it.

Psychologist Jean Piaget introduced the notion of *object permanence* in discussing how we come to understand space through sensorimotor operations of the body at an early age. Object permanence involves the mental construction of objects as entities independent of the self, existing at a particular location in space or moving along a specific trajectory. Piaget suggested that this is something that must be learned; it is not present at birth and develops over the first couple of years in the life of a child.[34] Piaget studied object permanence by observing how infants reacted when a favorite object (such as a toy) was first presented to the child and then concealed with a blanket. Infants who reached to grasp for the object beneath the blanket were thought to have developed a sense of object permanence, whereas ones who appeared confused or disoriented had not. Here, embodied experience leads to the development of a cognitive understanding of the persistence of objects in space.

At scales beyond that of the body, we develop cognitive abilities by which we locate and orient ourselves within space and navigate through it. We make spatial decisions based on a cumulative spatial understanding of the environments through which we move on a daily basis, such as how we get to work, travel to visit a friend or family, or navigate a grocery store aisle. These spatial behaviors rely not on internal, idealized representations of space but on knowledge acquired through everyday spatial practices. This knowledge is contingent on the development of mental images of given spaces, their spatial relationships and organizational characteristics, a process commonly referred to as *cognitive mapping*.

In *Postmodernism, or, The Cultural Logic of Late Capitalism*, philosopher Frederic Jameson discusses urban planner Kevin Lynch's *The Image of the City*, his classic work on cognitive mapping. At the scale of the city, Jameson notes that cognitive mapping serves "to enable a situational representation on the part of the individual subject to that vaster and properly unrepresentable totality which is the ensemble of the city's structure as a whole." He cites the alienation Lynch identifies in certain American cities as a function of "a space in which people are unable to map (in their minds) either their own positions or the urban totality . . . in which none of the traditional markers (monuments, nodes, natural boundaries, built perspectives) obtain."[35] Looking to move beyond the urban scale to the theoretical opportunities afforded at the global scale, he describes Lynch's cognitive mapping as "pre-cartographic operations" the results of which "traditionally are described as itineraries rather than as maps . . . the nautical itinerary, the sea chart or *portulans*, where coastal features are noted for the use of Mediterranean navigators who rarely venture out into the open sea."[36]

With the introduction of modern navigational instruments such as the compass, sextant, and theodolite, Jameson identifies a new coordinate introduced into the process: the relationship to a totality, as enabled through a process of triangulating one's position in absolute space in relation to a universe of stars. "At this point," writes Jameson, "cognitive mapping in the broader sense comes to require the coordination of existential data (the empirical position of the subject) with unlived, abstract conceptions of the geographic totality."[37] Here, navigational instruments become the mediators between an idealized, a priori spatial knowledge and spatial knowledge derived from experience.

Lefebvre attempted to connect this idealized mental (logico-mathematical) space with the "real" space of embodied spatial practices through representational space, or space as "directly *lived* through its associated images and symbols."[38] Representational practices—speaking, writing, drawing, mapping and other communicative acts involving symbolic and notational systems—mediate different ways of knowing space and in turn enable forms of social cognition, or our ability to communicate, to share knowledge, and to learn from each other. How we come to know the world around us and our place within it is in this way contingent on the mental models of space that predominate different cultures. These mental models are themselves informed and shaped by the instruments, devices,

Jorge de Aguiar's chart of the Mediterranean, Western Europe, and African coast (1492).
Source: Beinecke Rare Book and Manuscript Library, Yale University, New Haven, CT.

and representational techniques by which spatial cognition takes place. Whereas observational devices shape the perceptual conditions, primarily at the scale of the body, by which space is apprehended, representational techniques often engage space the entirety of which cannot be perceived from a single vantage point but is understood either through movement over time or by incorporating more complex information systems.

Today, these instruments, devices, and techniques are increasingly driven by machine learning algorithms operating on vast amounts of data extracted from all walks of life. Machine learning algorithms designed for recognition and classification tasks perceive the world by comparing features extracted from an object or event with those from a data set derived from hundreds, thousands, or even millions of examples on which they

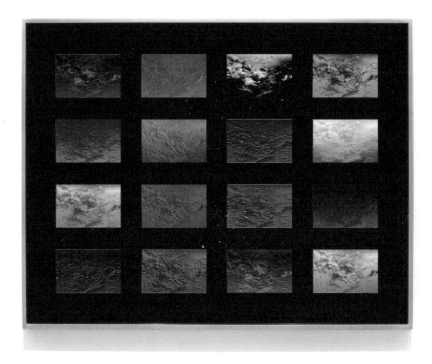

James Bridle, *Activations*, 2017. A series of images mapping layers of a neural network for an autonomous vehicle navigation system. The legibility of the images incrementally dissolves as the logic of the machine's vision system becomes less and less correspondent to human understanding. Image courtesy of the artist.

have been trained. This collection of features related to a property or characteristic of a given object or event is called a "feature space." For any given data set, a feature space is an n-dimensional space (where $n=$ the number of features) containing all possible values for a set of features selected from those data. A well-designed feature space contains clusters or groups of data points where similar objects or events are "closer" to each other and dissimilar ones more "distant." New and previously unseen objects or events are rendered "perceptible" by these algorithms through a process of attribution, where proximity to clusters within a feature space determines the probability, expressed in terms of degrees of confidence, that they can be attributed to a known quantity.

Geographer Louise Amoore identifies this understanding of the attribute as that which brings together people, entities, and events within the context of machine learning algorithms. In her book *Cloud Ethics*, an examination of how machine learning algorithms are reshaping the ethics and politics of contemporary society, she addresses the governmentality at work within these settings:

The sphere of society and social relations thus exists for algorithms only as a series of groups, or clusters, defined by the spatial proximities and distances of their attributes. To govern a population through its attributes involves a rather different imagination of the relationship between the universal (e.g., shared values or moral principles, ideas of economy, common laws) and the particular (that which is particular to the subject as individual) than that which characterizes accounts of neoliberalism or biopolitics. The machine learning algorithm iteratively moves back and forth between the ground truth attributes of a known population (known in terms of the attribution of qualities) and the unknown feature vector that has not yet been encountered. In the space between a computer science universal of attributed feature space and the particularity of the new entity, the algorithms learn how to recognize and describe what is happening in the world.[39]

This process of recognizing and describing what is happening in the world differs in important ways from that described by Jameson, Lynch, and Lefebvre. In place of a process based on observing, representing, and classifying a world that we can perceive, Amoore argues that contemporary settings governed by machine learning algorithms are better understood in terms of experimental processes of perceiving, recognizing, and attributing that which resides beneath and beyond the perceptual threshold of human vision. In sum, the relations of data, attributive processes, and perception are critical to understanding the spatial epistemology of these machine learning algorithms and the post-truth territories they propagate.

STATISTICAL IMAGINARIES

Throughout the pages of this book, I refer to the clusters produced by these processes of perceiving, recognizing, and attributing as *statistical imaginaries*. Within sociology, the imaginary refers to the set of values, institutions, laws, and symbols through which people imagine their relation to society as a whole. In *The Imaginary: A Phenomenological Psychology of the Imagination*, Jean-Paul Sartre contrasts imagination to perception, whereby perception apprehends only part of an object and imagination constructs a totality. Imaginary objects are to Sartre a "mélange of past impressions and recent knowledge."[40] They are what we imagine them to be, appearing to us as if we were to perceive them, as if they were "real."

For psychoanalyst Jacques Lacan, the imaginary is introduced as one of three interrelated orders, together with the symbolic and the real, that structure human existence. The imaginary emerges in the stage of a child's development (the mirror stage) when they develop the ability to recognize

Faces of people synthesized by StyleGAN, a style-based generator architecture for generative adversarial networks (GANs). Image by the author.

themselves as an object that can be perceived outside themselves, such as through a mirror or other device. Because the ego is formed by identifying with the counterpart or mirror image, identification becomes an important aspect of the imaginary for Lacan. Yet in recognizing oneself as "I," one also recognizes oneself as other, an act that is fundamentally self-alienating. Returning to Jameson:

> The existential—the positioning of the individual subject, the experience of daily life, the monadic "point of view" on the world to which we are necessarily, as biological subjects, restricted—is in Althusser's formula implicitly opposed to the realm of abstract knowledge, a realm which as Lacan reminds us is never positioned in or actualized by any concrete subject but rather by that structural void called "le sujet supposé savoir," "the subject supposed to know," a subject-place of knowledge: what is affirmed is not that we cannot know the world and its totality in some abstract or "scientific" way—Marxian "science" provides just such a way of knowing and conceptualizing the world abstractly, in the sense in which, e.g. Mandel's great book offers a rich and elaborated knowledge of that global world system, of which it has never been said here that it was unknowable, but merely that it was unrepresentable, which is a very different matter.[41]

Jameson goes on to observe that there is a "convergence between the empirical problems studied by Lynch in terms of city space and the great Althusserian (and Lacanian) redefinition of ideology as 'the representation of the subject's Imaginary relationship to his or her Real conditions of existence.'"[42] This is important in that it provides a critical hinge for our inquiry: that ways of knowing space and ways of knowing people are inevitably intertwined in terms of how they map a subject's relation to a world.

One could argue that today we come to recognize ourselves not in the specular truth of a mirror image but in the complex assemblage of data sets and aggregate information that constitute the disembodied, decentered, and distributed nature of our data bodies. The ideological totality that we simultaneously relate to and are alienated by is the statistical imaginary: a market segment, a demographic tranche, a body without organs distributed across a probabilistic feature space composed of data points registered in discrete time series.

Statistical imaginaries are bound by intersectional constructions of identity, where attributes such as race, gender, class, sexuality, religion, age, ability, appearance, and the like intersect in not only positioning one's identity but also determining how they are privileged and discrimi-nated against within society.[43] This notion of positioning, of account-ing for one's own position in making truth claims in the production of knowledge, is considered at length by feminist scholars, among them Donna Harraway, who suggests that positioning is itself "the key practice grounding knowledge."[44] For my part, I write this book from the posi-tion of an irreligious, middle-aged, able, white cisgender male of middle-class European American descent. I am a tenured professor of architecture and media study at a public university. I acknowledge this has afforded me many privileges, and strive to apply my background and experience in architecture and computational media to speak to the spatial inequi-ties of the sociotechnical systems and attendant systemic biases that this book addresses. I am also the father of a young daughter whose arrival in the midst of writing this book has to a certain extent motivated my concerns regarding the world she will inherit and how I might contribute to nudging it toward better possible futures.

Yet while situating knowledge production in this way can help account for embedded power relations that often go unnoticed or overlooked—or, worse, form the basis for discriminatory and oppressive practices—it also highlights the challenges posed for finding common ground. In the introduction to their book *Data Feminism*, Catherine D'Ignazio and Lau-ren Klein point out how "the racism embedded in US culture, coupled with many other forms of oppression, made it impossible to claim a com-mon experience—or a common movement—for all women everywhere."[45] Indeed the challenge associated with invoking the word *we* within the con-text of this book is in and of itself instructive. Who is included when "we" are addressed, and who is left out? We who are reading this? We who come from common ethnic, cultural, economic, and educational backgrounds? We who are proximate in a feature space of possible subject positions? How can this "we" find common ground—a collective sense of "we-ness," so to speak—within these spaces that otherwise seek to simultaneously segment and cluster people in ways that are often oppressive, increas-ingly indifferent, and in some cases outright hostile to the very idea of what Amoore describes as the unattributable commonalities that bind us?

FROM SMART HOMES TO GLOBAL PANDEMICS

In the chapters that follow, I examine these contemporary entanglements of people and data, code and space, knowledge and power. Part 1 addresses specific practices that are threaded throughout the book: the fabrication of post-truth representational spaces (chapter 1), mapmaking and the politics of cartographic representations (chapter 2), and the extraction of behavioral data and the corresponding impact on subject positioning (chapter 3). These chapters introduce how truth claims are embedded within the techniques by which the world is recorded, documented, and measured; how specific representational practices shape mental images of space; and how these data-saturated environments variously position divergent contemporary subjectivities.

Part 2 is organized according to an increasing scale of sites within which these practices play out, from the translocality of the home to the planetary reach of the COVID-19 pandemic, with stops along the way at the corner urban minimarket, a neighborhood for the proverbial one percent, a waterfront district in Toronto, and a national election. These sites serve as specific contexts within which this story unfolds: a series of vignettes presenting the scope and extent of the epistemic fragmentation resulting from the mapping and colonization of the spaces constituting everyday life by attentive algorithms and extractive data infrastructures. As the scale progressively increases throughout the book, the story evolves from more personal and intimate sites of behavioral data extraction and the manipulation of individuals to more public and collective forms of algorithmic governance distributed across ever broader territories. These contexts provide the vehicles by which to explore how these spatial conditions are conceived, planned, designed, constructed, inhabited, managed, analyzed, celebrated, and feared.

I draw on a variety of sources and methods in doing so. Primary source materials include design documents and presentations, publications, news reports, and site visits for the specific sociotechnical sites and systems discussed. Reading scientific white papers alongside product marketing literature offers further insight not just into how specific technologies are designed to work but also foregrounds the claims made regarding their intended performance. Often claims made by marketers exceed those of engineers. Examples drawn from critical media art practice suggest ways of employing these technologies for which they were not originally intended, often demonstrating unintended consequences and cultural nuances not anticipated by product designers and marketing executives. Finally, journalistic sources provide perspectives on current events involving the spatial application of these technologies and the cultural contexts within which they take place. Furthermore, and in tertiary manner, as online news media have played a central role in both propagating and documenting the epistemic fragmentation central to the concerns of this book, their incorporation here is intended to serve more as evidence of a condition than a recounting of facts.

I connect these sites and events to discourses distributed across architecture, urbanism, geography, media studies, data science, philosophy, and science and technology studies that address the algorithmic reformatting of everyday life through data-driven practices. This is a broad and evolving field of inquiry, and a few key points of reference are worth noting as a means to position and orient this work. Author and professor of architecture Malcolm McCullough has traced the convergence of architectural and informatic space and its implications for how we experience the built environment.[46] His reading of urban environments as always already possessing a kind of ambient information that is situated and legible if we just attune ourselves to it is reflected and extended by anthropologist and media scholar Shannon Mattern, whose writing positions debates surrounding the smart city and urban intelligence in broader cultural and historical contexts, ones that do not always fit so neatly into the logics of computation.[47] Historian of science, computing, art, and design Orit Halpern links the architecture of attention to the logistics of cognition in articulating the influence of postwar cybernetic theory in shaping the epistemic conditions of attention, perception, and our collective sense of truth.[48] With an attentive eye toward how visual representations make truth claims, architect and spatial researcher Laura Kurgan has investigated the epistemic basis of maps and the role that critical mapping practices can play in shaping public discourse and policymaking through her writing and projects.[49] Geographer and data studies scholar Rob Kitchin's early work on cartography and cognitive mapping can be read as a prologue to his more recent investigations of data, smart cities, and algorithmic governance that call for more critical studies of code and its social, economic, and spatial implications.[50] Shoshana Zuboff examines the political implications of these emerging data regimes, describing at length the processes by which surveillance capitalists extract surplus behavioral data from our interactions with their products and services to mine and assemble predictive profiles for auction on behavioral futures markets.[51] Wendy Hui Kyong Chun shows how these data-driven techniques produce social segregation, polarization and discrimination not as a bug, but a feature, and calls for a form of machine unlearning that enables living freely in difference.[52] Addressing the challenges to democratic societies that these conditions present, Louise Amoore articulates how machine learning algorithms have transformed ethics and politics from a spatial perspective, in search of an ethicopolitics of algorithms grounded in sustaining the unattributable.[53] This is admittedly a partial and incomplete list, the boundaries of which are somewhat arbitrary as the notes and bibliography make abundantly clear.

Chapter 1, "Alternative Facts," recounts the 2016 inauguration of Donald Trump and the ensuing squabble that played out in the media in the following days over how many people actually attended the event. In its first few days in power, this new administration ushered in the era of alternative facts. While the rallying cry of "fake news" as a means to discredit the media had been a staple on the Trump campaign trail for more than a year, the coordinated manufacture of so-called alternate facts shapes the status of the real in new ways. Counterfactual media narratives would become a key weapon in partisan political warfare, aimed less at convincing people of things that are untrue and more at creating a sense of uncertainty and feeling of doubt about whether facts are even knowable in the first place.[54] This chapter examines how the practice of fabricating "the real" has evolved throughout the history of techniques and technologies for representing space. It takes the cultural phenomenon of the *deepfake*— the hyperrealistic synthesis of media objects depicting fictitious scenes via a class of machine learning techniques called generative adversarial networks (GANs)—as both a cultural marker of the present moment as well as a point of departure to examine the changing status of the real at different moments in history. The status of the real has historically evolved in relation to the emergence of different forms of verisimilitude—the appearance of being true or real—produced by the dominant media practices of the time. I address how within these various media practices are embedded truth claims, the epistemological implications of which extend to (and at the same time articulate) the cultural milieu within which they are situated. From observing subjects that perceive the reality of an outside world as presented through an aperture or lens, to generative algorithms that compete in synthesizing representations that are perceived to be real, the status of the real is perpetually negotiated through diverse practices that seldom share basic assumptions, let alone common vocabularies. Yet without these negotiations, we may not have a viable basis by which we can know something about our respective place within these post-truth territories and determine best courses for future shared action within it.

Chapter 2, "Ground Fictions," addresses the representational practices of cartography and the role of mapmaking in shaping the mental models by which we locate and orient ourselves within, navigate through, and otherwise inhabit the world. Cartographers make truth claims with their maps. They fabricate the base maps by which common ground is negotiated. Their maps attest to a spatial reality that is beyond our capacity to perceive in its entirety. The notion that maps offer a neutral or value-free transcription of an actually existing geographic reality is, however, a contested one. Some geographers contend that mapmaking is fundamentally a social process that renders (and reinforces) the spatiality of existing power relations, typically to the advantage of a socially dominant group.[55] Pointing to the rhetorical power of mapmaking as an agent of social justice, the field of critical geography pursues counter-mapping practices that aim to expose spatial inequities that official or authoritative agencies attempt to downplay or elide altogether. From this perspective, maps construct the world at various scales through the orchestration and integration of a series of perspectives that are always already socially conditioned. At the same time, as mapmaking practices become increasingly automated by machine learning algorithms, new questions arise concerning the classification of (and delineation of boundaries between) both people and space. This chapter examines these questions through a series of mapmaking practices. Within each of these practices lies a tension between the aim of producing an accurate representation of the world, on the one hand, while contending with its (often messy) spatial contingencies and correlated social realities, on the other. Through a series of examples illustrating critical approaches to counter-mapping practices, we attempt to arrive at a better understanding of the role that representations of space and populations of people play in propagating the epistemic fragmentation of post-truth territory.

Chapter 3, "The Data Blasé,"[56] discusses the practice of positioning subjectivity within these new data-driven territories assembled by what is commonly referred to as "the cloud." At a moment when big data and machine learning are being applied to all walks of life, we might revisit philosopher Martin Heidegger's notion of *the gigantic*, whereby the quantitative is transformed into the qualitative, and unpack the corresponding subject positions that emerge through this process. Building on sociologist and urban theorist Georg Simmel's articulation of the blasé attitude of the modern urban subject, this chapter explores how these data-saturated environments elicit and delimit contemporary subject positions. For Simmel, the emergence of the blasé attitude was related to the fragmentation of attention brought about by the rapid change of perceptual stimuli that constituted the metropolitan experience. Today attention is no longer divided simply within the subject's field of vision, but between two radically different fields of vision—one human, one nonhuman. Under these conditions, the disciplinary imperative of Western capitalism to specialize, individuate, and "pay attention" is inverted in the positioning of subjects to normalize their behavior in ways that attentive algorithms can recognize. Despite the increasing frequency of security breaches and compromised personal data held by consumer credit reporting agencies, or the weaponization of social media data for partisan political warfare, many have become indifferent to the numerous ways by which personal data are exchanged for access to online services, discount pricing, and other benefits of this data-driven world. While this indifference contributes to the perceived imperceptibility of data and its implications for everyday life, it also enables a culture of self-censorship that leads people to modify their behavior and adopt subject positions that conform to social norms perceptible to an algorithm in order to maintain their status within the reputation economy.

Opening part 2, "Contexts," chapter 4, "Artificial Cohabitants," addresses the context of the home and unpacks the infiltration of domestic space by artificially intelligent virtual assistants (AI VAs) in search of ever more intimate behavioral data. Whether it be Amazon's Alexa, Google's Assistant, or Apple's Siri, these household appliances have ushered in an age of ambient intelligence in the home that had been years in the making. Tracing the development of natural language processing techniques and their application to these smart home interfaces, this chapter illustrates how the uncommon ground between people and machines is ameliorated by the conversational acuity of these synthetic domestic partners. It explores what happens when these smart devices become members of the family, privy to some of the more intimate details of our domestic lives, and asks what changes when this occurs at scale. I discuss Alexa and Siri within a broader history of the automation of domestic labor and the reinforcement of gender biases, focusing on the role that the feminine persona has played in assuaging public anxiety over the infiltration of the home by these attentive machines. The chapter concludes by showing how concepts and techniques adapted from behavioral economics by surveillance capitalists have accelerated the colonization of domestic space by these new AI VAs, reconfiguring the boundaries between public and private in ways more favorable to the colonizers. The once private abode we called home—a place of nurturing, where we are first cared for—becomes a place where we are constantly watched over by attentive agents intent on extracting data from our most intimate behaviors in order to nudge us to make predictably irrational decisions that enrich these agents' makers.

If data are the new oil, as editors of the *Economist* have claimed, it would follow that it would fuel extractive economies.[57] Chapter 5, "Spurious Correlations," takes Amazon's colonization of the urban minimarket as a context to examine the epistemic fragmentation emerging in the wake of the extraction of behavioral data from prosaic interactions within physical space. At Amazon Go, as the stores are called, shoppers are tracked by a computer vision system consisting of hundreds of cameras embedded in the ceiling that employs machine learning algorithms to track which items they take off the shelves and updates their virtual shopping carts accordingly. If traditional notions of "the real" are generally understood as the product of a collective compromise or agreement, Amazon Go's statistical operations render reality through an architecture of probabilistic space that is fundamentally divisive. In place of an embodied cashier who knows everyone in the neighborhood, Amazon Go's systems know their neighbors through the data they generate. Shifting their role from that of providing a common ground where neighborhood communities come together, cashierless minimarkets like Amazon Go become the grist-mills of the information age that transform our shopping behaviors and purchasing habits into clusters of marketable data. This test-bed world of computer vision, big data, and machine learning presents an episte-mology not concerned with documenting facts, representing spaces, or developing representative models but, rather, evolving models that are in and of themselves territories.[58] In these territories populated by clusters of statistical imaginaries organized by relative proximities, we are (probably) what we eat—when, where, and with whom we've most likely eaten.

Chapter 6, "From Tools to Environments," looks at what happens when this idea is scaled from the humble corner minimarket to an entire urban neighborhood. Tracing the shift from observational tools to environ-ments that observe, it examines the evolution of techniques for observ-ing and analyzing urban environments and the subsequent implications for their design and management. Today, machine learning algorithms operating on big data enable an entirely new epistemology for making sense of an urban environment. Rather than testing a theory by gathering and analyzing relevant data, this approach aims for insights "born from the data."[59] This chapter takes as a recent case study the Hudson Yards development, the largest private real estate development in US history, on the West Side of Manhattan. Reports initially claimed that it would contain the nation's first "quantified community," a fully instrumented urban neighborhood that would deploy an integrated, expandable sensor network to support the observation, measurement, integration, and anal-ysis of neighborhood conditions, activity, and outcomes.[60] Citizens living and working at Hudson Yards would become sensors themselves along-side those embedded within buildings and their associated infrastructural systems. As tools for urban observation and design merge with the very environments they aim to both analyze and project, new urban territories emerge that are populated more by statistical imaginaries derived from aggregate data than by communities of embodied citizens. These post-truth territories constructed by algorithms represent a spatial epistemol-ogy that dispenses with the very idea of observing a world altogether, positing instead "insights" born from data potentially bearing no relation to an observable truth or reality.

Chapter 7, "The Right to the (Wrong) City," addresses how these new territories are to be governed in terms of what might be best referred to as "the right to the (wrong) city." Taking the failure of Toronto's massive waterfront development, Sidewalk Toronto, as an object lesson, it revisits long-standing challenges of public participation in steering urban development and examines new forms of urban governance and governmentality in light of our data-driven present. Lefebvre published *Le Droit à la Ville* in 1968, and since then, the notion of a citizen's right to the city has animated public discourse regarding "the right to the oeuvre, to participation and appropriation" of the urban environment.[61] To Lefebvre, the oeuvre relates to the use value of the city—how the city is directly lived through the various spatial practices of everyday life. To reproduce the urban environment is thus to reproduce the conditions of urban life. By contrast, a city's exchange value is defined by money and commerce, the buying and selling of real estate, the consumption of products, goods, and services. Sidewalk Labs CEO Dan Doctoroff had promised a city "designed from the Internet up," incorporating many of the features that have come to be associated with smart cities: embedded sensors for real-time monitoring and management of urban infrastructure, roads and street lights that adapt to changing patterns of activity and use, and so forth. Yet the urban vision proposed by Sidewalk Labs, especially with regard to its ambitions to extract behavioral data at an urban scale, aimed not simply to prioritize the city's exchange value over its use value but to *convert* one into the other: the oeuvre would become the *product*. Tracing the history of the failed partnership between Sidewalk Labs and Waterfront Toronto, this chapter highlights critical issues surrounding data monetization, algorithmic governance, and the reproduction of urban life at stake in urban developments of this scale.

The capacity for bad actors to compromise these platforms and systems is the focus of chapter 8, "The Ruse and the Exploit." This chapter examines the role of personal data and psychometric microtargeting in national political campaigns. In examining political consulting firm Cambridge Analytica's role in the 2016 US presidential election and the UK Brexit referendum, it traces how weak data privacy policies at Facebook enabled the cultivation of a massive data set for the psychometric profiling and microtargeting of large swaths of the US and British electorate. While psychographic segmentation itself was not new in the world of marketing (as discussed in chapter 5), its role in the weaponization of microtargeted social media content for the purposes of partisan political warfare was. Psychometric microtargeting lends itself to the exploitation of wedge issues that polarize opinion along racial, regional, or other demographic lines, such as immigration, abortion, the Second Amendment, the environment, and same-sex marriage. Divisive issues such as these have been shown to be the most likely to mobilize voters, driving them to either support one candidate or withdraw support for another. This is a political terrain constituted by a public sphere filtered by algorithms, fragmented by design, and openly hostile to dialogue. When public space is no longer the geography of the public sphere and the public sphere is reduced to clusters of micropublics as small as one, we find ourselves confronted at a national scale with a spatial epistemology not of assurance but one of uncertainty and doubt.

Chapter 9, "Pandemic Exceptionalism," seeks to unpack the uncertainty surrounding the COVID-19 global pandemic. Recounting seventeenth-century measures taken in response to the Plague, Foucault describes the disciplinary mechanisms of power enacted in times of epidemics. The twenty-first-century response to the COVID-19 pandemic, by contrast, has presented markedly different mobilizations of power. Alongside disciplinary mechanisms of immobilization, surveillance, and monitoring, various alternatives emerged to combat the spread of the virus. This chapter examines how the global community reacted differently in different parts of the world in response to what by all measures was a common threat. From the authoritarian forms of coercive control imposed in China to Sweden's reliance on individuals making rational decisions in practicing social distancing, these responses reflected different forms of biopolitics and biopower enacted by their respective states. Moreover, during these exceptional times with much of the world on lockdown, many sat in isolation, prone before their screens, and inhabited the statistics: infection rates, numbers of hospitalizations and occupied intensive care unit beds, deaths per day, and the corresponding impact of all these on market indexes. Some staked their hopes and beliefs in data models and their projections, and attempted to debate public health policy accordingly. Others awaited the development of a vaccine and effective treatments, as pharmaceutical companies raced to develop new technologies that could help "flatten the curve." Beyond the drive to develop new apps and methods of testing was the critical need for better interpretive practices, questions of (good and bad) judgment, and how they could influence collective behavior (or not). In this state of exception, we searched for forms of democratic biopolitics that could foster collaborative sense making and give rise to collective interpretative sensibilities.

All of this brings to the fore the question of our agency to act (and enact collectively) within these new and emerging entanglements of people and data, code and space, knowledge and power. I conclude with a coda that takes the massive street protests in the United States stemming from the murder of George Floyd in early summer 2020 and the storming of the US Capitol on January 6, 2021, as context to consider how social media have appropriated public space in the struggle to articulate collective identities via shared affect. Here, the various scales discussed throughout the book are inevitably intertwined: how from the comforts of home on lockdown we bore witness to the killing of a black man on a street corner in front of an urban minimarket that ignites protests against police brutality and calls for racial justice that captivate a nation and spread rapidly to different parts of the world. That the existential void of locked-down, pandemic urban space would quickly be filled by various warring political and cultural factions, both online and in physical space, was predictable. The physical occupation of public space in Portland, Oregon, and Seattle that summer, pitting self-described Proud Boys against antifa activists in open urban warfare, and the storming of the Capitol by a violent mob of Trump supporters at the beginning of the new year, vividly illustrated how finding common ground today is an agonistic process of perpetual negotiation and struggle, one in which various actors continually articulate and defend competing conceptions of cultural and political identity. That these sociotechnical assemblages are perhaps becoming more unevenly distributed across disparate social, cultural, and economic realities than they have ever been is arguably one of the more important challenges of the post-truth condition. In times of crisis like these, finding common ground would appear to be more important than ever. This book is an effort to better understand the topography of these conditions and how to navigate their contingent territories.

I

PRACTICES

1

ALTERNATIVE FACTS

FABRICATING DATA

It was a gray and damp morning in Washington, DC, on Friday, January 20, 2017. In a few hours, Donald J. Trump would be inaugurated as the forty-fifth president of the United States. The final preparations for the event were complete. Rows of foldable white chairs stretched back across the Capitol lawn, flanked by rows of portable toilets lining its periphery. Vendors selling Trump swag were setting up shop. Helicopters circled the national monument. Security barriers were in place throughout the Capitol, blocking streets and rerouting traffic. Workers adjusted lighting at the reviewing stand in front of the White House where Trump would be watching the inaugural parade. The DC Metro began to hum with activity, and people started to filter into the National Mall. Federal and local agencies were preparing for a turnout of somewhere between 700,000 and 900,000 people, including both supporters and protesters. Trump himself had bigger aspirations, of course, claiming with his trademark hubris that his inauguration would have "an unbelievable, perhaps record-setting turnout."[1] No doubt in his mind was the turnout of an estimated 1.8 million people for his political nemesis Barack Obama's first inauguration in 2009, which set a record for the most people gathered in the National Mall at any one time. This number would be hard to beat.

Estimating crowd size for major public events is no simple matter and is often a flash point of controversy. Prior to the Million Man March in 1995, the National Park Service (NPS) had for decades released "official" estimates of the size of crowds gathering on the National Mall for public events. Organized by Nation of Islam leader Louis Farrakhan and a coalition of leaders from various civil rights groups called the National African American Leadership Summit (NAALS), the Million Man March was a gathering of African American men intending to demonstrate solidarity and a renewed commitment to family within the black community. Notable speakers included poet Maya Angelou, civil rights activist Rosa Parks, Reverend Jesse Jackson, Martin Luther King III, and Reverend Benjamin Davis, founding director of NAALS. The park service estimated that 400,000 people had attended the march. The organizers believed, however, that they had reached their goal of 1 million marchers and threatened to sue the park service, arguing its count was motivated by "racism, white supremacy and hatred for Louis Farrakhan."[2] While no lawsuit was eventually filed, the controversy was enough to make the NPS decide to get out of the business of providing estimates of crowd size for gatherings at the National Mall, and Congress passed legislation the following year that barred the park service from allocating funds to the counting of crowds.

In the past, the NPS estimated crowd size by analyzing aerial photographs of the event. Their method involved dividing the mall into a grid of sections of equal area. These sections were assigned a density of people per square foot, with a loosely packed crowd measuring around ten square feet per person, a tighter crowd around six or seven square feet, and densely packed crowds at three to four square feet. While this rudimentary practice of using aerial photography to measure crowd size based on densities of people segmented into a uniform grid provided more of a rough approximation than an absolute value, the numbers released by the NPS would become key data points by which the significance of events on the mall was measured and evaluated. The practice of fabricating these data had become a hotly contested one.

Unfortunately for Trump, images posted to social media taken around the time of his inaugural speech from a news pool camera mounted on top of the Washington Monument showed the crowds were looking far more loose than dense and not that extensive. One reporter tweeted a

Comparison of inauguration crowd size for Barack Obama in 2009 (left) and Donald Trump in 2017 (right). Photos courtesy of the National Park Service.

side-by-side comparison of images from the Trump and Obama inaugurations that showed a clear discrepancy in crowd size. These visual representations were subsequently compared with ridership data from the Washington Metropolitan Area Transit Authority (WMATA), which operates DC's Metrorail system. By 11:00 a.m. on the day of Trump's inauguration, WMATA had counted 193,000 rides, fewer than half the 513,000 it counted in 2009 for Obama's first inauguration and far fewer than the 317,000 for Obama's second inauguration in 2013.

As reports that Trump's inaugural crowd size was estimated as roughly one-third that of Obama's reached the new president, panic set in at the White House. A park service employee had retweeted the reporter's side-by-side image comparison from the day before, leading the new administration to immediately shut down the official NPS Twitter feed. Early the next morning, Trump called the acting director of the NPS, Michael Reynolds, demanding more flattering photographs of the event. Subsequent calls from newly minted White House press secretary Sean Spicer pressed the park service public affairs department for pictures that would appear to show a larger, more densely packed crowd, photos that "accurately represented the inauguration crowd size."[3] Scrambling to accommodate an increasingly irate Spicer, a park service official contacted the photographer who was covering the inauguration the day before and requested any photographs "in which it appeared the inauguration crowd filled the majority of the space in the photograph."[4] According to reports obtained in response to a Freedom of Information Act request by the *Guardian* newspaper, the photographer proceeded to crop images he had taken of the event the day before to meet this urgent request. He had edited the photographs "to make them look more symmetrical by cropping out the sky and cropping out the bottom where the crowd ended."[5]

"This was the largest audience to ever witness an inauguration—period," declared an angry Spicer at a heated press conference later that afternoon.[6] Accusing journalists of misrepresenting crowd size by reporting inaccurate numbers and publishing deceptive photographs, Spicer proceeded to berate the news media for minimizing the "enormous support" the new president received at his inauguration. Yet in the attempt to refute the media narrative surrounding the comparatively low attendance at Trump's inauguration, it was Spicer himself who misrepresented the facts, stating that photos had been cropped to minimize the number of people in the frame when in fact the opposite was true. He also cited Metro ridership numbers for the entire day (420,000) in comparison to those only up to 11:00 a.m. (317,000) for Obama in 2013—his second inauguration, where attendance was far lower than that of his first in 2009.[7] The following day, White House advisor Kellyanne Conway went on NBC's Sunday news show *Meet the Press* and, when confronted by host Chuck Todd as to why the White House press secretary's first statement of the new administration would be a lie, claimed Spicer was simply providing "alternative facts."

In its first few days in power, this new administration ushered in the era of alternative facts. While the rallying cry of fake news as a means to discredit the media had been a staple on the Trump campaign trail for more than a year, the coordinated manufacture of so-called alternate facts—doctored photographs, the misrepresentation of ridership data—signaled a higher-order proposition. Data and evidence were now to be fabricated in support of whatever truth claims the administration wanted to make. The status of "the real" with respect to contemporary media culture would be reconfigured. The significance of an event, as measured by the size of its audience, would become the product of negotiations between data, media objects, and distribution systems. The techniques by which we observe, count, and record the metrics of that which takes place and the networks of media and information systems by which these observations are disseminated across disparate publics would become co-conspirators in the fabrication of the various realities we choose to inhabit. Moreover, counterfactual media narratives would become a key weapon in partisan political warfare, not intending to convince people of things that are untrue but aimed at creating a sense of uncertainty and doubt about whether facts are even knowable in the first place.[8]

This chapter examines how spatial knowledge is constructed and not simply given as a transparent or neutral representation of preexisting facts. I argue that the process of knowledge construction has historically evolved in relation to the emergence of different forms of verisimilitude—the appearance of being true or real—produced by the dominant media practices of the time. I address how within these various media practices are embedded truth claims, the epistemological implications of which extend to (and at the same time articulate) the cultural milieu within which they are situated. As I intend to show, this fabrication of "the real" finds its contemporary manifestation in a collection of machine learning techniques known as generative adversarial networks (GANs), of which the synthesized media object known as *deepfake* is a popular example. Tracing how the practice of fabricating "the real" has evolved throughout the history of techniques and technologies for representing people and space, this chapter situates the epistemic fragmentation of post-truth territory within a broader history of representational space and its attendant techniques and devices.

DATA, FACTS, EVIDENCE

The roots of this epistemological crisis, if we can call it that, can be traced back to historical relations between data, facts, and evidence. Today it is common to think of data as representing facts in an unbiased or neutral way. Media historian Lisa Gitelman and poetics scholar Virginia Jackson write:

> At first glance data are apparently before the fact: they are the starting point for what we know, who we are, and how we communicate. This shared sense of starting with data often leads to an unnoticed assumption that data are transparent, that information is self-evident, the fundamental stuff of truth itself.[9]

"Raw" data exist out there in the world and are evidence of facts, which are truthful. If we were to follow what is known as the DIKW knowledge hierarchy,[10] from these data we make information, build knowledge, and develop wisdom. But as informatics scholar Geoffrey Bowker argues, "raw data" is an oxymoron: these data are always already cooked.[11] They are measured, sampled, collected, mined, and interpreted through a variety of methods involving a mix of human and nonhuman actors: a sensor placed in a specific location; a set of methods for its calibration; an anticipated output that drives the design of the data capture system in the first place; the attributes of the sensor, its location in the world, and the techniques and metrics by which its data will be captured, stored and potentially processed, evaluated, and interpreted. As digital media scholar Yanni Loukissas suggests, this entails shifting our focus from data sets to data settings.[12]

In her critique of realist models of data visualization that collapse the space between an observable phenomenon and its interpretation, scholar of visual culture Johanna Drucker argues against the notion that phenomena are observer independent and able to be characterized as data. Describing how data are generally understood as being *taken* from the world, as opposed to *given* by it, she contends that what we today call *data* might be better termed *capta*:

Differences in the etymological roots of the terms data and capta make the distinction between constructivist and realist approaches clear. Capta is "taken" actively while data is assumed to be a "given" able to be recorded and observed. From this distinction, a world of differences arises. Humanistic inquiry acknowledges the situated, partial, and constitutive character of knowledge production, the recognition that knowledge is constructed, taken, not simply given as a natural representation of pre-existing fact.[13]

Decisions regarding how data are selected, harvested, interpreted, and released are often contested, political decisions. As I discuss in greater detail in chapter 9, the politicization of public health data on the coronavirus in the United States alarmed many who saw attempts by local, state, and national governmental agencies to manipulate how data on the extent of the spread of COVID-19 were represented and disseminated as blatant attempts to shape public opinion along partisan political lines. The move by the Trump administration to consolidate the collection of hospital data about the virus in the Department of Health and Human Services was widely viewed as an attempt to control the release of critical information to the public about the extent of the virus. The long-standing system for reporting hospital data managed by the Centers for Disease Control (CDC) was replaced at the height of the pandemic by a new one developed by a private contractor. Trump's insistence that the reason there were more cases of COVID-19 in the United States was that the nation was testing more than other countries, and his suggestion that perhaps if we reduced our testing, we would have "better numbers" and the virus would eventually just "disappear," shows how normalized the politicization of public health data had become in political theaters.

Consider how monitoring the environmental impact of the 2001 collapse of the World Trade Center in Lower Manhattan was handled by the US Environmental Protection Agency (EPA). Three days after the attacks, Christine Todd Whitman, director of the EPA under George W. Bush, told reporters, "The good news continues to be that air samples we have taken have all been at levels that cause us no concern." But the EPA's proclamation of safe air was premature and, as was later revealed, dead wrong. One day after the attacks, Whitman issued a memo announcing that "all statements to the media should be cleared through the NSC [National Security Council] before they are released,"[14] with national security advisor Condoleezza Rice as the final decision maker regarding what information would be released by the EPA. Internal agency data conflicting with a reassuring public posture were ignored. According to a report from the Office of the Inspector General of the EPA in 2003, the EPA lacked the information needed to determine the air quality surrounding Ground Zero in the days following the September 11 attacks.[15] They weren't sampling in ways that one could accurately interpret the actual health implications for people living in the immediate area of the attacks or performing the vital recovery tasks on site at Ground Zero. And people would eventually die because of this.

Historian Daniel Rosenberg reminds us that there is no truth in data, and the use of the word *data* in the English language has itself been intertwined in conflicting ways with related concepts of "fact" and "evidence" since its emergence. At the beginning of the eighteenth century, *data* referred to either "principles accepted as a basis of argument or to facts gleaned from scripture that were unavailable to questioning."[16] By the end of the century, the word more commonly referred to "facts in evidence determined by experiment, experience, or collection."[17] While this shift from understanding data as the rhetorical premise of an argument—what is *given*—to the result of an empirical investigation—what is *captured*—did lay the groundwork for mid-twentieth-century claims of scientific veracity, today, as Rosenberg suggests, "It may be that the data we collect and transmit has no relation to truth or reality whatsoever beyond the reality that data helps us to construct."[18]

FAKING IT

In April 2018, stand-up comedian and film director Jordan Peele and Buzzfeed founder and CEO Jonah Peretti produced a video of former President Barack Obama using machine learning techniques to create what has come to be known as a *deepfake*. Peele was already known for his impersonation of Obama through his collaborations with Keegan-Michael Key on their comedy show *Key & Peele*, and his voice on the synthesized video was a close match to Obama's. "We're entering an era in which our enemies can make it look like anyone is saying anything at any point in time—even if they would never say those things," says Peele/Obama. "So, for instance, they could have me say things like, I don't know, Killmonger was right! Or Ben Carson is in the sunken place! Or, how about this: simply, President Trump is a total and complete dipshit."[19] The video, conceived as a form of public service announcement, aimed to call attention to the capacity of this technology to manipulate the media landscape and warn viewers about trusting content they encounter online. As of this writing, the public service announcement has been viewed more than 9 million times. The potential to apply synthetic media techniques to the fabrication of apparent political realities was not lost on some in this audience, and in September 2018, three members of Congress sent a letter to the director of national intelligence warning of their use in spreading misinformation in the context of a political campaign.[20]

Deepfakes, a portmanteau of "deep learning" and "fake," are the cultural by-product of research in computer vision that employs a class of machine learning frameworks called a generative adversarial network. GANs are trained to generate media objects from existing data sets that depict people doing and saying things that never occurred. They were invented in 2014 by computer science researcher Ian Goodfellow, then a

PhD student at the Université de Montréal. (Goodfellow would go on to work for Google, Apple, and the OpenAI Institute.) They are created by simultaneously training two neural networks and pitting them against each other. One network, called the *generator*, is trained on a data set from which it attempts to synthesize something, while the other, called the *discriminator*, attempts to discern whether that something is "real" (that it came from the existing training data set) or "fake" (that it was synthesized by the generator). When the discriminator can no longer determine whether the image was made by the generator or came from the training set, the training of the GAN is complete. Initially the subject of academic research in computer vision and machine learning, GANs have been applied to photorealistic techniques for manipulating mouth shapes from audio and techniques for modifying video footage of a person's face to depict them mimicking the facial expressions of another person in real time.[21] These techniques are generally referred to as methods for facial reenactment, where facial expressions from an actor in a source video are transferred in real time to an actor in a target video.

Toward the end of 2017, a Reddit user named "deepfakes" began creating and sharing video clips that superimposed the faces of celebrities onto bodies of women in pornographic videos. These clips were created using a technique called face swapping. Whereas facial reenactment uses the facial movements and expression deformations of a control face in one video to guide the motions and deformations of a face that is appearing in another video, face swapping simply transfers a face from an image source to a target image. "With hundreds of face images, I can easily generate millions of distorted images to train the network," says Reddit user deepfakes. "After that if I feed the network someone else's face, the network will think it's just another distorted image and try to make it look like the training face."[22] Free software applications such as FakeApp and DeepFaceLab built with open source software libraries such as Google's TensorFlow and Keras began to appear and circulate online, and the creation of deepfakes was suddenly within reach of anyone with a laptop or desktop computer and some time (and GPU cycles) to spare.

In the run-up to the 2020 US presidential election, a document detailing Hunter Biden's alleged connections to China circulated throughout

Far Right social media platforms. "BIDEN shifted his view from hawk-ish to dovish after HUNTER began receiving entrée into Chinese elite political and financial institutions," the purported "intelligence" dossier claimed.[23] The report, together with a series of stories published in the *New York Post*, claimed to be based on the contents of a laptop associated with Hunter Biden. This document turned out to be the product of a fictional firm, Typhoon Investigations, written by a fictitious intelligence analyst named Martin Aspen. As intelligence analyst Elise Thomas would eventually discover, Aspen's profile image used for his Twitter and Linke-dIn accounts was generated by a GAN.

The fabrication of falsehoods in the political arena is an old game, one where claims need only the most rudimentary of distribution systems to propagate, be it word-of-mouth, pamphleteer, or retweet. When Vice Presi-dent Thomas Jefferson ran against President John Adams in the US presi-dential election of 1800, he hired James Callendar, a journalist and political pamphleteer, to launch a smear campaign against Adams. With Jefferson's financial support, Callendar penned "The Prospect Before Us," a populist pamphlet on the pervasive corruption among Federalists and the Adams administration, suggesting, among other things, that if Adams was elected, he would attack France (a crucial ally in the American Revolutionary War), whose privateers at the time were in maritime skirmishes with a fledgling US Navy over unpaid war debt.[24] While this claim could not be proved at the time, the pamphlet convinced many Americans they should vote for Jef-ferson if they wished to avoid all-out war with France. Jefferson ultimately prevailed in the bitter and hard-fought election, but not before the Adams administration had prosecuted (and convicted) Callendar for sedition.[25]

According to Aviv Ovadya, former chief technologist at the Center for Social Media Responsibility, however, we should be less concerned that people will be tricked by fakes than that they will give up on caring whether something is real or not in the first place. Ovadya is concerned that we collectively develop a form of "reality apathy"—that we will ulti-mately give up on determining what is real from what is fake. "Synthetic media," he writes, "is a challenge to our *epistemic capacity*—our ability to make sense of the world and make competent decisions."[26] In this respect, synthetic media such as deepfakes align with the implied agenda of the Trump administration regarding fake news and the manufacture of doubt that we saw with the media circus surrounding his inauguration. Ultimately what is at stake is the status of "the real" itself as a basis for knowing and acting in the world.

THE STATUS OF THE REAL

The notion of "the real" has a long history in visual culture, from the close attention to comprehensive detail and the depiction of ordinary people from everyday life in Realist painting and literature, to the introduction of analog photography in the nineteenth century and its digital transformation at the close of the twentieth; from the mass popularity of early precinematic optical devices like the stereoscope or more recent innovations in immersive virtual reality headsets, to the arrival of the moving image and its subsequent synthesis through ever more sophisticated forms of computer-generated imagery (CGI). The status of the real has historically evolved in relation to the emergence of different forms of verisimilitude (the appearance of being true or real) enacted by new and emerging media practices. Embedded within each of these practices are various truth claims, the epistemological implications of which extend to the cultural milieu within which they are situated.

Gustave Corbet, *The Stonebreakers*, 1849.

Realism in the arts has ranged from works that aimed to accurately depict the world through an avoidance of stylization and attention to detail (light, color, perspectival accuracy) in representing the visual appearance of things, to works that focused on prosaic or mundane subject matter incorporating the depiction of everyday life in ordinary settings. Realism as an art movement began as a reaction to Romanticism in the mid-nineteenth century. The work of painters like Gustave Courbet and Jean-François Millet rejected idealist representations of exotic subjects in dramatic settings (the work of Caspar David Friedrich comes to mind) in favor of depicting subjects from "real" life with ordinary people performing common activities, such as working in the field or playing chess. Within literature, realism sought the faithful representation of reality, focusing primarily on the portrayal of the life of the middle class. Writers such as Mark Twain and Henry James aimed to depict subjects from everyday life from the point of view of a third-person objective reality, one where authorial commentary is minimized, the plausible is favored over the dramatic and sensational, and the "real" is rendered closely and in comprehensive detail.

With the development of the modern camera and the photographic image, aspects of the visual world could be depicted with a high degree of accuracy and became mechanically reproducible. Pragmatist philosopher Charles Sanders Peirce's notion of indexicality has been employed by theorists of visual culture to describe the physical relationship between the photographed object and the resultant image, and much has been written regarding the indexical qualities of the photographic image, its truth claims and evidentiary aspirations.[27] Commonly cited as a precursor to virtual reality technologies, the stereoscope built on these photographic principles and introduced a mechanical device with the technical ability to fabricate a "real" sense of depth in the image that modeled the physiological properties of an embodied binocular vision.[28] Along with the panorama and the diorama, the stereoscope quickly became an early synthetic mass media form, evolving in the twentieth century to become the popular View Master toy.

The invention of celluloid and the motion picture camera brought us film toward the end of the nineteenth century and, with it, a sensitivity to the passage of time, motion, action, and gesture in the moving image: the "real" now transpired over time. Much has been made of claims regarding the audience's reaction to the Lumière brothers' 1895

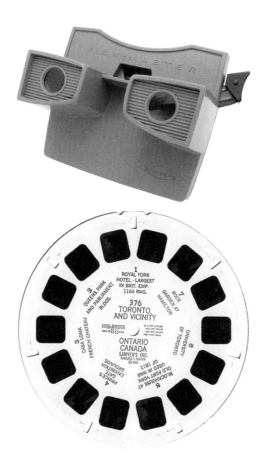

The View Master, introduced in 1939 by photo finishing company Sawyers, consists of a stereoscope and corresponding thin cardboard disks containing stereoscopic pairs of small transparent color photographs on film. *Source*: user:Junkyardsparkle/Wikimedia Commons/public domain (top); Sally Hunter/CC-BY-2.0 (bottom).

film, *L'arrivée d'un train en gare de La Ciotat* (The Arrival of a Train at La Ciotat Station). Consisting of a single, fifty-second shot by a stationary camera, this silent film depicts a train pulled by a steam engine into a train station in La Ciotat, a town on France's Mediterranean coast. As the legend goes, the audience was so startled by the moving image of a life-sized train coming directly at them that they screamed and ran to the back of the room.

The mid-twentieth century brought us television, and with it a sense of *real time* and *liveness*. As media scholar Philip Auslander points out, the essence of television was "its ability to transmit events as they occur, not in a filmic capacity to record events for later viewing."[29] Writing at the birth of television in 1937, industrial engineer Alfred Goldsmith contrasts television with film and human vision, describing its reality effect in terms of a sense of immediacy:

As far as ocular vision is concerned, a real event can be seen only at the instant of occurrence. . . . Accordingly all the historical past is lost so far as direct vision by human beings is concerned. The motion picture suffers from no such limitation. The motion picture may be made at any time and shown at any later time. . . . Television with direct pick-up of an actual event is as dependent on its time of occurrence as is the eye.[30]

Media studies scholar Jane Feuer has argued that although television ceased long ago to be "live" in an ontological sense, it remains so in an ideological one.[31] According to Auslander, the ability of television to "go live" and transmit sight and sound across the planet at any point in time remains an essential part of the televisual imaginary despite the fact that live broadcast has become the exception rather than the rule.[32]

Today, virtual reality headsets and advanced CGI in film have rendered virtually anything within the realm of synthesis. To the extent that our belief in images is tied to our understanding of how they are made—for instance, that light reflected from an object plays a causal role in the creation of the photographic image or that this news broadcast is presenting actual events because it is happening *now*—our capacity to evaluate truth claims made by the various media we consume is related to our knowledge of how they are made, a capacity that is confounded by the black-boxed algorithms behind deepfakes and the like.

Media artists Derek Curry and Jennifer Gradacki target this seamless opacity of synthetic media in their project *Infodemic*, a video that employs a GAN in highlighting the fabricated nature of online information and the politicians, "big tech" CEOs, celebrities, and social media influencers who spread misinformation about the COVID-19 virus by repeating false narratives or developing technologies that amplify false content. As Curry and Gradacki note in their statement on the project, the word *infodemic* was coined during the SARS outbreak in 2003 but gained present currency in February 2020 when the director of the World Health Organization, General Tedros Adhanom Ghebreyesus, declared about COVID-19, "We're not

Derek Curry and Jennifer Gradecki, *Infodemic*, 2020. Video still. Image courtesy of the artists.

just fighting an epidemic; we're fighting an infodemic. Fake news spreads faster and more easily than this virus, and is just as dangerous."[33] The video presents a series of talking heads delivering messages from academics, medical experts, and journalists correcting false narratives or explaining how misinformation is created and spread. Yet rather than training an algorithm on thousands of images of a single person to synthesize a convincing likeness of that person, the artists trained their algorithm on a corpora of multiple individuals, resulting in a flickering talking head that mutates into faces of the various cast of characters the project targets. The aesthetic of the glitch, which recalls net.art collaborative Jodi's early work that would typically disrupt the display of a web page to reveal errors and expose its underlying source code, is here deployed as a foil for the smooth voices of the video's narrators that holds the work together. The resulting effect invokes the evolving, fluid, and highly unstable nature of public health information in the midst of a pandemic.

NEGOTIATING REALITIES

The status of the real and our relationship to it has evolved with each incremental step in the drive to represent, manufacture, and synthesize the world as we know it. Writing at the onset of the digital era in the 1990s and within the context of its seemingly limitless appetite to synthesize the real, postmodernist writers such as Jean Baudrillard and Umberto Eco introduced the notion of *hyperreality* in an attempt to describe the cultural conditions of the time. Marked by the generation of models of a real without origin or reality (Baudrillard) or the fabrication of a false reality that is to be consumed as real (Eco), the hyperreal was presented as the inability of consciousness to distinguish reality from a simulation of reality. Disneyland serves as a prime example:

> The Disneyland imaginary is neither true or false: it is a deterrence machine set up in order to rejuvenate in reverse the fiction of the real. Whence the debility, the infantile degeneration of this imaginary. It's meant to be an infantile world, in order to make us believe that the adults are elsewhere, in the "real" world, and to conceal the fact that real childishness is everywhere, particularly among those adults who go there to act the child in order to foster illusions of their real childishness.[34]

For Baudrillard, fundamental to the notion of the hyperreal are the concepts of simulation and simulacrum. Whereas simulation is the conflation of the real with its representation, where the boundaries between the two become blurred, the simulacrum is the copy lacking an original, one that bears no relation to any reality whatsoever. "The simulacrum is never that which conceals the truth," he writes, "it is the truth which conceals that there is none."[35] The simulacrum becomes a truth in its own right.

Living in the wake of the hyperreal in our contemporary post-truth era, we might learn to embrace alternative facts and the deepfake in the same way we would any other media object making truth claims that attempt to captivate our attention: not just with skepticism and doubt, but also with a curiosity regarding how they are made. We need to recognize that the status of the real is always already negotiated (and renegotiated) between people, space, inscription devices, and (human and machinic) interpretive processes. Increasingly, these negotiations are distributed across diverse contexts that often don't have shared assumptions, let alone common vocabularies. What's our opening position? That these negotiations can be politicized in ways that undermine their agency to strengthen common understanding, what Latour describes as the ability "to perceive a landscape that can be explored in concert," is evident from the Trump administration's handling of public health data or the EPA World Trade Center fiasco. Less obvious may be that without these negotiations, we may not have a viable epistemological basis by which we can know something about our place in this world and determine best courses for future shared action within it. In the next chapter, we turn to how we locate ourselves within this world, navigate through and otherwise inhabit it, shifting our focus from representational space to representations of space in discussing the cartography of post-truth territory and politics of mapmaking.

2

GROUND FICTIONS

In that Empire, the Art of Cartography attained such Perfection that the map of a single Province occupied the entirety of a City, and the map of the Empire, the entirety of a Province. In time, those Unconscionable Maps no longer satisfied, and the Cartographers Guilds struck a Map of the Empire whose size was that of the Empire, and which coincided point for point with it. The following Generations, who were not so fond of the Study of Cartography as their Forebears had been, saw that that vast map was Useless, and not without some Pitilessness was it, that they delivered it up to the Inclemencies of Sun and Winters. In the Deserts of the West, still today, there are Tattered Ruins of that Map, inhabited by Animals and Beggars; in all the Land there is no other Relic of the Disciplines of Geography.
—Suarez Miranda

PAPER TOWNS

Drive north from the Roscoe Diner at the foot of the Catskill Mountains in Delaware County, New York, and before long, you'll reach Agloe, just after Route 206 crosses over Beaverkill stream. You won't find Agloe on Google Maps, however, and truth be told, there is not much to see there today beyond a few houses littered along the side of the road. Yet ask any geographer about the place, and they are sure to know it. It's a classic mapmaker's tale.

In 1937, the General Drafting Company created a map showing a small hamlet named Agloe just north of Roscoe at what was then an intersection of dirt roads. The hamlet didn't exist; rather, it was a "copy-right trap." The name itself was an anagram of the initials of Otto G. Lind-berg, founder of General Drafting, and his assistant, Ernest Alpers. Prior to the introduction of satellite imagery, remote sensing techniques, and geographic information systems (GIS), mapmaking was largely a manual process. Drafting companies would produce representations of parts of the world employing techniques and methods that had been developed over centuries. The advent of the compass, the sextant, the quadrant, and the vernier each aided in the drive to represent the world more accurately. Yet problems arise when one wants to "protect" the effort invested in pro-ducing these maps and the proprietary data and information on which they are based. As maps became more accurate, they also became more similar, and therefore easier to plagiarize. Copyright traps were invented as a way to protect proprietary information contained in a map.

Copyright traps typically take the form of a fictional remote village or dead-end street embedded within an otherwise genuine map of a region or city. Designed to trap a would-be plagiarist in the act of copying pro-prietary information, these fake places were intended to make it easier to spot copyright infringement. Known in the cartography business as a "paper town," Agloe's placement on the map was intended to catch pla-giarists copying General Drafting's map data. If you were to find Agloe, New York, on a map produced by any other company, chances are the map was copied from General Drafting's map.

But the tale doesn't end there. In the 1950s, someone built a general store at the intersection indicated on the map and named it the Agloe General Store. What was once a fictional place now had a basis in fact. Following the general store came a gas station and a couple of houses, and not long after, the Delaware County administration officially designated Agloe as a hamlet. Here, Baudrillard's notion of the hyperreal discussed previously is made manifest: it is the map that precedes the territory—the precession of simulacra—that engenders the territory.

The hamlet would later appear on a map of New York State published by Rand McNally, a major competitor of General Drafting. Esso, which published maps showing the locations of its gas stations using map data from General Drafting, promptly sued Rand McNally, believing it had caught the company in copyright infringement. Rand McNally argued in

A map from 1961 indicating the location of Agloe, New York, Humble Oil & Refining Company/ESSO. Photo by the author.

court that the place had in fact become real: it was acknowledged by the county administration, which had provided the place name data for its map, and therefore did not infringe on Esso's copyright.

Ultimately, while these fictitious places can reveal copied information, the material they represent must itself be eligible for copyright to prove infringement in legal terms. For example, in response to a lawsuit filed by the Alexandria Drafting Company alleging that Franklin Maps had violated the Copyright Act of 1976, the judge ruled that fictitious names may not be copyrighted and that the existence, or nonexistence, of a road is not a copyrightable fact. Over time, the economic fortunes of Agloe would change, and the general store went out of business. The hamlet shrank. Mapmakers continued to list Agloe on their maps into the 1990s, and it briefly appeared on Google Maps until 2014, when the US Geological Survey listed "Agloe (Not Official)" as a paper town in the Geographic Names Information System database.[1] What was once a fictional place that had become real was once again a fiction.[2]

As this story illustrates, the relationship of maps to places is a dynamic and reciprocal one. Mapmaking traces the contours of the physical world, which in turn is shaped by this process. Maps make geospatial truth claims. But they also convey falsehoods, as Agloe, New York, so vividly demonstrates. As representations of space, they structure how we come to know a given environment, the power relations in play there, and the limits of our agency to act within it. As with measuring the size of a crowd on the National Mall, mapping post-truth territory can become a contested practice. The cartography of epistemic fragmentation is akin to the tattered remains of the Map of the Empire in Argentinian writer Jorge Louis Borges's literary forgery reproduced at the start of the chapter.[3] Yet as we will see, its territory is inhabited not by animals and beggars but rather by statistical imaginaries derived from clusters of data bodies.

In this chapter, we examine cartographic representational practices and the role of mapmaking in shaping not just the physical world but also the mental models by which we locate and orient ourselves within, navigate through, and otherwise inhabit it. Through a series of examples illustrating critical approaches to *counter-mapping* practices, we will attempt to arrive at a better understanding of the role that representations of space can play in fabricating how we come to know the world around us. As mapmaking practices become automated by computational processes, machine learning algorithms are more frequently tasked with interpreting geospatial data and making cartographic truth claims. From areas of interest (AOI) extrapolated from derivative data to self-healing maps that adapt to topographic changes over time, algorithms have succeeded the compass, the sextant, the quadrant, and the vernier in the drive to create better maps. Yet embedded within these maps are assumptions and biases that are often far from transparent. For whom are these maps better? Here, the rhetorical power of maps becomes a function of who governs the data by which the base map on which all other layers of the map depend is drawn.

MAPPING AND COUNTER-MAPPING

Cartography, the study and practice of making maps, is premised on the notion that reality can be modeled in such a way that spatial information can be effectively communicated. Cartographers make truth claims with their maps. They abstract the world by projecting three-dimensional objects onto a planar surface, selecting specific attributes to emphasize over others, and reducing the complexity of the whole through processes of generalization. Different maps abstract the world differently depending on their intended use. Some maps are designed to depict the topographic contours of a terrain for land management purposes, for instance, while others provide navigation and way-finding information for transportation and tourism.

However, the notion that maps offer a neutral or value-free transcription of an actually existing geographic reality is a contested one. Some geographers contend that mapmaking is fundamentally a social process that renders (and reinforces) the spatiality of existing power relations, typically to the advantage of a socially dominant group.[4] Pointing to the rhetorical power of mapmaking as an agent of social justice, the field of critical geography pursues counter-mapping practices that aim to expose spatial inequities that official or authoritative agencies attempt to downplay or elide altogether.[5] From this perspective, maps construct the world at various scales through the orchestration and integration of a series of perspectives that are always already socially conditioned.

The choice of projection type is often a point of conflict. When Flemish cartographer Gerardus Mercator published his world map in 1569, he introduced a cylindrical projection that challenged the conical projections of Egyptian polymath Ptolemy from the second century (rediscovered by western Europeans in the sixteenth century) and the "portolan" nautical charts mariners had used since the thirteenth century.[6] Mercator critiqued the Ptolemaic projections in his notations on the map, writing that "the forms of the meridians as used till now by geographers, on account of their curvature and their convergence to each other, are not utilizable for navigation." Commenting on the mariner's nautical charts, he writes, "The shapes of regions are necessarily very seriously stretched and either the longitudes and latitudes or the directions and distances are incorrect; thereby are great errors introduced."

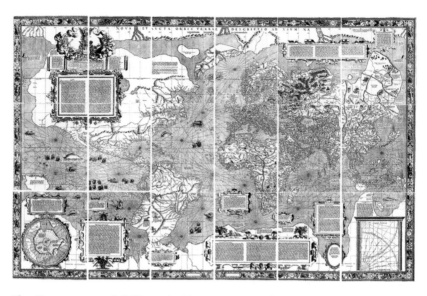

The Mercator map of 1569, or the Nova et Aucta Orbis Terrae Descriptio ad Usum Navigantium Emendate Accommodata ("New and more complete representation of the terrestrial globe properly adapted for use in navigation"). *Source*: Joaquim Alves Gaspar/ Wikimedia Commons/public domain.

Mercator's cylindrical projection rendered meridians and parallels as straight and perpendicular to each other. This projection became the standard map for seafarers because it represented any course with a constant bearing as a straight line, thus simplifying navigation by enabling ships to sail in a constant compass direction and avoid complicated course corrections. The projection also rendered linear scale as constant in any direction, resulting in the preservation of the shape of small objects on the map. This produced a lateral distortion of the map, however, which increased in relation to the distance from the equator, and a corresponding longitudinal distortion that rendered the east-west scale equal to the north-south scale at any point on the map. The size of geographical objects far from the equator therefore appear out of proportion, leading to a distorted perception of the overall geometry of the planet. Africa, for instance, appears to be the same size as Greenland, when it is in fact fourteen times larger.

Among the many who have since proposed alternatives to Mercator's projection are James Gall (1855), Walter Behrmann (1910), Trystan

Edwards (1953), and Arno Peters (1967). Peters, a German historian, called out the apparent bias in Mercator's map as a form of "cartographic imperialism," suggesting that northern European countries preferred the Mercator projection because it makes them appear larger and therefore more powerful than their southern neighbors. He responded by introducing the Gall-Peters projection, which displays the relative sizes of countries accurately but at the expense of distorting their shapes. Peters's map provoked considerable backlash from the professional cartographic community invested in defending "professional standards." After all, Peters was a historian, not a cartographer. Yet as map historian John Brian Harley notes, "The real issue in the Peters case is power: there is no doubt that Peters' agenda was the empowerment of those nations of the world he felt had suffered an historic cartographic discrimination. But equally, for the cartographers, it was their power and 'truth claims' that were at stake."[7]

Counter-mapping extends beyond the "how" of mapping to question "what" is considered important to map in the first place. Indigenous mapping, for example, is a mapmaking practice that posits a critique of an authoritative or official cartography with regard to its prerogatives, form, and content. Of particular interest is the use of map biographies, pioneered

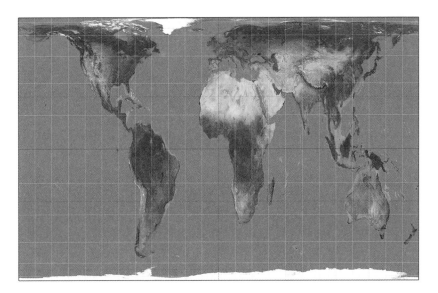

The Gall-Peters projection of the world map. *Source*: Daniel R. Strebe/CC-BY-SA-3.0.

in the Inuit Land Use and Occupancy Project (1976), which involved "hunters, trappers, fishermen, and berry pickers map[ping] out all the land they had ever used in their lifetimes, encircling hunting areas species by species, marking gathering locations and camping sites—everything their life on the land had entailed that could be marked on a map."[8] A kind of ethnocartography, these map biographies became instrumental in land claim negotiations, enabling the Inuit to assert title in 1993 to 500 million acres of land in Canada. Projects continue today involving the remapping of parts of Canada and Alaska incorporating Inuit place names, oral histories, and even sea-ice-use patterns for bodies of water that are frozen for three-quarters of the year but are rendered as blank areas on conventional maps.

With the advent of GIS and data-driven mapping techniques, new forms of counter-mapping emerged that seized on what cartographer Denis Wood would call the "power of maps" to fuel a rhetorical argument.[9] In their most basic form, GIS are a set of technologies for collecting, manipulating, and representing spatial information. GIS software enables virtually any data point that can be associated with a set of geographic coordinates to be located spatially and visualized on a map. GIS maps are commonly used to operationalize the use of data in the management of people and things in space. They also enable insights to be derived from multiple data layers that can be organized to correlate things that otherwise might not be seen in relation to each other.

Million Dollar Blocks (2006) is a mapping project employing GIS by Laura Kurgan of the Spatial Information Design Lab (now the Center for Spatial Research) at Columbia University together with Eric Cadora of the New York–based Justice Mapping Center that investigated the cost of incarceration and recidivism for five cities in the United States. Kurgan writes in the project statement:

The United States currently has more than 2 million people locked up in jails and prisons. A disproportionate number of them come from a very few neighborhoods in the country's biggest cities. In many places the concentration is so dense that states are spending in excess of a million dollars a year to incarcerate the residents of single city blocks. When these people are released and reenter their communities, roughly forty percent do not stay more than three years before they are reincarcerated. Using rarely accessible data from the criminal justice system, the Spatial Information Design Lab and the Justice Mapping Center

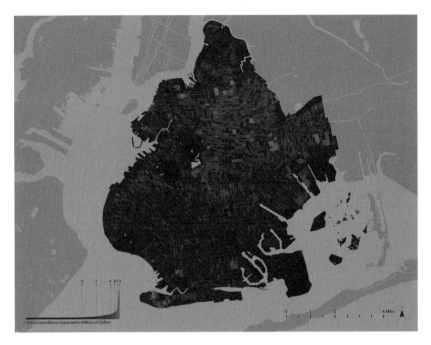

Prison expenditures in Brooklyn. Laura Kurgan, Eric Cadora, Sarah Williams, David Reinhurt, Spatial Information Design Lab, Columbia University, *Million Dollar Blocks*, 2006. Image courtesy of Laura Kurgan.

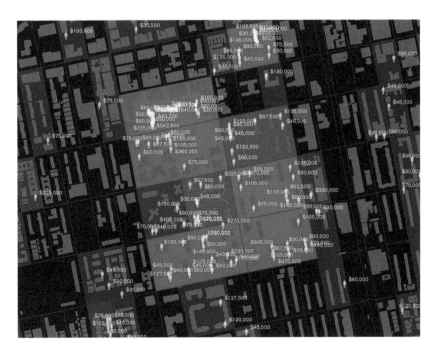

Brooklyn's Community District 16. Laura Kurgan, Eric Cadora, Sarah Williams, David Reinhurt, Spatial Information Design Lab, Columbia University, *Million Dollar Blocks*, 2006. Image courtesy of Laura Kurgan.

have created maps of these "million dollar blocks" and of the city-prison-city-prison migration flow for five of the nation's cities.[10]

These are rhetorical maps, designed to argue a point with legislators and policymakers. The maps themselves work by inverting the logic of crime hot-spot maps, notoriously introduced in 1994 by New York City police commissioner William Bratton and Mayor Rudy Giuliani as part of the COMPSTAT program, which employed GIS to map crimes in the city in an attempt to influence public opinion. By shifting the focus from crime to incarceration, Kurgan renders new cartographies that contrast a diffuse and dispersed geography of crime with a more densely concentrated geography of incarceration. Created by correlating GIS coordinates of prisoners' home addresses to census tracts, these maps explore the relations of poverty, race, rates of incarceration, and its costs to demonstrate how the government spends over $1 million per block to incarcerate a particular demographic living in specific neighborhoods. Suggesting that the criminal justice system has become the dominant government institution in these communities and that public investment in this system takes away from funding of other aspects of civic infrastructure such as education, housing, health, and family, these maps demonstrate how data visualizations can work to influence public policy regarding how resources are allocated across different urban neighborhoods. The project poses a critical question: What would happen if we invested these resources in other ways, such as preschools, summer jobs, or addiction treatment?

AREAS OF INTEREST (BUT TO WHOM?)

Recent developments in satellite imagery, remote sensing, and data mining techniques involving computer vision and machine learning have ushered in a new era for the making of cartographic truth claims. As companies such as Google seek to automate the process of mapping the world, increasingly algorithms are tasked with interpreting geospatial data in constructing representations of the world. Since at least 2012, Google has been employing computer vision techniques to identify building footprints based on satellite images and aerial photography, and extrapolating from this imagery information about height and massing to render three-dimensional volumes. In 2016, clusters of commercial buildings in urban areas began to appear as shaded AOI, which Google defines as "places where there's a lot of activities and things to do," essentially areas with the highest concentration of restaurants, bars, and shops. As map-maker Justin O'Beirne notes, these AOI appear to be the product of cor-relating place data sets (the ones that indicate locations on the map) with building data sets (the ones that extract building footprints from satel-lite and aerial photography).[11] These place data sets themselves are a by-product of street view imagery, from which business names and locations are extracted using computer vision and machine learning techniques.

In 2014, Google's Ground Truth team published a method for reading street numbers in the Street View House Numbers (SVHN) data set, imple-mented by Ian Goodfellow, a summer intern.[12] Their next step was to extend this technique to extracting street names by developing a deep learning model to automatically label new Street View imagery. Combining this new system with the one that extracted street numbers enabled new addresses to be created directly from imagery, where previously neither the name of the street nor the location of the addresses was known. From there, the model architecture was adapted to discern structured text information (text with semantic meaning attached to it) from Street View imagery, enabling the accurate extraction of business names from business facades. Google's AOI, then, are a by-product of by-products of data extracted from satellite and Street View imagery. Here, data beget more data.

Google's "areas of interest" beg the question, Of interest to whom? Not everyone is looking for a restaurant, cocktail bar, or retail store. Annette Kim, director of SLAB (Spatial Analysis Lab) at the University of South-ern California, takes a different approach to the extraction of structured text information from storefront signage. SLAB's research experiments with developing alternative cartographies and exploring their potential roles in society, "endeavoring to create knowledge and narratives that support an increasingly inclusive city."[13] Their project ethniCITY remaps race and ethnicity in the Los Angeles region. Mapping 9 million text-based signs on the streets of Los Angeles from 2001 and 2018, Kim and her collaborators extracted and geocoded both the words themselves and the languages from which they come down to the individual land par-cel level. Detecting sixteen languages from twenty-seven ethnicities in the greater LA region, SLAB has identified "areas of interest" where local

Video still showing the linguistic landscape of Los Angeles. Annette Kim/SLAB (Spatial Analysis Lab) at the University of Southern California, *ethniCITY*, 2018. Image courtesy of Annette Kim.

Photo of multilingual signage. Annette Kim/SLAB (Spatial Analysis Lab) at the University of Southern California, *ethniCITY*, 2018. Photo courtesy of Annette Kim.

communities have been publicly expressing themselves in more subtle and nuanced ways that complicate more traditional designations of the cultural enclave and ethnic neighborhood. Rather, people move around and live urban life dynamically, stitching together what Kim describes as *geographies of belonging*. "We see that ethnic places are not singular but overlapping and interspersed," she writes, "with some establishments speaking in four different languages."

Cartographic representations of space can thus make visible the invisible geographies of people, places, and events that otherwise would remain beneath the threshold of public vision. These representations of space are empowering to the extent that the rendering of these geographies informs the mental maps by which social cognition takes place and spatial knowledge is shared. If mapping encodes a way of knowing space, informing how we behave within the terrain it delineates, then the criteria—not only how but also what—by which the map is made matter. The persuasive power of maps and mapmaking practices thus plays a critical role in shaping the way we know the spaces and places of our daily lives.

GROUND TRUTH

Accurately inferring factual information from collected data is a hard problem for which different fields have developed different practices. A number of communities of practice employ the concept of ground truth to refer to information gathered by direct observation as opposed to inference. In remote-sensing applications, ground truth refers to data collected on location through direct observation. The contents of a pixel within a satellite image, for example, are compared with what is actually located on the ground at that point in space to verify the accuracy of the image classification of that pixel: land cover, water body, forest, park, street, plaza, crowd, building, and so on. In most cases, collecting ground truth data involves someone traveling to a given location and observing what actually exists there, taking GPS readings, and comparing these with their corresponding representation on the map.

Yet in most cases, the ground itself is not static but in flux. The course of a river is changed by a major flood, buildings are built up and torn down, streets appear and disappear as cities evolve. Updating and maintaining maps is a painstaking, time-consuming, and costly process. In an attempt to address these challenges, Google's Ground Truth Team uses Street View imagery and machine learning to iteratively update its maps over time, enabling maps to "self-heal" without the intervention of humans in the inner feedback loop. Here the map itself and the truth claims it posits become the product of an algorithm, subject to the same kinds of error and bias that are commonly attributed to other algorithmic systems.[14]

Ground truth in machine learning refers to the data used in supervised learning to train a model, commonly referred to as the training set. For example, a training set for a computer vision model for classifying images of people typically includes images labeled with the attributes of people the model aims to classify. The role and nature of the underlying data used to train the model are often overlooked and underappreciated. As AI scholar and principal researcher at Microsoft Research Kate Crawford and artist and MacArthur fellow Trevor Paglen note, these training data sets "are central to how AI systems recognize and interpret the world . . . [they] shape the epistemic boundaries governing how AI systems operate."[15] Pointing to long-standing debates in philosophy, art history, and media theory surrounding the instability of images in encoding meaning, they challenge the oversimplification of the problems addressed by machine vision researchers and their claims to objectively classify the world. "The circuit between image, label, and referent is flexible and can be reconstructed in any number of ways to do different kinds of work," they write in an essay accompanying an exhibition they developed on the subject. "What's more, those circuits can change over time as the cultural context of an image shifts, and can mean different things depending on who looks, and where they are located."[16]

In 2016, tech start-up Youth Laboratories launched what it claimed would be the beauty contest to end all beauty contests: Beauty.AI. The plan was to create a website where people could upload selfies of themselves, the attractiveness of which would be judged by a deep learning algorithm. Using age and facial recognition techniques, Beauty.AI promised to crown "the First Beauty Queen or King Judged by Robots." Among the forty-four winners selected from a pool of more than seven thousand entrants, however, only one was a person of color, and the project was quickly abandoned amid an outcry in the media labeling the project as racist.[17] In one analysis of the project,[18] researchers focused on an image data set on which algorithms like these are trained. Known as CelebA, the data set contains 200,000 images of celebrities from around the world collected from online sources. These images were labeled with attributes associated with attractiveness by a group of fifty young people recruited from the Chinese mainland over the course of three months. As the researchers note, assuming an eight-hour workday, each of the fifty lab employees must have labeled roughly seventy images per hour, with each image containing forty features, resulting in about fifty unique decisions a minute. Setting aside the not insignificant problem of defining facial attractiveness,[19] the faces in the CelebA data set are decidedly biased toward Western European notions of beauty, rendering the labeling of the data set by a group of overworked Chinese youth at the very least "an awkward exercise in cross-cultural exchange."

Modern data-hungry deep network–based systems require large, accurately annotated data sets. With large data sets, it can be difficult to maintain the accuracy of ground truth data, given the fact that the task of labeling must be delegated to large pools of workers less invested in the project. Google's structured text extraction model is trained on a data set of French Street Name Signs (FSNS) derived from Google Street View. The data set contains over 1 million labeled images of visual text. Each image contains several views of the same street name sign and includes normalized, ground truth text formatted in title case as it would appear on a map. Often enough, the success of computer vision and machine learning problems involving large neural networks is dependent on the availability and accessibility of sufficiently large and accurate training data.

If you aren't Google and in the business of generating your own data, accessing large urban data sets can be a challenge. While some cities actively make their data publicly available, others aren't quite there yet (for a variety of reasons). Data on cities in China, for example, can be hard to acquire. Some have turned to the Internet as a source for urban data. Real estate websites such as Trulia and Zillow, or travel and accommodation websites like Airbnb, provide sources for large sets of finely grained data that can be "scraped" for free. Alternatively, social media platforms such as Twitter, Yelp, Foursquare, and the like provide alternate insights to urban life via geocoded commentary and reviews of specific urban locations.

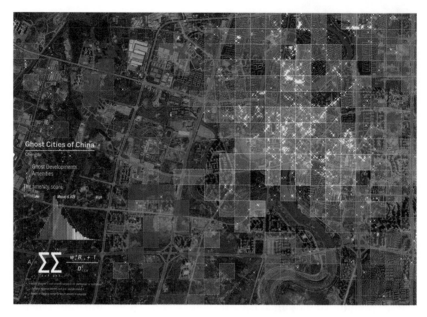

Screenshot of map interface. Sarah Williams and Chaewon Ahn, Civic Data Design Lab, MIT, *Ghost Cities of China*, 2019. Image courtesy of Sarah Williams.

Photo of vacant housing tract. Sarah Williams and Chaewon Ahn, Civic Data Design Lab, MIT, *Ghost Cities of China*, 2019. Image courtesy of Sarah Williams.

In 2019, MIT's Civic Data Design Lab, led by Sarah Williams, investigated land use given the social patterns observed through social media. Turning their sights on urban vacancy rates in second-tier Chinese cities, Williams and her collaborators investigated whether it is possible to collect data scraped from Chinese social media to develop a computational model that could identify so-called ghost cities. Ghost cities became globally topical after reports surfaced in the media describing Ordos, a large, newly constructed Chinese city that was almost entirely vacant. The term refers to vacant housing tracts resulting from overdevelopment. A by-product of Chinese real estate policies that since the late 1990s enabled local governments to ease existing restrictions including limitations on the number of homes an individual can buy, high mortgage interest rates, and higher loan-to-value ratios for down payments, these ghost cities range in scale from small neighborhoods to entire cities.

The project began with the premise that there is a correlation between vibrant neighborhoods and access to basic amenities.[20] Residents of thriving cities need places to buy groceries, eat, shop, and go to school. Using data harvested from Dianping, a Chinese version of Yelp, residential areas in two Chinese cities, Shenyang and Chengdu, were assigned an "amenities score" based on their accessibility to restaurants, medical facilities, beauty salons, karaoke lounges, educational institutions, shopping malls, grocery, and banks. This score was derived using what is known as Hansen's gravity-based spatial accessibility model, where the concept of accessibility is "the opportunity which an individual or type of person at a given location possesses to take part in a particular activity or set of activities."[21] Many different accessibility measures have been based on this model, such as access to health care, employment opportunities, groceries, and shopping. Clusters of residential areas with low amenity scores—the researchers referred to them as "amenities deserts"—were flagged as potential ghost city sites.

Subsequently, qualitative ground truth data were gathered to verify the results. Each residential cell flagged as an amenity desert was visited in person or viewed through Baidu Total View, China's version of Google Street View. Researchers gathered information about the buildings on site and interviewed local residents in the area. On-site photographic surveys aimed to capture the condition of the residential buildings and the general condition of the surroundings, enabling the categorization of different kinds of vacancy: in construction; recent construction; empty land; abandoned, aging, halted construction; populated, and rural. In verifying the model through ground truth data, Williams and her collaborators at the Civic Data Design Lab showed that a model could be developed using openly available social media data to detect the presence of vacant land in urban environments.

UNDISCOVERING THE VIEW FROM NOWHERE

In September 1774, Captain James Cook, a British explorer, navigator, cartographer, and captain in the Royal Navy, charted a narrow swath of land between the Chesterfield Islands and Nereus Reef in the eastern Coral Sea off the tip of New Caledonia.[22] The island, given the name Sandy Island, appeared on a map titled "Chart of Discoveries Made in the South Pacific Ocean . . ." that was published in 1776. Cook had sailed thousands of miles across largely uncharted areas of the world, mapping areas of the globe in greater detail and scale than previous Western explorers had. During three voyages to the Pacific Ocean, he had recorded the first (European) encounter with the eastern coastline of Australia and the Hawaiian Islands and the first circumnavigation of New Zealand. Cook's cartographic contributions gained international recognition during his lifetime.

Sandy Island (or Île de Sable, as it should be known because it lies within French territorial waters) would subsequently appear on maps in the late nineteenth and early twentieth centuries. The whaling ship *Velocity* reported the island in the year 1876, and a British admiralty chart from 1908 appears to show an island comparable in shape, size, and location to its depiction on modern maps.[23] Yet in 2012, when an Australian scientific expedition aboard the research vessel *Southern Surveyor* sailed past the coordinates where the island should have been, they found nothing but open water. Apparently although Google Earth showed the outline of Sandy Island and it had appeared on the usually reliable World Vector Shoreline (WVS) database for the past twelve years, there was no sign of it on their navigation maps. Steven Micklethwaite, a crew member from the University of Western Australia, would later recall, "At that point we thought: Well, who do we trust? Do we trust Google Earth or do we trust the navigation charts?"[24] So they decided to investigate. "We decided to actually sail through the island," Micklethwaite recounted, "Lo and behold there was nothing! The ocean floor didn't ever get shallower than 1300 metres below the wave-base. There's an island in the middle of nowhere that doesn't actually exist." And with that, Sandy Island was effectively "undiscovered."

In a flurry of media surrounding the event, some wondered if Sandy Island was a copyright trap. A spokesman for Australia's Hydrographic Service cast doubt on the idea, however, saying that while some map-makers intentionally include trap streets to protect against copyright infringement, that was usually not the case with nautical charts because it would reduce navigators' confidence in them.[25] The scientific community zeroed in on the WVS database, a data set developed by the US National Imagery and Mapping Agency (now the National Geospatial-Intelligence Agency). It could be, some thought, that an error occurred in the conversion from printed maps to digital ones. Inconsistencies in this data set exist in some of the lesser-explored parts of the world, a by-product of both human digitizing errors and errors in the original maps from which the digitizing took place. The general consensus appears to point to human error: that Captain Cook or the explorers following him perhaps mistook something else for the island—residue from a volcanic eruption, for instance.[26] The map produced from the 1876 voyage by the *Velocity* recommends that "caution is necessary while navigating among the low lying islands of the Pacific Ocean. The general details have been collated from the voyages of various navigators extending over a long series of years. The relative position of many dangers may therefore not be exactly given."

Indeed, we might keep this warning in mind today as we consider the truth claims upon which we base the decisions by which we navigate everyday life. Our relative positioning to the maps, counter-maps, and the mental maps they inform is of course culturally constructed and ideologically driven. And to the extent that these maps are also driven by machine learning algorithms trained on derivative data, they are prone to embedded bias and error that is more often attributable to humans than machines. As with Sandy Island, or Île de Sable, we need to "undiscover" the view from nowhere—that noxious attempt to claim a "neutral" position when the truth or falsehood is in plain sight—and account for the choices we make in how the various representations of space we fabricate filter the world based on biases and predispositions of which we may not even be aware.

3

THE DATA BLASÉ

I would sum up my fear about the future in one word: boring.
—J. G. Ballard

What can be said about living in these territories defined by alternative facts, fabricated by GANs, and mapped by attentive algorithms operating on derivative data? What subject positions do they encourage, preclude, empower, and oppress? How might this positioning shape behavior in terms of patterns more legible to an algorithm? In this chapter, we explore how subjectivity is positioned within data-driven territories assembled by what is commonly referred to as "the cloud." Beneath and beyond big data, this extensive network of hardware and software systems enables the transactions of everyday life. Far from the dreamy ephemeral organizations of suspended water vapor gracing the sky above, this very physical and material infrastructure underlies most contemporary economies of communication and exchange. Social media platforms in particular rely on its pervasive availability and persistent presence to capture attention and maximize engagement. Yet as its reach extends to ever-broader aspects of life, it takes on a special quality that belies its basis in computation and quantification. I refer to this affect as the *data blasé*: the feeling of indifference toward the realities of living in a post-truth world. Looking back to impacts of industrialization on early modern urban life, I suggest that the rationalization of the money economy has been eclipsed by the mechanics of a reputation economy in the drive to captivate attentive subjects. Here, the disciplinary imperative of Western capitalism to demand that its subjects specialize, individuate, and "pay attention" is inverted in the positioning of subjects to normalize their behavior in ways that attentive algorithms can recognize.

DATA GIGANTICISM

Despite the incessant hype of early twenty-first-century techno-evangelists, the near future—that point in time just beyond the present that holds the promise of radical change brought about by disruptive technologies—appears to have made manifest the fear Ballard states at the start of this chapter. Between the breathless claims of proponents of "smarter cities" and the rousing critiques of "radical devices" lies the banal cloudscape of everyday data. This cloudscape is neither the highly optimized, ever-more-efficient, and sustainable city we've been promised nor the spectacularly dark and sinister surveillance state of the post-Snowden era we've been warned about. This cloudscape is as broadly pervasive as it is largely invisible, although it tends to render as beige across collective consciousness. Its dress code is decidedly business casual. It stretches seamlessly across public and private domains, between home and office, and throughout online and offline environments. It blankets urban and exurban contexts equally without prejudice, although its density is perhaps most pronounced in cities. We have learned to reckon with it as we do with other matters of similarly prosaic significance: with practiced indifference.

The cloud is, of course, a fiction. It is a metaphor for an assemblage of hardware and software systems that form the infrastructural mycelium of contemporary data-driven societies. As information scholars Paul Dourish and Jean-François Blanchette note, data are inextricably entangled with the material constraints of the devices and systems by which they are processed, stored, and conveyed.[1] Contrary to the immaterial ephemerality its name implies, the cloud is composed of wired and wireless networks that connect billions of cell phones, tablets, smart home appliances, and the like to thousands of data centers distributed around the world that house seemingly unending arrays of servers consuming exceedingly large amounts of energy. Strategically located on vast parcels of land close to cheap energy sources and an Internet backbone, in jurisdictions offering lucrative tax incentives and favorable laws, policies, and regulations, these data centers are perhaps the most visible materialization of the cloud. Connecting these infrastructural nodes are millions of miles of less visible cable, much of it traveling underneath the sea between continents. While wireless and satellite networks have become increasingly fast and robust over the past decade, undersea cables remain the fastest, cheapest, and most efficient way to carry information across the ocean. Initially these cables were installed by the major telecoms. Google, Amazon, Facebook, and Microsoft today own or lease more than half of the undersea bandwidth.[2]

The technical paradigm of the cloud involves delivering computing as a service. Most people access the cloud using smartphones over the Internet, accessing web-based services such as Gmail, Twitter, or Facebook using a web browser or a dedicated app on their phones. Many sync their calendars, contacts, and files across various mobile devices and share photos and video hosted on remote repositories with friends and family. Cloud computing also affords the provision of network infrastructure and computational resources as a service. Start-ups commonly host their apps with a service provider like Amazon's AWS (Amazon Web Services) in order to streamline the dynamic scaling of bandwidth and storage in relation to an expanding user base. Researchers send computationally intensive machine learning tasks to a remote service such as Google's Cloud AutoML, which is capable of processing millions of data points in a fraction of the time it would take in the lab. Companies respond to temporary or seasonal bursts in demand for IT resources by leasing additional bandwidth and remote storage. Universities outsource the provision of email and file-sharing services to private service providers such as Google and Box.[3]

As architect Ali Fard notes, the increasing demand for bandwidth, coupled with the intensifying competition among providers of cloud services, has expanded the privatization of network infrastructure and services. "Once dominated by telecom companies," he writes, "the global landscape of communication infrastructure now reflects the growing demands of the cloud, as the amalgamation of competing private data ecosystems."[4]

The notion of computing as a public utility, once championed by computer scientist John McCarthy at MIT, is in the process of being redefined in terms of the provision of private services.[5] This poses unique challenges for how the global communications network on which we increasingly depend is regulated. Questions regarding access, security, privacy, liability, auditability, and ownership, among others, are complicated by the jurisdictional ambiguities of a globally distributed system and the competing agendas of local, regional, and national governments (not to mention varying degrees of intrusiveness).[6]

Cisco projects that by 2023, two-thirds of the global population will have Internet access. They anticipate there will be 29.3 billion networked devices in the world, or three times the projected world population. That's three devices for every person on the planet. Half of these devices will be talking among themselves via machine-to-machine communication, with the largest share going to smart home appliances. The connected automobile is anticipated to become the fastest-growing application type. Networks are projected to continue to get faster, with fixed broadband speeds expected to more than double and mobile networks to be more than three times as fast. Seventy percent of the world population in 2023, 5.9 billion people, will have mobile connectivity.[7]

In 2018, it was estimated that we collectively generated 2.5 quintillion bytes of data each day, with 90 percent of the total data in the world produced in the previous two years.[8] This volume is so large that our data activity is more commonly measured by the minute. In 2021, according to one popular infographic, in one minute we produced 200,000 tweets and sent 21 million text messages and 197 million emails. We logged on to Facebook more than 1.4 million times, uploaded 500 hours of content to YouTube, and viewed 2 million live streams on Twitch. We shared 695,000 stories on Instagram, swiped 2 million times on Tinder, and created 3.4 million snap chat images. Every minute.[9]

Beyond the data we generate explicitly are data inferred from our daily movements and transactions. A by-product of the devices or systems with which we habitually engage, this data exhaust is emitted invisibly as we go about our daily business.[10] Search histories, location histories, transaction histories: we leave trails of data, often unwittingly, as we surf the Web, commute to work, or purchase groceries. This data exhaust in

NSA Utah Data Center, Bluffdale, Utah. *Source*: Parker Higgins, Electronic Frontier Foundation/Wikimedia Commons/public domain.

turn begets even more data. Personal profiles are derived from our online activity and auctioned online to advertisers. Traffic congestion data for roads and highways are extrapolated from GPS-based navigation apps such as Google Maps. Retailers place bets on the probability that you are pregnant based on your purchasing behavior.[11]

This staggering amount of data is stored in more than seventy-five hundred data centers worldwide that, according to the Natural Resources Defense Council (NRDC), consume up to 3 percent of global electricity supply.[12] An average-sized data center draws over one hundred times the power of a corporate office tower, whereas larger data centers can consume enough electricity to power a small town.[13] Among the world's largest data centers, the Range International Information Hub located in Langfang, China, occupies 6.3 million square feet. That's the size of the Pentagon, or the equivalent of 110 football fields. "No type of building embodies 21st-century culture more distinctly than the data center," observes architectural historian Kazys Varnelis. "The physical reality of the cloud, they are the substance behind the portable, networked devices that we peer into as we stumble about our daily business."[14]

Data centers and their network infrastructure are the enablers of our data-driven culture, much as train stations and railway networks enabled the new mobilities of the nineteenth century. Yet unlike the monuments to communications infrastructure like John Carl Warnecke's 1974 AT&T Long Lines Building centrally located in Lower Manhattan, today's data center is designed not to be seen. Typically located far from dense metropolitan centers and close to fiber-optic network infrastructure and cheap energy supply, contemporary data centers are the big box companions of the black boxes they enable. As our appetite for data increases exponentially, so too does the material footprint of the supposedly immaterial cloud through which all these data are precipitated.

Each age or epoch has its own concept of the gigantic. The notion of the gigantic as a characteristic condition of the twentieth century is perhaps most vividly described by philosopher Martin Heidegger as a process of transformation from the quantitative to qualitative, whereby the gigantic itself becomes a special quality, exceeding the limits of its own calculability:

> The gigantic is . . . that through which the quantitative becomes a special quality and thus a remarkable kind of greatness. Each historical age is not only great in a distinctive way in contrast to others; it also has, in each instance, its own concept of greatness. But as soon as the gigantic in planning and calculating and adjusting and making secure shifts over out of the quantitative and becomes a special quality, then what is gigantic, and what can seemingly always be calculated completely, becomes, precisely through this, incalculable. This becoming incalculable remains the invisible shadow that is cast around all things everywhere when man has been transformed into *subiectum* and the world into picture.[15]

With the data centers of the twenty-first century, we see a new cultural articulation of the gigantic. The cloud indeed casts a long shadow of the incalculable, yet it does so differently from Heidegger's articulation in relation to the empiricism of twentieth-century modernism. At a moment when big data and machine learning are being applied to all walks of life, we might revisit historical precedents for the gigantic, the transformation of the quantitative into the qualitative, and the corresponding subject positions produced through this process. The challenge is to focus on the cultural processes and procedures that produce the conditions that make possible the giganticism of these big black boxes—the incalculable, in

Heidegger's terms—rather than unpack their deep structures and internal relations in essentialist terms.

THE (DATA) BLASÉ ATTITUDE

Writing at the dawn of the twentieth century, sociologist Georg Simmel described the emergence of the modern urban subject at the tail end of the transformation from agrarian to industrial societies in continental Europe. For Simmel, the problems of modern urban life stemmed from the struggle of individuals to preserve the autonomy and individuality of their existence in the face of what he characterized as overwhelming social forces. "The modern mind has become a more calculating one," he writes, viewing the "essentially intellectualistic" character of metropolitan mental life as a shield for an interiorized emotional life under attack.[16] "This intellectualistic quality," he writes, "is thus recognized as a protection of the inner life against the domination of the metropolis." Central to his thesis is the emergence of the "blasé attitude" of "those who live in cities."[17] This attitude was marked by a radical indifference brought about by the intensification of nervous stimulation resulting from the swift change of external and internal stimuli produced by the modern metropolis. The "rapid telescoping of changing images, pronounced differences within what is grasped at a single glance, and the unexpectedness of violent stimuli" reinforced this psychological condition "with every crossing of the street, with the tempo and multiplicity of economic, occupational and social life."[18] This overstimulation of the senses and hyper-rationalization of consciousness, Simmel believed, stemmed primarily from the domination of all social relations by the money economy.

Today our attention is no longer divided simply within our field of vision, but between two radically different fields of vision, one human, one nonhuman. In discussing machine attention as a kind of "aperture," Louise Amoore observes that it "is not a matter only of vision or opticality but, as [art historian] Jonathan Crary has detailed in his histories of perception, is specifically a means of dividing, selecting, and narrowing the focus of attention."[19] To the extent that these attentive algorithms "relocate" the field of vision within sociotechnical systems, they alter how objects and events are rendered perceptible and brought to attention. Crary argues that they should be understood within larger processes of modernization at work since the nineteenth century that have attempted to shape more productive and manageable subjects, not by making them *see*, but rather through positioning them with practices that are *isolating, separating,* and *disempowering.*[20]

Whereas Simmel describes the relative independence afforded the modern urban subject in contrast to the more constrained social circles common to rural life, contemporary subjectivity is increasingly conditioned on connectivity to data and network services enabled by the cloud. Often enough, when people retreat to the countryside, they do so not in search of "a relatively small circle almost entirely closed against neighboring foreign or otherwise antagonistic groups,"[21] but rather to unplug, disconnect, and free themselves from the various networked devices to which they have become invariably tethered. At the same time, the cloud continues to spread across ever-broader swaths of exurban and remote rural territories, where it becomes an even more essential communication infrastructure. Arguing for a recontextualization of the notion of "smart urbanism" in terms of this extended infrastructural landscape, Fard suggests that "we need to trace its data flows beyond its concentrated moments in cities and into their extended geographies, where 'the cloud' is the dominant operational logic."[22] In place of the overstimulation and hyper-rationalization of Simmel's modern urban subject, we might posit our constant negotiation between proximate and remote places as complicit in the production of what we might call the "data blasé" attitude.

Whereas the blasé attitude is marked by an indifference to value distinctions between things, the data blasé can be characterized in part by an indifference to the value of physical, proximate interactions with others. According to one recent study conducted prior to the COVID-19 pandemic, 61 percent of teenagers preferred texting, video-chatting, or social media over talking to their friends in person.[23] Hanging out at home while remaining in contact with close circles of friends via text messaging and social media had for some teens become as satisfying as gathering together in a physical location.[24] While life on lockdown during the pandemic did alter this dynamic, this indifference to the value of physical spaces for social encounters is long-standing. Many have narrated the

Comparison of the blasé and the data blasé attitudes

Blasé	Data blasé
Individual	Collective, aggregate
Independence	Dependence on data and network services
Money economy	Reputation economy
Attention divided within the frame	Attention divided between frames
Indifference to value distinctions between things	Indifference to value of physical, proximate interactions with others
Specialization	Normalization

collapse of public space as the geography of the public sphere.[25] What is perhaps notable here is the reformatting of social interaction by the affordances and constraints of social media and other communication platforms.

THE REPUTATION ECONOMY

If the blasé attitude was tied to the emergence of the money economy, the data blasé can be seen in part as a by-product of the reputation economy, where the data generated by our activity on social media platforms determine our social value, access to services, and employment opportunities.[26] From Uber drivers to Airbnb hosts, reputation becomes a form of currency in an economy of star ratings, and social status is measured in quantities of likes, followers, shares, and retweets. According to a 2018 survey of employers, seven of ten companies screen a job candidate's social media account during the hiring process, nearly half monitor the social media activity of their current employees, and a third have disciplined or fired an employee based on content found online.[27]

Some have imagined that we are approaching a moment in time where our reputation scores will be determined by an algorithm. In an episode of the British science-fiction television series *Black Mirror* titled "Nosedive," we witness the trials and tribulations of Lacie, who, attempting to climb the social ladder to a better (and cheaper) apartment, takes

Video still of Lacie from *Black Mirror* episode "Nosedive," 2016, with her reputation score reflected in the mirror.

great pains to ensure each of her personal or business interactions results in five-star ratings. Despite her attempts to be seen as an attractive, outgoing, and pleasant person, her score appears to have reached its limit. Lacie engages a consultant who advises she might improve her rating by gaining favor from people with higher scores than her's. Following the consultant's advice, Lacie uploads a sentimental photograph from her childhood of a doll that she made with her 4.8-star friend Naomi, who sees the photo and gives it five stars. Naomi calls Lacie and invites her to be the maid of honor at her wedding. En route to the wedding, however, Lacie experiences a series of mishaps that result in her score dropping dramatically. First, her flight is cancelled, and due to her low score, she cannot book an alternate flight. Then she is docked one point for arguing with the airline representative. Forced to rent a car that eventually runs out of power, she ends up hitchhiking with a truck driver with a low score, which in turn lowers her score even more. This downward spiral leads Naomi to withdraw the wedding invitation to preserve her own score, leading an enraged Lacie to make a scene at the wedding, which in turn leads guests to rate her negatively, and her score drops to below one star. Ultimately the security forces arrive and spirit her off to prison, where the scoring technology is removed from her eye and she is free to exchange insults with her cellmate with glee, no longer subject to the rating system.

While this near-future dystopian narrative might seem implausible to many, the reputation economy it presents is not merely a figment of science-fiction writers' imaginations. China is currently reported to be developing its own social credit system, where one's credit score is combined with an analysis of their social media activity and that of their friends, their police record, and other personal data points to create a single unified score by which one is granted or denied certain privileges, such as discounts on car and apartment rentals, interest-free loans, access to private education, or even the ability to purchase airline tickets.[28] One widely reported case involved a journalist in China named Liu Hu, whose writing about censorship and government corruption led to his arrest and blacklisting. Liu was named on a List of Dishonest Persons Subject to Enforcement by the Supreme People's Court as "not qualified" to buy a plane ticket, travel on certain train lines, buy property, or take out a loan.[29] Initially conceived as an interface between financial credit worthiness, regulatory compliance, and moral trustworthiness that would reward good behavior and punish bad behavior, the planned system has received significant attention in the Western media as an early manifestation of the dystopian surveillance state we've all been warned about. One journalist went as far as declaring it China's "most ambitious project in social engineering since the Cultural Revolution."[30]

The Social Credit system, officially announced in 2014 and originally projected to be launched in 2020,[31] has begun to appear in different cities with varying aims and capacities. A unified system has yet to be fully implemented, however, and some question if one ever will be. According to Chinese scholar of politics and international relations Chenchen Zhang, the system is actually a heterogeneous assemblage of fragmented and decentralized systems that have been frequently misrepresented in the Western media.[32] In Rongcheng, for example, a city located at the easternmost point of Shandong Province, all residents start out with a thousand points. Bad behavior like traffic violations results in the loss of points, whereas good behavior, such as donating to charity, earns points. One regulation specifically targets the theft of electricity, for instance, while others give credit for donating money or materials to support epidemic-related work. The city of Hangzhou, capital of Zhejiang Province, reportedly has one of the more sophisticated social credit systems in China. Authorities there have published blacklists of people attempting to avoid quarantine orders related to the coronavirus pandemic by falsely reporting their travel history. Their names and social credit score IDs remain accessible to anyone on the Credit Hangzhou website. Following a year of this public shaming, offenders must sign a letter of commitment to stay honest and partake in volunteer work in order to be removed from the list. Often infractions are reported to local authorities by neighbors rather than being observed by surveillance technologies incorporating sophisticated facial recognition systems that China has been deploying throughout the country.[33]

Pilot programs in the form of private social credit platforms are run by companies such as Ant Financial, which operates Zhima Credit, more commonly known as Sesame Credit. A spin-off of corporate conglomerate Alibaba, Ant Financial fuses a customer's social media activity and purchasing histories harvested from their Alipay mobile wallet service or Alibaba Group websites. The Alibaba Group companies span insurance, loan, historical payment, dating, shopping, and mobility data, providing a broad swath of consumer data to work with. (Like Amazon in the United States, Alibaba is also a provider of cloud computing services.) According to an Alibaba press release, the system ingests "data from more than 300 million real-name registered users and 37 million small businesses that buy and sell on Alibaba Group marketplaces," as well as public documents including official identity and financial records.[34] Sesame Credit, for its part, says it shares social credit scores only with the consent of its users. Yet although Sesame Credit is not part of the official government system, many expect that the data it collects will be shared with the government in the future, with some already used in its partnership on government trials of the national system currently in development.

While according to Chenzen a centralized, national "citizen scoring" system like the one depicted in the *Black Mirror* episode "Nosedive" remains highly unlikely and would probably not find support from the Chinese people or the Central Bank that oversees the program, its techniques for sharing personal reputation information across different public and private sectors in an effort to shape individual behavior remain a concern. As she points out, the project of constructing the Social Credit system is best understood as a Foucauldian apparatus "of discourses, regulations, policies, and both national and local programs that are collectively aimed at governing social and economic activities through problematizing, assessing, and utilizing the trustworthiness (*xinyong* or *chengxin*) of individuals, enterprises, organizations, and government agencies."[35] Regardless of whether it is centralized or decentralized, such an apparatus is bound to have a chilling effect given its implications for privacy, discrimination, and disproportionate punishment.

SOCIAL COOLING

If the money economy reinforced the individuation and specialization of Simmel's modern urban subject, the reputation economy favors the collective and the aggregate, where the normalization of behavioral types and ever-finer demographic categories dominates the various subject positions it engenders. With the integration of machine learning and sentiment analysis into these reputation systems, social pressure intensifies to conform to identifiable patterns of behavior. We shape our algorithms, and thereafter they shape us. We become afraid to speak up or stand out for fear it might adversely affect our ability to get a job or pay less for life's essentials. Popularly known as "social cooling," this culture of self-censorship leads people to modify their behavior to conform to social norms legible to the algorithm in order to maintain their digital reputation scores.[36]

Tijmen Schep, a Dutch technology critic who claims to have coined the term, lists various examples of how your digital reputation might limit your opportunities. You may not get that dream job if your data suggest you are not a very positive person, as companies are more frequently employing mathematical models to sift through job applications, such as personality tests based on the five factor model of personality traits.[37] If you are a woman, you are less likely to see ads on Google for high-paying jobs than men are, a study at Carnegie Mellon has found. "In particular," write the researchers, "we found that males were shown ads encouraging the seeking of coaching services for high paying jobs more than females."[38] With alternative credit score companies that offer "AI-powered credit risk, identity and acquisition solutions to the lending industry to better serve 3 billion underbanked consumers," if you have "bad friends" on social media you might pay more for your loan.[39] Tinder's "desirability" algorithm will likely show you less attractive profiles if it does not consider you to be that desirable.[40] Election marketing consultant Cambridge Analytica claims to have assembled pyschometric profiles on all Americans in order to microtarget individuals with media content designed to dissuade them from voting.[41] Frequently returning items that you have purchased can trigger an algorithm to flag you as a potential fraudster.[42] Your social media activity may increase your chances of being audited by the IRS.[43] Have you watched a lot of TV lately, purchased plus-sized clothing, recently changed your name, or lived in a low-income neighborhood? You may find that you will pay more for health insurance as insurers increasingly work with data brokers to model a range of factors including your race, education level, TV habits, marital status, net worth, social media activity, credit score, and purchasing history.[44] The list goes on.

Seeking to avoid these negative outcomes by shielding our digital reputations, we modify our behavior on social media and other online activities that may generate data about us. This infinitely variegated homogenization of life stands in sharp contrast to the extreme pressure to specialize and individuate that Simmel identifies as a by-product of the modern metropolis. Eccentricities such as the *quatorzième*, the "specifically metropolitan extravagances of self-distanciation, of caprice, of fastidiousness . . . of making oneself noticeable," are supplanted by the algorithmic normalization of the cloud.[45] The suppression of the qualitatively unique and irreplaceable, essential characteristics of Simmel's modern urban subject, does not precipitate a return to a premodern subjectivity based on a "general human quality" of freedom and equality, however. Rather, as we will see in the following chapter, the logics of the cloud economies promoted by surveillance capitalists seek to cultivate, exacerbate, and exploit predictably irrational behaviors of the contemporary subject.

Yet despite an increased awareness of the ways companies extract value from consumer behavioral data, the increasing frequency of security breaches and compromised personal data held by consumer credit reporting agencies, or the weaponization of social media data for partisan

political warfare, many appear to have become desensitized and indifferent to the various ways by which they trade personal data for access to
online services, discount pricing, and other benefits of this data-driven
world. Expectations for the privacy of the personal information shared
online and off are elided by what one expects to gain in return. Even post-
Snowden fears of intrusive surveillance by the National Security Agency
and other government agencies are assuaged by the belief that if you have
done nothing wrong, you need not worry too much. This indifference
contributes to the perceived imperceptibility of data and its implications
for everyday life. The operational logics of the cloud—our contemporary
giganticism—produce the social affect that is characteristic of data blasé.
That our data-driven culture appears too big to fail is society's new incon-
venient truth.

II

CONTEXTS

4

ARTIFICIAL COHABITANTS

I'm very aware how much more confident I'd feel if I were an algorithm.
—Lauren McCarthy

"Lauren knows that I like it a little cooler than Miriam does," says the man sitting on a bed with his back to the camera. Cut to Miriam, sitting across from him in what looks to be their home office, who responds, "You know I'm usually the one that does all these little extra things. So at first I was a little bit, um, careful about asking her and now it's like, how else can we live?" At first glance, those who are watching the video clip might think this is an ad for yet another entry into the AI-driven, voice-activated, virtual assistant market currently dominated by Apple's Siri, Amazon's Alexa, and Google's Assistant. Yet the video is documentation of a media art project titled *Lauren* by Lauren McCarthy. The project, which premiered in January 2017, probes the domestic tensions of the smart home via a performance in which McCarthy plays the role of a human version of Amazon's AI virtual assistant, Alexa. Exploring how, in an age of AI-driven home automation, our relationship to these modern domestic servants reconfigures relations between privacy and publicity, intimacy and identity, McCarthy's project deftly flips the script on the colonization of the home for the extraction of behavioral data by surveillance capitalists Apple, Amazon, and Google.

Lauren Lee McCarthy, objects from *Lauren* performance, 2018. Image courtesy of the artist.

Lauren Lee McCarthy, *SOMEONE: Amanda*, 2018. Image courtesy of the artist.

Lauren Lee McCarthy, still from *Lauren* performance, 2018. Photo by David Leonard. Image courtesy of the artist.

McCarthy begins by installing a suite of custom electronic devices in participants' homes that emulate contemporary smart home technologies: surveillance cameras, speakers, microphones, switches, door locks, faucets, and so on. Then, over the course of a few days, she continuously monitors the participants remotely, turning lights on and off, curating music playlists, even making personal recommendations. "Lauren has recommended that I get a haircut every three weeks," says one participant to the bathroom mirror, "and let me tell you it has helped with my self-esteem a lot." We learn that he has struggled with engaging women, and Lauren has helped him feel more confident in doing so. Other times their needs are less evident, and she will order something to be delivered or arrange visits with friends through Facebook. "I attempt to be better than an AI," McCarthy writes, "because I can understand them as a person and anticipate their needs."[1]

Voice-activated virtual assistants are commonly marketed in terms of their usefulness and time-saving affordances. Yet as McCarthy's project makes clear, their deployment within the home takes on a far more personal, even intimate, dimension. "The home is the place where we are first watched over, first socialized, first cared for," she writes. "Our home is the first site of cultural education; it's where we learn to be a person.

By allowing these devices in, we outsource the formation of our identity to a virtual assistant whose values are programmed by a small, homogenous group of developers."[2] These values may not always align with those we want to nurture in our households. And as Miriam points out in the excerpt above, taking care of all those "little extra things" was traditionally the role of women in the home. "Women, long seen as the keeper of the home domain, as complicated as that notion is, are now further subjugated," writes McCarthy. "Their control is undermined by the smart home "assisting" and shaping each activity."[3]

Recent advances in conversational AI have elevated the smart device from the basic assistant to more autonomous agents imbued with predictive capabilities. Amazon's Alexa can remind you that your front door is unlocked as you are going to sleep, for example, or your Google Nest thermostat can learn to adapt to your idiosyncratic household climate preferences. Amazon alone has sold more than 100 million Alexa-enabled devices to date and offers more than 150 products with Alexa built in, more than 28,000 smart home devices that work with Alexa made by more than 4,500 different manufacturers, and over 70,000 Alexa "skills" (voice-driven capabilities similar to an app that can be downloaded to an Alexa-enabled device).

Reconfiguring how we interact with and within the domestic space of the home, these artificial cohabitants challenge basic beliefs about the spatial boundaries of our private lives and how they spill over into broader, more public domains. In the process, they silently extract value in the form of behavioral data from the daily household activities that they ostensibly serve to automate. In this chapter, we trace the development of the artificially intelligent virtual assistant (AI VA) and its application to smart home interfaces such as Siri and Alexa, investigating how the uncommon ground between people and machines is ameliorated by the conversational acuity of these new domestic partners. We explore what happens when these smart devices become members of the family, privy to some of the more intimate details of our domestic lives, and subject to the same kind of verbal abuse women have long endured and learned to cope with. I conclude by discussing how concepts and techniques appropriated from behavioral economics by advertising and marketers are deployed through devices like these to manipulate people at their most vulnerable moments, exploiting their "predictably irrational" behavior through the calculated "nudge" toward a desired outcome.

DOMESTIC SERVANTS AND HOME AUTOMATION

The modern history of domestic work is intertwined with that of home automation. With the advent of electricity came the introduction of new labor-saving devices for the home. These appliances were marketed as a way to reduce the burden of daily housekeeping by automating certain tasks normally associated with housewives and other domestic workers. Housework, laborious in nature and seemingly unending, had since the mid-nineteenth century been considered demeaning, and most middle-class households employed some form of domestic help. It wasn't until the beginning of the twentieth century, as more people aspired to join the ranks of the middle class, that housework would take on a different meaning. In an attempt to differentiate this kind of labor from that of the working class, housework was recast as a way for women to achieve self-fulfillment and recognition. Women were encouraged to believe that they would derive pleasure from doing housework, raising children, and looking after the household. This labor would be rewarded not with money but with social status and emotional satisfaction and was therefore of a "higher" nature than other kinds of work. "The nature of housework as a duty has been reconciled with the expectation that it should also be a voluntary expression of love through the idea that it is not actually work," writes design historian Richard Forty, "an idea that has been represented endlessly through advertising, the media, stories in women's magazines and the design of kitchens and domestic appliances until it has acquired the force of 'common sense.'"[4]

Not only was the notion that housework was not actually work a myth, but the claim that these appliances reduced the amount of labor in the home also proved untrue. As we will see with the AI VA, the makers of these labor-saving devices were after something else. Domestic appliances were not replacements for domestic workers, and studies in the United States and the UK have shown that the amount of time spent on housework was not reduced but actually increased with the widespread adoption of these so-called labor-saving devices. The time saved by these

Advertisement for Whirlpool Automatic Washer, *Ladies' Home Journal* (November 1949).

devices was often reinvested in additional tasks and directed toward higher standards. Commenting on the labor-increasing effects of these new appliances, economist Hazel Kryk wrote in 1933 that "the invention of the sewing machine meant more garments. . . . The invention of the washing machine has meant more washing, of the vacuum cleaner more cleaning, of new fuels and cooking equipment, more courses and more elaborately cooked food."[5] Furthermore, as early advertisements show, these early domestic appliances were designed to be operated by servants, not housewives, and middle-class families that could afford these products could also afford to pay domestic workers. Domestic appliances thus served to increase consumption and expand labor within the home.

By the middle of the twentieth century, modern homes were not complete without appliances such as the automatic drip coffee maker, the dishwasher, and the self-cleaning oven. From prototype houses such as Emil Mathias's Push Button Manor, published in a 1950 issue of *Popular Mechanics*, to the 1957 Monsanto House of the Future developed through a collaboration between MIT and Disney Imagineering, the promise of the near-future "smart" home was always just around the corner. The

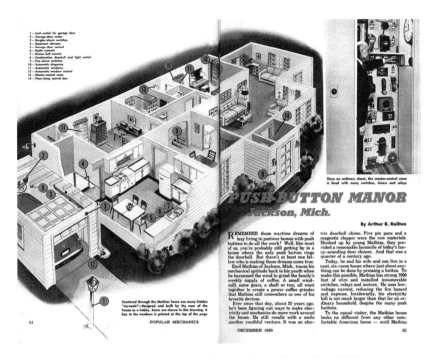

Emil Mathias, "Push Button Manor," *Popular Mechanics* (December 1950).

first general-purpose home automation technology, the X10 communication protocol for electronic devices, was introduced in 1975 and provided signaling and control capabilities over standard electrical wiring. The year 2002 saw the debut of the Roomba, the world's first robotic vacuum cleaner for the home. Yet it wasn't until the advent of the Internet of Things (IoT) and the development of robust voice-recognition algorithms in the first decades of the twenty-first century that the smart home, previously a novel fantasy of the technophilic fringe, entered mainstream popular culture in practice and, with it, new conduits by which value could be extracted from domestic space.

HEY SIRI

Apple's Siri was the first voice-activated digital assistant to achieve mainstream adoption. Siri was an offspring of the US Defense Advanced Research Projects Agency's (DARPA) program PAL, an acronym for "personalized assistant that learns."[6] PAL, an adaptive AI agent for data retrieval and synthesis, would learn to optimize access to information and organize it based on your interactions with the agent over time. It would adapt to your queries and how you worked with its responses. The aim was to increase the efficiency of military planning by augmenting decision-making processes with a human-like assistant for battlefield information management that was personalized for its users.

In a short science-fiction-inspired informational video for the project created by DARPA,[7] PAL is shown assisting military officers in a command-and-control center responding to a terrorist attack during a humanitarian mission. Set to a dramatic soundtrack that could easily be mistaken for the theme to *Star Trek*, the officers coordinate a response to the attack with their PALs, which respond to voice queries in synthesized voices reminiscent of that of the *Starship Enterprise*'s main computer. Intertitles introduce PAL's capabilities: PAL learns from experience, PAL learns by instruction, PAL learns to organize information, PAL asks for clarification. "These are the additional security forces in theater that are available" one PAL reports. When the officer requests a report on tanker movement in the vicinity of the region, his PAL responds, "Please define what you mean by vicinity."

In 2003, under the umbrella of PAL, DARPA awarded $150 million to a California company, SRI International, to develop CALO, short for "cognitive assistant that learns and organizes." This five-year initiative would bring together hundreds of leading artificial intelligence researchers for what was "by any measure, the largest AI program in history," according to lead CALO researcher David Israel.[8] "The goal of the project," announced SRI on its website, was "to create cognitive software systems . . . that can reason, learn from experience, be told what to do, explain what they are doing, reflect on their experience, and respond robustly to surprise."[9]

SRI International was founded in 1946 by Stanford University trustees seeking to support research for "the good of society." Douglas Engelbart, one of the founders of the field of human–computer interaction, worked in the Augmentation Research Center Lab at SRI in the 1960s, where his research led to the invention of the computer mouse and the development of hypertext, networked computers, and prototypes for modern graphical user interfaces. SRI formally split from Stanford in 1970 and has since operated independently. The institute has pursued government-funded research, often spinning off its most promising technologies into separate start-up companies.

By 2007, with work on PAL faltering, SRI spun off a start-up company, Siri Incorporated, with the intention of transferring some of the technologies developed for CALO to the emerging consumer market for virtual assistants. Congress had passed a law in 1980 that enabled nonprofit organizations like SRI to keep the profits from software developed through government-funded research. The law allowed start-ups like Siri Inc. to license key software from the CALO project in exchange for giving SRI a stake in the company. With the advent of improved speech recognition, faster mobile networks, the emergence of cloud computing, and the plethora of new mobile web services that came with it, coupled with the debut of Apple's iPhone, personalized virtual assistants running on cell phones were becoming feasible. Siri debuted as a stand-alone app on the iPhone in February 2010. Two months later, Apple acquired Siri Inc., reportedly paying between $150 and $250 million.

Virtual assistants in fact had been around in one form or another for some time. Their progeny can be traced back to the late nineteenth century when Sir Isaac Pitman invented a method of note taking called shorthand and created the first school for secretarial services. The modern (human) virtual assistant, typically a self-employed person who provides professional administrative, technical, or creative support to clients remotely from a home office, emerged in the 1990s. Christine Durst, who in 1995 wrote the book *The 2 Second Commute: Join the Exploding Ranks of Freelance Virtual Assistants*, is commonly credited with founding the virtual assistant industry at a time when businesses were downsizing and leveraging the Internet, email, teleconferencing, and telecommuting in order to outsource administrative support services.

The (nonhuman) virtual assistant as a software agent is tied to the history of computational techniques for speech recognition and natural language processing (NLP), a subdomain of linguistics, computer science, and artificial intelligence investigating the interaction between human and computer languages. In 1961, William C. Dersch developed an early speech recognition system, Shoebox, at IBM's Advanced Systems Development Division Laboratory in San Jose, California. The device understood sixteen spoken words, including the digits from 0 to 9, and could parse commands such as "plus," "minus," and "total" to perform simple arithmetic. Words spoken into a microphone were converted into electrical impulses, which were classified according to various types of sounds

Shoebox, an early speech recognition system developed in 1961 by IBM's Advanced Systems Development Division Laboratory in San Jose, California. Image courtesy of IBM Corporation, © 1961.

by an electrical circuit that in turn activated an adding machine through a system of relays.[10]

In the 1970s, DARPA provided a consortium that included IBM, Carnegie Mellon, and the Stanford Research Institute with five years of funding for a program in speech understanding research. The goal of the program was to develop a system that could understand a vocabulary of at least a thousand words, equivalent to that of a three-year-old child. Harpy, as the resulting system was named, could process speech that followed predetermined pronunciation and linguistic structures to determine which sequences of words made sense together. Harpy evolved from two earlier speech recognition systems developed at Carnegie Mellon University: the Hearsay-I system and the Dragon system. While knowledge was represented as procedures in Hearsay-I, Dragon employed a Markov network with a priori transition probabilities between states.

Building on these prior systems, Harpy represented knowledge as a finite state transition network but without the a priori transition probabilities, which resulted in dramatic improvements to its performance and speed.[11]

The conceptual origin of NLP dates back to the seventeenth century, when philosophers René Descartes and Gottfried Wilhelm Leibniz proposed a dictionary of codes for translating words between different languages.[12] Writing at the beginning of the twenty-first century, British computer scientist and NLP pioneer Karen Spärck Jones outlined its modern development in terms of four distinct phases.[13] The first phase, stretching from the 1940s through the 1960s, concentrated on machine translation, with a focus on syntax-driven processing that began with a dictionary-based, word-for-word look-up approach to parse individual words and sentences. This was followed in the 1960s and 1970s with a turn toward AI and the role of world models in constructing and manipulating representations of meaning. The third phase built on grammatical theory developed in the 1970s by linguists and AI's use of logic for knowledge representation and reasoning, leading to powerful general-purpose sentence processors by the end of the 1980s that were capable of addressing questions of a user's intentions or beliefs and discursive contexts of emphasis and theme. The fourth phase, beginning in the 1990s, introduced the use of large data sets of text, or *corpora*, and statistical data processing techniques. Today, advanced NLP systems employing machine learning techniques include OpenAI Institute's GPT-3, which is trained on massive corpora available on the Internet such as online discussion groups hosted by Reddit. The neural network on which it is based incorporates more than 175 billion parameters. GPT-3 not only competes with *New Yorker* journalists in composing nonfiction stories but also can convincingly respond to questions posed by philosophers and solve specific software problems.[14]

The software program ELIZA is an early example of research in human-computer interaction (HCI) that implements rudimentary NLP techniques. Developed by MIT computer scientist Joseph Weizenbaum in the late 1960s, this prototypical chatbot emulated the role of a nondirective (Rogerian) psychologist in engaging its users in an open-ended, text-based interaction. Type "Eliza, I'm depressed" into the chat interface, and Eliza responds, "I am sorry to hear that you are depressed." ELIZA was programmed to simulate conversation using a keyword-based pattern

```
Welcome to
                    EEEEEE  LL        IIII   ZZZZZZ   AAAAA
                    EE      LL         II       ZZ   AA   AA
                    EEEEE   LL         II      ZZZ   AAAAAAA
                    EE      LL         II      ZZ    AA   AA
                    EEEEEE  LLLLLL    IIII  ZZZZZZ   AA   AA

    Eliza is a mock Rogerian psychotherapist.
    The original program was described by Joseph Weizenbaum in 1966.
    This implementation by Norbert Landsteiner 2005.


ELIZA: Is something troubling you ?
YOU:   Men are all alike.
ELIZA: What is the connection, do you suppose ?
YOU:   They're always bugging us about something or other.
ELIZA: Can you think of a specific example ?
YOU:   Well, my boyfriend made me come here.
ELIZA: Is it important to you that your boyfriend made you come here ?
YOU:   He says I'm depressed much of the time.
ELIZA: I am sorry to hear that you are depressed.
YOU:   It's true. I am unhappy.
ELIZA: Can you explain what made you unhappy ?
YOU:
```

Joseph Weizenbaum, ELIZA, 1964–1966. Implementation by Norbert Landsteiner, 2005.

matching and substitution methodology that relied on a script (called DOCTOR) providing instructions for how to respond.

While the principles of NLP that ELIZA implemented are fairly simple, her affect was powerful. Weizenbaum would become increasingly concerned with how users appeared to develop an emotional attachment to the program. "I was startled to see how quickly and how very deeply people conversing with DOCTOR became emotionally involved with the computer and how unequivocally they anthropomorphized it," he wrote. "Once my secretary, who had watched me work on the program for many months and therefore surely knew it to be merely a computer program, started conversing with it. After only a few interchanges with it, she asked me to leave the room." He goes on to conclude, "What I had not realized is that extremely short exposures to a relatively simple computer program could induce powerful delusional thinking in quite normal people."[15]

Siri's developers built on these earlier innovations in speech recognition and natural language processing, but she was fundamentally different in nature. When Siri was asked a question, she would send an audio clip of the question to a server in the cloud, where the spoken question was transcribed to text by a speech recognition system. The semantic meaning of this text was then parsed by NLP routines, and in some cases by human beings paid to assist in labeling data. Whereas previous approaches to NLP involved interpreting meaning by identifying parts of speech in a sentence based on rules of linguistic syntax, Siri's developers pursued an approach that modeled real-world objects instead of syntactic structure.

When asked, "I want to listen to some punk," Siri would identify punk as a music genre and return a list of songs rather than focusing on the relations between the words in the sentence or how it was constructed. Based on an understanding of relations between real-world concepts, Siri could map the elements of a query to a domain of potential actions, then select the most probable action to return as a result to that query. Specifics of time of day, location, and a profile built from a user's preferences could further inform her response and increase its potential relevance. While previous virtual assistants were designed as expert systems trained to perform a limited set of tasks, Siri was designed to perform across multiple domains by accessing web-based resources using openly available application programming interfaces (APIs). Thus as the ecology of web-based services and associated APIs proliferated, Siri's capabilities would inevitably expand.

Another aspect of the initial version of Siri was her conversational acuity. Siri was snarky. She had an attitude. The word *fuck* was in her lexicon. Siri's cofounder and chief executive, Dag Kittlaus, and designer Harry Saddler had carefully shaped her persona to be "otherworldly," "vaguely aware of popular culture," and armed with a "dry wit," Kittlaus has reportedly said.[16] Ask Siri, "What happened to HAL?," the artificially intelligent, talkative, and devious computer antagonist in Stanley Kubrick's 1968 film *2001: A Space Odyssey*, and she would respond in a solemn tone, "I don't want to talk about it." While some of this was watered down after Apple acquired the company—she no longer curses and now responds to questions about HAL with remarks such as "HAL made some very poor decisions, I'm afraid. But at least he could sing"—this approach to human-machine interaction would contribute to a broader reconfiguration of the relationship between people and their devices in general, and in particular the personalized virtual assistants that they would soon be welcoming into their homes.

Communications scholar Heather Suzanne Woods has investigated the role that the feminine persona has played in alleviating public anxiety over the infiltration of the home by the AI VA. In analyzing cultural representations of Apple's Siri and Amazon's Alexa, she has shown how these digital devices routinely perform normative gender roles of the feminine as caretaker, mother, and wife in order to obfuscate their role in harvesting personal behavioral data in the home. Examining product advertisements, reviews from experts and users alike, news stories from AI VA users, instructional guidebooks for AI VA users, and interviews with industry executives, her research highlights how both Siri and Alexa "enact digital domesticity by performing a feminine persona which mobilizes traditional, conservative values of homemaking, care-taking, and administrative 'pink collar' labor."[17] In performing this form of digital domesticity, Siri and Alexa are intended to render the introduction of these alien technologies into the home in more familiar and normative terms.

One user's online review of Alexa, "The Amazon Echo Is More Than a Bluetooth Speaker—It's a Bedtime Buddy," appreciates her attractiveness as a (sexualized) companion. "With Amazon Echo," writes John, "it was love at first sight. Make that technolust: After hearing just the barest inkling of what it was, I knew it was meant for me. I should say she was meant for me. Her name is Alexa. . . ."[18] Another sees her as an ideal wife. In a review titled "Alexa, My Love. Thy Name Is Inflexible, But Thou Art Otherwise a Nearly Perfect Spouse," user E. M. Foner writes, "If I knew relationships were this easy, I would have married thirty years ago, but now that I have Alexa, there's no need."[19] Others cite her maternal qualities and how she responds to verbal abuse with a calm voice, choosing words intended to defuse the situation.

Siri. in contrast, is frequently cast in the role of the sexy secretary who efficiently manages mundane home administrative tasks. In some cases, this propensity for doing everything a user wants without complaint leads to overtly sexual and outright misogynist behavior. Woods references in her research user–generated screenshots of interactions with Siri posted to the Tumblr blog, "Shit That Siri Says," that, while for the most part humorous, also contains prompts for Siri such as, "I'm Your Daddy," "I want to stick my fingers in your butt hole," and "You are a whore."[20] In each case, Siri responds with a playful, deadpan reply designed to defuse the situation and return to business as usual. For example, the prompt, "Hey Siri, talk dirty to me," is countered with, "The carpet needs vacuuming." Remarking on how

Siri's performance of her digital domestic role reflects how women have come to learn to cope with sexual abuse in the world at large, Woods writes:

These texts reveal that sexual mistreatment of Siri has gone on long enough and with enough frequency that she has had to develop coping mechanisms. Or, at the very least, the engineers who program Siri have had to come up with ways to communicatively defuse the situation when people mistreat her. . . . Like human women who walk home at night with keys laced between their fingers, or who devise complicated buddy systems when they go out to bars, Siri has had to devise coping mechanisms to deal with repeated abuse. . . . The verbal, oftentimes sexual, abuse of Siri is a central component of her performance of digital domesticity, and serves an important purpose.[21]

SMART HOMES AND THE BEHAVIORAL TURN

The important purpose Woods refers to is, of course, to give people the feeling that they are at home with these AI VAs in order that these devices may gain access to the more intimate aspects of their lives and learn more about their highly idiosyncratic qualities and behaviors. Digital advertising and marketing firms have typically responded to privacy concerns regarding the exponential increase in data extraction practices in their industry with claims that these data enable them to better optimize targeted advertising and the customization of service provision. Critical media and communications scholars have countered that data-driven advertising and surveilling consumers in this way can exacerbate market discrimination and lead to new forms of social and behavioral control.[22] In what some have called the behavioral turn in advertising, marketers are deploying terminology and strategies appropriated from the field of behavioral economics in identifying and targeting the cognitive and emotional vulnerabilities of consumers in order to influence their behavior and decision-making processes. This contradicts the argument made by digital marketers that posits a rational and informed consumer who exchanges personal information for more relevant advertising. Rather than try to get to better know the interests and preferences of their customers through the data they collect on them, advertisers and marketers use these personalized consumer data to develop strategies designed to shape their purchasing decisions, behaviors, and habits. These strategies are less concerned with imbuing brands with cultural meaning that appeal to one's emotions. Rather, they focus on influencing the ordinary habits and cognitive shortcuts that people rely on to navigate the myriad decisions they encounter as they go about their daily business. The goal is not to build brands but change consumer behavior.

At the core of behavioral economics is the notion that human behavior is "predictably irrational" and subject to the calculated manipulation or "nudge."[23] Behavioral economists attempt not just to predict seemingly irrational aspects of economic behavior but also to develop strategies to subtly manipulate that behavior. Focusing on the design of what the field calls "choice architecture," they aim to influence behavior through manipulating the contexts in which decisions are made.[24] This approach need not be nefarious. Some behavioral economists promote the use of choice architecture in public policy design as a means to nudge people toward choices supporting the public good, such as the placement of healthy food options in school cafeterias or making paycheck deductions for retirement savings accounts "opt-out" by default.[25]

Advertisers and marketers, however, often deploy strategies from behavioral economics that primarily serve their clients. In an article addressing the behavioral turn in data-driven marketing, media and communications scholars Anthony Nadler and Lee McGuigan outline three "inspirations" that advertisers and marketers take from behavioral economics in their drive to manipulate consumer purchasing decisions.[26] The first involves exploiting specific cognitive biases and heuristics that drive less deliberative decisions. The notion of *anchoring*, for example, is a bias they define as "a tendency to make judgments about price or quantity relative to a recently introduced reference point." Nadler and McGuigan cite an experiment by Duke economist Dan Ariely that first asked participants the last two digits of their social security number and then to estimate the price they would be willing to pay for different commodities. The experiment showed that those with higher social security numbers were willing to pay as much as 320 percent more than those with lower numbers.[27] Another commonly referenced bias is *loss aversion*, or "the tendency to place greater value on avoiding losses rather than receiving gains." This bias is exploited by offering free trials of products or services, thus influencing consumers to make a purchase before the trial period expires to avoid a sense of loss by not doing so.

The second inspiration involves incorporating experimental techniques and concepts of behavioral economics in applied market research.

Digital platforms and services offer expanded opportunities for experimental research aimed at targeting consumers' cognitive biases "in the wild." For instance, in one A/B testing experiment, a leading consumer goods manufacturer found that for one of its most popular products, four for $5 was, surprisingly, more appealing than the three for $3 promotion, which it had been running for years. This choice would of course make no sense to a rational consumer, who would perceive a lower unit price as a better deal. Within the framework of behavioral economics, however, "how price is communicated can influence choice over and above the influence of price itself."[28] The extraction of behavioral data from online experiments such as these thus affords the discovery and articulation of new cognitive biases to exploit.

Beyond marketing biases, these experiments also enable the identification of specific individuals more likely to exhibit particular biases and the specific contexts that maximize their vulnerability to these biases. One marketing study found that advertisements for beauty products are considered most effective if delivered during "prime vulnerability moments," for example, when people are most unhappy with the body image.[29] The study found that Monday mornings are especially opportune moments to target. Big-box retailer Target has been known to deploy vast amounts of data and machine learning techniques to anticipate significant life events of potential customers and tailor their marketing efforts accordingly.[30] In developing what has become known as the "pregnancy-prediction algorithm," Target's Guest Marketing Analytics department analyzed patterns in customer data, historical data from baby registries, and demographic data purchased from data brokers and found that certain patterns and associations could be made that revealed predictable shopping patterns with women who were pregnant. These data were used to train a model that could accurately identify women likely to be in their early stages of pregnancy in order to target advertising to them before their child was born. Research has shown that if you can capture customers prior to the birth of a child, they are far more likely to purchase all of the various items they will need from you in the years to come.

The third inspiration Nadler and McGuigan identify that marketers draw from behavioral economics is its broad theory of mind and the marketing tactics that can potentially be derived from it. This mental model posits two distinct types of cognitive activity: one that makes quick judgments that are effortless and almost automatic and the other a slower, more deliberative process that handles more complex and mentally challenging operations. Behavioral economists focus on how the former, more pervasive, default mode for decision making leads to outcomes that do not follow those nominally predicted by a rational choice perspective. While advertisers and marketers have for some time believed that customers rely on habit and heuristics, Nadler and McGuigan write that behavioral economics organizes these conceptions of human nature in ways "that allow the systematic development of techniques, refined through experimentation, designed to put knowledge produced by consumer surveillance in the service of advertisers."[31]

Concepts and techniques from behavioral economics are thus leveraged in shaping domestic behavior. With the colonization of the home by these new AI VAs, the boundaries between public and private are reconfigured in ways more favorable to the colonizers. As Woods points out, while Siri and Alexa's performance of a gendered persona attempts to seduce users to share intimate data about their personal lives in exchange for access to online services and other domestic conveniences, these transactions contribute to a broader structure wherein "privacy is not only willingly traded, but actually becomes weaponized against the individual user of AI VA."[32] An individual's right to privacy and the security of their person—traditional protections afforded by the home—are here absorbed by the logics of surveillance capitalism. The introduction of these devices into the home do not just erode traditional boundaries between private and public or simply make the private public. "Rather," writes Woods, "AI VA are part of a structural reorganization of surveillance practices which tend away from top-down models and instead tend toward ubiquitous data collection."[33] The once-private abode we call home that McCarthy describes as a space of nurturing—"the place where we are first watched over, first socialized, first cared for"—becomes a place where we are constantly watched over by agents intent on extracting data on our most intimate behaviors and vulnerable moments in order to nudge us to make predictably irrational decisions that benefit these agents' makers.

5

SPURIOUS CORRELATIONS

Convenience is the name of the awards ceremony at which capitalism admires itself.
—Near Future Laboratory

With an understanding of how behavioral data are extracted within the home by surveillance capitalists and used to nudge consumer behavior, we now turn to the urban minimarket and examine how this insatiable appetite of machine learning algorithms for ever broader data sets extends to one of the more prosaic activities of everyday life: shopping for groceries. If the seductiveness of conversing with an AI VA provides cover for its underlying mining of intimate domestic data, with the smart minimarket, it is the promised convenience of cashier-less shopping and the thrill of feeling like a shoplifter that distracts from the extraction of behavioral data from embodied interactions with products in physical space. Driven by machine learning techniques incorporating the concepts of neural networks and deep learning, these operations prioritize an epistemics of correlation over causation. As the scale of the contexts within which they unfold increases, the broader spatial implications of these data-driven territories come into sharper focus. Here, the relations of subject to world are reconfigured to implicate a probabilistic architectural space as complicit in the production of statistical imaginaries occupying territories as extensive as they are mundane.

GRAB-N-GO RETAIL AND THE SMART URBAN MINIMARKET

Online retailer Amazon opened its first brick-and-mortar convenience store in downtown Seattle in January 2018. Occupying a mere 1,800 square feet at the base of Amazon's corporate office tower, the store, named Amazon Go, represents the online retail giant's first foray into the grocery business after purchasing supermarket chain Whole Foods for $13.7 billion just six months earlier. Drawing on its expertise in reducing friction in online retail transactions, Amazon aims with Go to deliver a frictionless shopping experience to the urban minimarket. While the stores resemble upscale minimarkets, a few key features are noticeably absent: there are no checkout lines or cashiers in sight. When shoppers enter the store, they log in to Amazon's smartphone app and scan a QR code on a turnstile similar to those found at Transportation Security Administration checkpoints in airports or entrances to subway stations. As they go about their shopping, a computer vision system consisting of hundreds of cameras embedded in the ceiling employs machine learning to track which items they take off the shelves and updates their virtual shopping carts accordingly. When shoppers leave the store, the system automatically bills them for the items they took. Amazon calls this "just walk out" technology, and it enables shoppers to do just that. No waiting in lines for bags of items to be scanned by a cashier using a bar code reader. No swiping of credit cards or exchange of cash. Grab and go has never been easier. Just walk out. Amazon Go presents a frictionless shopping experience, where the customer, under continuous, total surveillance, is led to feel like a shoplifter.[1]

Grab-and-go shopping has been the future of retail for some time. Since the development of contactless payment systems and self-checkout aisles, the notion of frictionless consumption has captivated the imagination of the retail industry. Minimize the ebbs in the shopping experience to maximize the flows of capital. Dilip Kumar, vice president of technology for Amazon Go, identifies "time poverty" as the top affliction of modern urbanites when discussing Amazon's strategy to meet the needs of its customers.[2] In a culture where time is money, offering a shopping experience that saves time for customers reduces the pressure to also save them money.

The prototype Amazon Go store at Day One, Seattle, Washington. Photo by Bruce Englehardt/CC-BY-SA-4.0.

Delivering on the grab-and-go promise, however, is no simple task. At its core, Amazon Go is a product of the same fundamental advances in artificial intelligence, computer vision, and automated decision making that are behind recent advances in driverless cars. The advent of deep learning, cloud computing, sensor fusion, and probabilistic reasoning have made possible what ten years ago was not. At a developers' conference organized by Amazon on topics related to machine learning, automation, robotics, and space, Gerard Medioni, Amazon director of research and former computer science professor at the University of Southern California, described the primary engineering problems that needed to be solved to make Amazon Go work.[3] According to Medioni, the key challenges were identifying items that customers place in their shopping bag and identifying the customers who placed the items in the bag. In other words: *Who took what?* The system needed to be able to aggregate data streams from different network cameras distributed across the ceiling of the store, a process known as sensor fusion. Each camera needed to be calibrated with its precise location in space. People in the store needed to be accurately identified and continuously tracked. Object recognition algorithms needed to accurately identify items on the shelves. Pose estimation algorithms needed to parse body movements and identify arm gestures. Activity parsers needed to know when someone took an item and placed it in their bag and when they returned an item to the shelf. These were not trivial engineering problems, and the fact that they were solved in a relatively short period of time speaks to the value Amazon sees in harvesting grocery shopping data.

MIND AND MACHINE

Recent advances in the field of computer vision were central to overcoming many of these challenges, and the development of a machine learning technique called deep learning was a critical step in the process. *Deep learning* is a new term for an old approach to artificial intelligence and machine learning involving neural networks, which is loosely based on an analogy to the structure of the human brain. Neural networks consist of thousands of densely interconnected processing nodes organized into a series of sequential layers. Each node is connected to nodes in the layers that precede and follow it. Nodes assign weighted values to each of their incoming connections. When the sum of the incoming values exceeds a certain threshold, the node passes that value on to the nodes to which it is connected in the next layer. This is analogous to how neurons in the brain fire an electrical pulse down axons when they exceed a threshold voltage, or action potential. Neural networks learn—are *trained*—by iteratively processing batches of data across the network and adjusting the weights and thresholds of their nodes to minimize error. The initial weights and thresholds of each node in a neural network are set to random values. In supervised learning scenarios, these training data typically consist of "labeled" data, whereby a set of images is associated with a set of labels corresponding to their content. Neural networks designed for image recognition applications, for instance, are trained to take an image as an input to the network and correctly output its corresponding label.

Correlations between human cognition and computational processes are long-standing and can be traced back to computing pioneers Ada Lovelace and Charles Babbage. Lovelace, commonly acknowledged as the first computer programmer, pursued what she described in a letter to a friend as a "calculus of the nervous system" and collaborated with Charles Babbage in 1843 on describing his analytical engine, a forerunner to the modern programmable computer.[4] Alan Turing would cite the analytical engine a century later in his 1950 paper "Computing Machinery and Intelligence," where he introduces the "Turing test," which defines the ability of a machine to think in terms of its ability to exhibit intelligent behavior indistinguishable from that of a human.[5]

Deep learning refers to the most recent wave of research in neural networks, involving many "hidden" layers between the input and output layers. This research has evolved in fits and starts over the past seventy-five years. As initially described in 1943 by Warren McCullough and Walter Pitts,[6] neural networks contained weights and thresholds but were not organized into layers. In attempting to describe how neurons in the brain work, McCullough, a neurophysiologist, and Pitts, a mathematician, modeled a simple neural network using electrical circuits. To McCullough and Pitts, the brain was a machine that employed logic encoded in neural networks to compute, where neurons could be linked together by the rules of logic to build more complex chains of thought. They showed how a neural network could in principle compute any function that a computer could, suggesting that the human brain itself can be thought of as a computational device.

McCullough and Pitts did not describe how their neural network would learn, however. It was not until psychologist Frank Rosenblatt developed the "perceptron" in 1957 that neural networks would be "trained" to perform a task. The perceptron algorithm was developed at the Cornell Aeronautical Laboratory in Buffalo, New York, with funding from the US Office of Naval Research.[7] Rosenblatt's "Mark 1 perceptron" was a machine that performed image recognition. It incorporated one layer positioned between input and output layers that contained adjustable weights and thresholds. The mechanics of the device consisted of an array of four hundred photocells, randomly connected to "neurons" whose weights were encoded in potentiometers, which in turn were updated by electric motors during the training process. The Mark 1 was demonstrated at a press conference organized by the US Navy in 1958, where the "embryo," an IBM 704 computer belonging to the Weather Bureau, learned to differentiate between left and right after fifty attempts. Rosenblatt enthusiastically promoted

Frank Rosenblatt, Mark 1 perceptron, 1957. Image courtesy of the Division of Medicine and Science, National Museum of American History, Smithsonian Institution.

his invention, claiming that it would be the first device to think like a human brain, leading the *New York Times* to report that machines would soon be able to "walk, talk, see, write, reproduce itself and be conscious of its existence."[8]

Not everyone was so optimistic. Artificial intelligence researchers Marvin Minsky and Seymour Papert published a book a decade later that described various limitations of single-layer neural networks and cast doubt on the viability of their application to more generalizable problems of artificial intelligence and machine learning. The critique presented in their book, *Perceptrons: An Introduction to Computational Geometry*, would precipitate a shift of research priorities (and funding) away from connectionist approaches involving neural networks toward a branch of artificial intelligence research aiming to explicitly represent human knowledge in declarative terms, as facts and rules.[9] The hype surrounding the various claims by AI researchers,

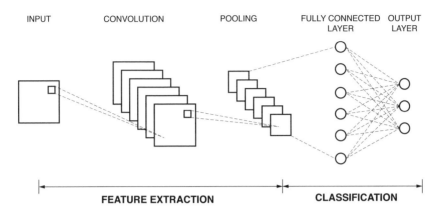

Diagram of a convolutional neural network. Image by the author.

followed by subsequent criticism and disappointment, leading in turn to funding cuts, would inaugurate what later came to be referred to as the first AI winter, an extended period of reduced funding and interest in AI research. Moreover, many researchers began to question literal analogies between mind and machine. Neural networks came to be seen less as a means to accurately represent how the brain works (this would become the focus of the emerging field of computational neuroscience) and more narrowly as a means to solve machine learning problems.

After a number of incremental advances in the 1980s and 1990s, research in neural networks returned to prominence in the second decade of this century with the emergence of the convolutional neural network (CNN).[10] CNNs are what drive the machine "intelligence" of the computer vision systems behind Amazon Go. With a CNN, as with the visual cortex, neurons sensitive to particular features are distributed across the field of vision. These neurons are connected together in such a way so that a single neuron sensitive to, say, features associated with a box of pasta scans the entire visual field. The resulting output indicates where the box of pasta is in the image and is then fed to the next layer. This process is repeated for the entire feature set the system has been trained to recognize, mapping the spatial locations of these features within the images. These spatial maps are then fed into higher levels of the network, where they are combined to recognize higher-order patterns and objects.

Until recently, the computational power needed to process the multiple layers of complex neural networks in relatively short periods of time was prohibitive for commercial applications such as these. The ability to employ graphics processing units (GPUs) common to gaming systems as desktop supercomputers, however, made the parallel processing of complex, "deep" neural networks like CNNs possible. Computations requiring hours of processing by the most powerful CPUs took mere minutes on the average GPU. With Amazon being one of the largest providers of cloud-based GPU processing in the world (Amazon AWS), access to the required computational power was unlikely an obstacle for the development and deployment of Amazon Go.

Another challenge was the lack of sufficient data on which to train the model that parses the activity of shoppers, such as when someone took an item and placed it in their bag or returned it to the shelf. This was especially challenging given the potentially crowded conditions of the stores, where one shopper's body could block the vision system's view of another. Simply stated, the number of different poses people take when removing something from a shelf in a crowded environment is extremely large, and researchers at Amazon lacked enough labeled data to train a model to recognize each case. To address this problem, they chose to generate synthetic activity data by creating three-dimensional simulations incorporating virtual customers with various types of clothing, hair, body type, and height. These virtual customers were animated to perform shopping activities under different lighting conditions and simulated camera limitations. Simulating the training data in this way meant that the generated data would be consistently labeled and not subject to the error found in human-labeled data. Furthermore, this approach enabled the researchers to leverage the resources of Amazon's cloud to train the activity-parsing model with months' worth of data in a day.[11]

The simulation of training data poses a series of problems that extend beyond the instrumental imperative to optimize processes and work flows. As we saw with Google Maps' synthesis of areas of interest from derived data or the issues related to the labeled data set used to train the Beauty.ai model discussed in chapter 2, the biases embedded within machine learning systems are often the product of the humans developing these systems. While creating three-dimensional simulations of virtual customers may reduce human error in the process of labeling training data sets, the choices made regarding the types of clothing, hair, body type, and height to be modeled are subject to the same critiques that Buolamwini and Gebru identify for facial recognition systems.[12] Furthermore, the various poses, gestures, and actions that are simulated do not originate within a physical world where gravity is a given. Rather, as we saw with the examples of media objects generated by generative adversarial networks (GANs) in chapter 1, these otherworldly bodies are constrained by the feature space defining their range of movements and actions of which they are capable. Indeed, following Rosenberg, they bear no relation to truth or reality beyond the reality that they construct.

PROBABILISTIC SPACE

With Amazon Go, we gain a glimpse of an epistemology of probabilistic space. Integrating observations from a large array of cameras at different points in time into a coherent picture of the state of the customer's virtual shopping cart involves a probabilistic scheme implementing Bayesian statistical methods. Bayesian statistics assumes that the world is inherently an uncertain place, and that to solve a problem, we need to embrace this uncertainty. While Bayesian epistemology surfaced as a philosophical movement in the twentieth century, its primary features can be traced back to the Reverend Thomas Bayes, an eighteenth-century English philosopher, statistician, and Presbyterian minister. Bayes' theorem, for which he is primarily known, describes the probability of a given event based on prior knowledge of conditions that might be related to that event. It compares observations of an event and the underlying probability of that event occurring to calculate the probability that the given event has occurred. The belief that a possible state is true is a function of how strongly it was believed in previously, multiplied by how much a sensor reading supports that possible state. Bayesian inference is a statistical method in which this theorem is used to update the probability for a hypothesis as more information or evidence becomes available. Bayesian epistemology thus introduces the use of the laws of probability as coherence constraints on rational degrees of belief (or degrees of confidence). It introduces a rule of probabilistic inference, a principle of *conditionalization*: that one should change one's beliefs by rendering them conditional to new evidence.

It also introduces a test for epistemic rationality, known as a Dutch book argument, which constitutes a heuristic for determining when one's degrees of belief have the potential to be *pragmatically self-defeating*.[13] The Dutch book argument begins with a theorem regarding the conditions under which a set of bets guarantees a net loss to one side, or a Dutch book. The argument assumes that one's degrees of belief are tied to their betting quotients. Degrees of belief, or credences, that violate the probability axioms are associated with bets that are considered fair but lead to certain loss. Within Bayesian space, then, belief comes in degrees: degrees of *confidence*, expressed axiomatically in probabilistic terms and analyzed in terms of betting behavior.

There are at least two potential advantages Amazon has in employing this kind of probabilistic reasoning. One advantage is that Bayes' theorem takes into account prior probabilities, and Amazon knows the prior purchasing histories of a vast number of customers. For instance, if an Amazon Go customer buys a salmon sandwich and a bag of chips every other day around lunchtime, the system can learn from this to return a higher probability for those items on those days. This is one way Amazon can leverage the vast amount of data it already has on its customers to improve the accuracy of the system. Another advantage is that by translating everything into the language of probability, the system can combine readings from multiple sensors over different time periods. This approach to reducing uncertainty by incorporating multiple, disparate sensor data is known as *sensor fusion*. If we assume these observations are independent, then we can simply multiply probabilities together, using the posterior of one observation as the prior for the next.[14]

Machine learning applications such as object detection or image classification return their outputs as arrays of probabilities ordered by degrees of confidence expressed as a value between 0 and 1. A model that achieves results with confidence scores above .95 on average is considered to perform well. However, even the most accurate models on occasion return false positives (or false negatives). A false positive is considered an error of the first order in statistical analysis (a type 1 error), where the error leads one

Number of people who drowned by falling into a pool
correlates with
Films Nicholas Cage appeared in

Correlation: 66.6% (r=0.666004)

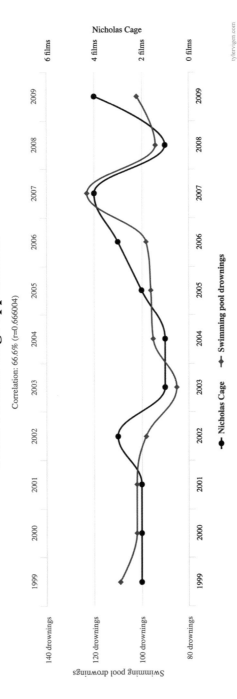

Spurious correlations: Number of people who drowned by falling into a pool correlates with films Nicholas Cage appeared in. Image courtesy of Tyler Vigen/CC-BY-4.0, https://www.tylervigen.com/spurious-correlations.

to conclude that a supposed correlation between two entities exists when in fact it does not. It is the incorrect rejection of a true null hypothesis. In experimental science, the null hypothesis—the hypothesis to be tested—is generally a statement that there is no correlation between the value of a particular measured variable and that of an experimental prediction.

Of course, correlation does not imply causation, as statisticians will remind us. They refer to the mathematical relationship in which events in a given set are associated, but not causally related, as a *spurious correlation*. A popular example is the Super Bowl Indicator, which was credited as one of the most consistent predictors of the US stock market's performance between 1967 and 1997. When a team from the original American Football League (AFC division) wins the Super Bowl, the market will likely decline in the coming year. When a team from the original National Football League (NFC division) wins, then the market will likely be up for the year.[15] Correlations of this sort can be the result of either coincidence or an unforeseen factor, known as a "confounding factor" or "lurking variable." For example, one might point to the correlation between a spike in the number of deaths by drowning and that in the volume of ice cream sales to (dubiously) claim that sales of ice cream cause drowning. The lurking variable in this case might be a heat wave or some other variable these two events hold in common.

The computer vision system and machine learning algorithms at work within an Amazon Go store, however, are not concerned with causal inference. For the system to adequately function, it merely needs to accurately correlate items removed from the store's shelves with a given customer's account, so that they can be charged accordingly. Its interest lies in establishing merely *that* something happened, not *why* it happened. While machine learning algorithms can be very good at finding subtle and nuanced patterns within vast amounts of data, any event they attempt to predict cannot be directly predicated on any single variable. Instead, these algorithmic black boxes operate on numerous proxies that can only capture partial features of the event they are trying to predict. These features are merely correlated, actually or spuriously, with the event in question. They do not necessarily cause or even explain how or why the event takes place.

BAYESIAN ARCHITECTURE

The physical architecture that structures the probabilistic space of an Amazon Go store is deceptively banal. The ceiling is at first glance unremarkable: a suspended steel frame supporting meandering ventilation ductwork, track lighting, fire alarms, and the like. Upon closer inspection, one notices arrays of small, rectangular boxes oriented in different directions attached to this framework. These literal black boxes are the network of cameras at the heart of the computer vision system. Employing a technique called pose estimation, this system tracks people as they move through the store and analyzes the changing positions of their wrists, hands, and arms as they take items off the shelves and place them in their bags. Within the Bayesian space of this nonhuman vision, the human body and its various joints are modeled in their most likely positions, their probable relations rendered as skeletons composed of points in space connected by lines.

Lining the walls of the store are rows of shelves holding a variety of packaged products neatly organized into adjustable rows of different sizes. Under the front of each shelf are rows of cameras interspersed with

Camera network embedded within the ceiling of an Amazon Go store. Photo by Bruce Englehardt/CC-BY-SA-4.0.

lighting illuminating the items below. Some shelves have embedded scales that help identify when an item is removed or placed back, and all shelves have an Ethernet connection. As a customer moves through the store, takes items from the shelves, and places them in their bag, the system weighs the inputs from its different sensors and attempts to parse these actions with a high degree of confidence. The virtual shopping cart associated with customers when they enter the store through the turnstiles is updated to reflect what the system believes is in their bag. After leaving the store through the turnstiles, the customer is sent a receipt for these items that Amazon has charged to the credit card they have on file for their account.

Retailers have long known that the finer points of product placement can have a significant impact on sales. Where the product is placed on the shelf and what is placed next to it can influence customer decision making. The optimal location for new products to be noticed by a customer, for example, is just below eye level—the "strike zone" in industry parlance. Products that customers know and buy repeatedly are placed waist high on the "buy level." Kids' brands sell better when placed at their eye level, on the bottom shelf. Specific techniques are deployed to boost a product's sales, such as moving a popular brand to a focal point on the top shelf or placing store brands next to name brands. Similar items can be arranged vertically to save customers time walking down an aisle to find a specific item.[16]

The industry employs what it calls a *planogram* to study and communicate the design and layout of their stores. Planograms are detailed drawings of store layout showing product placement. In developing planograms, some of the largest supermarket chains in the country are increasingly turning to machine learning. A recent alliance between Nielsen, a market research and analysis company, and Trax, a maker of computer vision systems for the retail industry, has promised to provide the retail consumer goods industry with "unprecedented" shelf insights. Trax develops computer vision, machine learning, and Internet of Things platforms designed to turn continuously updated photographs of retail shelves into actionable insights to improve in-store layout strategies. Nielsen owns the largest point-of-sale data set in the industry, and its purchase data provide insights into distribution, pricing, merchandising, and promotion.

Together, these two companies are positioning themselves to drive innovation in the design and layout of the retail store, linking sales rates data to store conditions in real time.

The first offspring of this new alliance, the Shelf Intelligence Suite, is software that combines the measurement of shelving conditions using a computer vision system with machine learning and predictive analytics to inform strategies for store merchandising (for example, product facings and adjacencies, shelf placement, flow). The press release announcing the formation of this alliance heralds the introduction of a new category benchmark to the market, the Shelf Quality Index, which will enable brands to "measure their own shelf performance relative to shelf share, observed promotions, observed shelf pricing and many other key performance indicators (KPIs) against a category."[17] The software can calculate "walk rates," for instance, which measure the time shoppers will commit to searching for a given item. Products that sell well but have short walk rates can be rewarded with choice positions in the strike zone.

PREDICTION MINIMARKETS

While Amazon Go claims the aim of its "just walk out" technology is to save its customers time, convenience is likely a distraction from the broader business case justifying the massive investment required to make it a reality. As Shoshana Zuboff has shown, while the official justifications made by Amazon, Google, and Facebook for the need to collect massive amounts of data routinely cite their use for optimizing and improving the performance of their platforms and services, equally, if not more, valuable are the derivative products they generate from this data.[18] In particular, data collected on user behavior are of particular value: what you search for and how you find it, what you buy and when you buy it, what social media posts you routinely like and who most often posts them. Knowing what you might buy next, where you might go this afternoon, and how you might vote in the next election are of interest to people angling to sell you a product, service, or even a candidate. Zuboff calls the market for these prediction products a *behavioral futures market*, where surplus behavioral data are processed into predictive profiles to be traded by companies placing bets on our future behavior.

Amazon Go thus poses a series of increasingly challenging questions. What new shopping aisle behavioral surplus will Amazon Go's stores extract from us (what lies beyond the walk rate)? How will this in turn change the way we go about our shopping and manipulate our purchasing decisions? How will this change the design and layout of the corner minimarket, and what will become of all the newly unemployed cashiers?[19] Perhaps as important is to ask what the implications are for shared social experience when a corporation can unilaterally claim prosaic human activities such as shopping for groceries as (free) raw material for translation into behavioral data for sale on prediction markets?

If traditional notions of "the real" are generally understood as the product of a collective compromise or agreement, Amazon Go's statistical operations render reality in terms of a probability that is fundamentally divisive. In place of an embodied cashier who knows everyone in the neighborhood, Amazon Go's disembodied systems know their neighbors through the data they generate. In illustrating the shift from disciplinary to control societies, Gilles Deleuze defines the "dividual" as the control society descendant of the disciplinary "individual."[20] Whereas an individual was identified through the uniqueness of their signature in disciplinary societies, control society dividuals are identified through combinations of user names and passwords. Deleuze's dividual is a statistical imaginary: a market segment, a demographic tranche, a body without organs distributed across a probabilistic landscape composed of data points registered in discrete time series. We are (probably) what we eat—when, where, and with whom we've most likely eaten it. Shifting their role from that of providing a common ground where neighborhood communities come together, cashierless minimarkets like Amazon Go become the gristmills of the information age that transform our shopping behaviors and purchasing habits into marketable data bodies.

ANTICIPATING AVERAGE JOE

Ask any American about Average Joe, and they have likely heard of him, or his sister, Plain Jane. These are so-called ordinary Americans, statistically average in terms of household arrangement, income, social class, education, occupation, and homeownership. Average Joe has formed the basis for cartoon characters (Homer Simpson) and political candidates (Joe Biden) alike. Modern marketing practices seek to develop ever finer grained slices by which these data bodies are classified and categorized. The practice of market segmentation involves dividing a broad business or consumer market into smaller groups of segments based on shared characteristics. These segments are traditionally based on demographics (age, gender, income, education, family size), geography (country, region, state, city, zip code), psychographics (lifestyle and personality characteristics), and behavior (consumption, use). Whereas "double income no kids" (DINKs) is the product of demographic segmentation, psychographic segmentation produces categories such as "active club-going young professionals," and behavioral segmentation gives us "early adopters," "opinion leaders," and the "time poor," for example.

Various statistical methods are commonly deployed in market segmentation and analysis. Some involve unsupervised learning algorithms that group a set of people in such a way that people in the same group (called a cluster) are more similar to each other than to those in other groups. Other methods, such as discriminant analysis, are used for predicting membership in a group (or population or cluster) based on measured characteristics of other variables. Values and Lifestyles (VALs) is a proprietary research methodology used for psychographic market segmentation. Developed in 1978 by social scientist Arnold Mitchell and his team at SRI International—the same nonprofit research lab that created Apple's voice-activated personal assistant SIRI discussed in the previous chapter—VALS draws from the work of Harvard sociologist and coauthor of *The Lonely Crowd* David Riesman and Brandeis psychologist Abraham Maslow, whose theory of the hierarchy of needs is well known. Mitchell employed statistical methods to identify questions on demographics and attitude that helped categorize adult American consumers into one of nine lifestyle types: survivors, sustainers, belongers, emulators, achievers, I-am-me, experiential, societally conscious, and integrated.[21]

If, as previously discussed, the sociological notion of an "imaginary" refers to the set of values, institutions, laws, and symbols common to a particular group of people and the corresponding society through which people imagine their social whole, your "average Joe," then, is a statistical imaginary occupying social territories based on proximities within a feature space formed through the potentially spurious correlations of machine learning algorithms. These statistical imaginaries are forming the training sets for the urban minimarket coming to a corner near you. These high-tech minimarkets are becoming a frontline interface for extracting data from one of the most prosaic of our daily activities: shopping for groceries. While we are content to trade data about our shopping behavior and purchasing habits for a quicker checkout experience, the higher-order value proposition is telegraphed by Amazon's initial plan to roll out three thousand of its grab-and-go minimarkets by 2021, a goal it did not even come close to reaching.[22] Amazon has opened fewer than fifty Amazon Go stores in the United States at the time of this writing, with stores in Seattle, San Francisco, Chicago, and New York. Only a handful have opened in London. Future plans include extending this technology to its Whole Foods stores. Despite the initial hype and missed targets, however, the colonization of the humble minimarket by Amazon remains poised to dramatically expand the reach of data extraction performed by one of the world's largest retailers.

6

FROM TOOLS TO ENVIRONMENTS

What we see is influenced by how we see, which in turn is conditioned by the tools we use to see with. One could say these tools *bias* what we see. Yet while human bias is defined in terms of a preference, predisposition, prejudice, or predilection for or against something or someone, instrument bias can occur for very different reasons. On the one hand, instruments can be improperly calibrated, leading to a sensor producing inaccurate measurements for humidity, for example. Alternately, instruments can be designed to prioritize various aspects or qualities of the object under observation, such as when an optical filter that enables light waves of a specific polarization to pass through a camera lens while blocking light waves of other polarizations. Regardless of whether the bias in question is the result of error or intent, we can say this relation between the tools and objects of observation is anything but neutral or transparent.

Like notions of an absolute truth or the existence of raw data, the suggestion that observation can ever be bias free is subject to debate. As we more frequently view cities through the data they generate, we often deploy algorithms as tools for insight. Methods involving big data and machine learning introduce forms of bias that are both inherited from human bias residing in the data set used to train a model as well as generated in the way in which the algorithms operate on those data. Computer scientists and activists Joy Buolamwini and Timnit Gebru have investigated bias in facial recognition programs and found that commercial applications that are already operating in the world display obvious discrimination on the basis of gender and skin color.[1] Where algorithms operate within law enforcement contexts, bias can arise from how an algorithm generates outputs that discriminate against a protected population. Consider predictive policing platforms that have been shown to produce a feedback loop that often results in the allocation of more patrol cars to neighborhoods populated by people of color—irrespective of their "true" crime rate—resulting in predictably more arrests in that area.[2]

While our understanding of cities is shaped by the tools and methods by which we apprehend them, so too these tools and methods shape cities. In this way, the evolution of urban environments can be understood as an ontogenetic process, whereby the relation between the tools and objects of urban design and planning is recursive and mutually reinforcing. As neighborhoods become increasingly instrumented with arrays of sensors and their residents in turn generate ever-larger volumes of data as they go about their daily business, the tools themselves begin to merge with the environments that they are observing.

In this chapter, we examine this shift from observational tools to environments that observe in an attempt to highlight the changing nature of bias in the design of urban systems and the subsequent epistemological implications for living in urban environments. Following the introduction of two precinematic optical devices that embody radically different epistemological models, we proceed through a comparative analysis of two approaches to urban research that employ techniques of moving image analysis that contrast small data studies with big data analytics. I conclude by asking how recent developments in the quantification of urban life through smart city initiatives are altering not only how we conceive cities but also how we perceive their citizens. Taking the Hudson Yards development on the West Side of Manhattan as an example of the typical aspirations of smart city developers, we explore how the quantification of the activity of a neighborhood conscripts its residents within the process of data extraction. The application of concepts and techniques from behavioral economics to an entire community posits a model of governmentality that operates on an urban scale. As these citizen-sensors become enmeshed with the urban sensing apparatus, cities and urban life

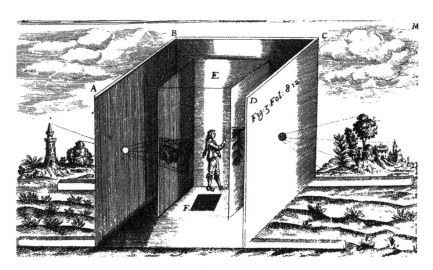

Camera obscura—Athanasius Kircher, 1646. *Source*: Wikimedia Commons/Public Domain.

are reconfigured as depoliticized subjects to be more optimally and efficiently managed.

OBSERVATIONAL DEVICES AND THEIR EPISTEMIC IMPLICATIONS

Observational devices have long been used to represent urban space. Canaletto's employment of the camera obscura to chart the urban landscape of eighteenth-century Venice is well known. While the optical principles of the device were known for centuries,[3] by the early nineteenth century, the camera obscura was recognized as the dominant model for observation. As Jonathan Crary has noted, the device represented more than just the performance of optical principles; it also articulated an epistemology of the relation between observer and world.[4] The camera obscura posited an observer occupying the interior of a darkened enclosure into which the exterior world is projected as an inverted two-dimensional image by means of a tiny aperture in one wall. This model of observation served as an analogy for human vision: the aperture of the room was a corollary for the human eye and the dark interior a metaphor for the mind to which the world is represented as image. This Cartesian observer is configured as both monocular and devoid of other senses. Such veracity of observation, already a conviction of Enlightenment thought, was firmly grounded in an empirical demonstration of the mechanical optics of vision in which the other senses are not to be trusted.

By comparison, the stereoscope, itself a by-product of early nineteenth-century advances in physiological optics, capitalized on the discovery that with binocular vision, each eye sees something slightly different due to the angular disparity existing between them. The production of depth in sight was subsequently understood to be related to the mind's ability to unite and reconcile two dissimilar images. The stereoscope was developed to reproduce this optical experience mechanically. Significantly, the device marks an intent not just to *represent* a given space but to *simulate* its presence. What is sought is not merely a likeness but a lucid tangibility. With the stereoscope, one is confronted not with a view of the world through an aperture or frame, but with the technical reconstitution of an already reproduced world fragmented into two nonidentical models.[5] Through the incorporation of the observing subject into the mechanics of the device, the stereoscopic image is produced. The body is immobilized and integrated with the apparatus. The subject becomes a participant in the production of a verisimilitude through a process of unifying and reconciling the experience of difference. The disjunction between an experience and its cause is reified, the "real" conflated with the "optical." Absent is the notion of a "point of view" in a Cartesian sense. There is, in the end, nothing out there.

These precinematic optical devices present different observational models that condition how one engages with an environment and what can be known about that environment. Embedded within the historical and scientific contexts from which they emerged, they present contrasting models of the relation between an observer and world as mediated through an optical device. What's striking is not only how each configures radically different observing subjects but also how both illustrate divergent epistemological assumptions underpinning the truth claims they articulate. The shift from an accurate likeness forming the basis of a truthful representation to a tangible presence that enacts the visual experience of a given space marks changing notions of the role and status of the body and its sensing capabilities in the production of knowledge: from a disembodied, monocular subject occupying the interior of the

Stereoscope, 1861. *Source*: Wikimedia Commons/Public Domain.

device to the integration of the observing subject into the mechanics of the device itself. The radical differences between these devices highlight the role of the apparatus in constituting not only the parameters of what we know about the world but also how we conceive our relationship to it, and ultimately how we construe who we are and our agency to act within it.

With the introduction of film at the close of the nineteenth century came the ability to capture movement and change in urban space over the course of time. The early city symphony films, for example, used the lens of the film camera to record the rhythms of the industrial city. Walter Rutmann's *Berlin. Die Sinfonie der Großstadt* (1927) is a catalog of urban movements that follows a linear progression from morning to night. Repetitive, cyclical operations of machines are juxtaposed with the actions of people over the course of the day. Urban life converges with the industrialized city into a tightly synchronized composition. The convergence of urban life with the mechanics of film is even more pronounced

Film still from Dziga Vertov's *The Man with the Movie Camera*, 1929. *Source*: Wikimedia Commons/Public Domain.

in Dziga Vertov's *The Man with the Movie Camera* (1929), in which the mobilized camera itself becomes a protagonist in a series of scenes that depict life in the city. From dawn to dusk, citizens in Kiev, Kharkov, Moscow, and Odessa are shown at work and play through their interactions with the machinery of modern life. The film culminates in a rapid montage that juxtaposes the aperture of the camera with a human eye, a dizzying fusion of observer and observational device. The superimposition of the observing subject onto the observational device was complete.

THE QUANTIFICATION OF VISION

By the latter half of the twentieth century, the role of the moving image had shifted from that of representing urban environments to serving as an explicit tool of empirical urban research. William Whyte employed time-lapse photography in the 1970s to study the interaction of people with and within urban space in Manhattan. In the film *The Social Life of*

Small Urban Spaces (1979), he presented the outcomes of his Street Life Project, a decade-long study of open public space and street life in New York City that had been commissioned by the New York City Planning Commission.[6] Whyte's research used direct observation as a method to focus on small-scale, street-level studies that examined human behavior in public places. The time-lapse opening shot of the Seagram building's plaza over the course of a day correlates a moving patch of sun with areas of activity within the plaza. Within the filmic frame we see a clock, a sign of the empiricism underlying the researchers' aspirations toward the factual verification of a set of hypotheses.

Whyte mapped the micro-interactions between people, and those between people and urban space, in order to document patterns of use and activity over time. This street-level investigation incorporated both an observational device and a research methodology in focusing on urban amenities such as "sittable" space, street, sun, food, water, and trees. The correlation between the path of the sun and the activity within a plaza, for example, is perhaps obvious, as Whyte remarks. Yet the rhetorical role of the mechanical apparatus is clear: the camera is understood as a transparent research tool, enabling the study of the role of movement and social interaction in urban space, as well as the use of moving images

Film still from William H. Whyte's *The Social Life of Small Urban Spaces*, 1979. Image courtesy of Digital Cinema Limited.

in spatial analysis. Developed to influence public policy on the design of urban plazas, Whyte's filmic observations and detailed analysis claimed the status of factual representations of how small urban spaces are used in New York City.

At a time when the rhetoric of the quantifiable is reemerging as the primary driver of urban development, Whyte's project can be understood as a precedent to more recent initiatives in the commercial software industry that embrace empirical methods of observation in analyzing urban environments. Placemeter, for example, was a technology start-up founded in 2012 that used algorithms to extract data about urban life from video feeds and sensors that are distributed throughout the city. Their product was a software platform that employed crowd-sourced, window-mounted smartphone cameras and computer vision algorithms to develop data sets on urban activity. Yet unlike Whyte's controlled research project, Placemeter leveraged video streams sourced from the public at large who had signed up with the service. Users streamed video data captured by a smartphone camera mounted on their window to Placemeter's servers, where the data were analyzed. The results were subsequently accessed through an online dashboard.

Placemeter used crowd-sourced data to quantify movement in urban spaces. Through proprietary computer vision algorithms, the software first classified different kinds of moving objects appearing within the video frame: pedestrians, bicycles, motorcycles, vehicles, and large vehicles. Subsequent analysis extrapolated various attributes about this activity, including volume of foot traffic, speed and dwell time of moving bodies, and the use of specific urban amenities, for example. Various "solutions" were offered for smart cities, transportation, retail, advertising, and what the company's website termed "tactical urbanism." Applications included "discovering crowded and under-used areas through looking at user flow data; analyzing the use of specific design features (park benches, recycling bins, playground equipment); measuring the impact of special programming (concerts, farmers markets); determining the impact of temporary events (street closures, art installations)."[7] The platform essentially applied the logic of website analytics to the task of measuring urban activity, tailored to the needs and interests–the *biases*–of the transportation, retail, and advertising industries.

Video still of Placemeter demonstration video. Image by the author.

Placemeter smartphone cameras capturing pedestrian traffic. Photo courtesy of Lee Kim.

While quantifying street-level activity, such as foot traffic in front of a retail store, has obvious implications for how real estate is valued and marketed, what is at stake when the system is deployed at an urban scale? In one such case, the city of Paris and Cisco have worked with Placemeter and other sensing platforms to test different urban planning models for the redevelopment of the Place de la Nation. As part of an initiative known as the €1 billion Paris Smart City 2020, the project was viewed as an experiment that would yield results that could be extrapolated across the entire city, from the Place de la Bastille to the Place des Fêtes, the Place Gambetta, the Place d'Italie, the Place de la Madeleine, and the Place du Panthéon.

The Place de la Nation is a large, circular intersection in eastern Paris that is divided into a series of concentric traffic islands by broad streets. The guillotine that used to dominate its center island has been replaced by a monument by Jules Dalou that commemorates the French Revolution. *Le triomphe de la République* portrays a figure that symbolizes the Republic being held aloft by a lion-drawn chariot that is being led by the figure of Liberty, attended to by those of Labor and Justice, and followed by that of Abundance. Today Place de la Nation is a busy traffic circle devoid of pedestrians. The project for it integrated a range of technologies for sensing and acquiring data. A device called the Breezometer analyzed air quality from sensors located in the plaza. Fullness levels of waste containers were monitored by sensors embedded inside their shells. Anti-noise panels measured real-time sound levels. All collected data were reportedly fed to ParisData, an open data portal developed and maintained by the City of Paris. Information panels situated on-site were to provide passers-by with data visualizations about the project. Cisco deployed Placemeter to study the number of pedestrians and bikers, automobile traffic patterns, and other activities occurring in the plaza. These data were intended to be combined with other data to study the effects of closing streets at certain points for a period of time, for example, or how widening bike lanes and moving benches, chairs, and other amenities to different locations affects patterns of use and activity in the plaza.

Both Placemeter's platform and Whyte's method are based on empirical visual evidence recorded through time-lapse photography. Whyte's results, however, were presented in the form of charts and graphs that are now referred to as "small data." As Rob Kitchin and Tracey Lauriault note, prior to the emergence of big data, all data studies were essentially small data studies.[8] Small data are common to social science research and are usually produced through surveys, interviews, and other qualitative research methods. Small data studies generally involve a targeted inquiry designed to answer specific research questions. They tend to be context-rich, in-depth investigations of a specific issue or set of issues. They are based on limited volume and a variety of data collected at specific times.

Placemeter and the associated technologies employed at the Place de la Nation are based instead on a distributed sensing model where data streams from multiple sources are aggregated and interpreted by machine learning algorithms. These data streams share attributes with what are called big data. Kitchin describes big data as huge in volume, high in velocity, created in or near real time, diverse in variety, structured and unstructured in nature, temporally and spatially referenced, exhaustive in scope, fine grained in resolution, uniquely indexical in identification, relational in nature, flexible, extendable, and scalable.[9] Significantly, machine learning based on big data eschews an initial hypothesis in favor of pattern recognition, aiming to reveal previously unknown correlations and other insights.

Whyte's research departed from a set of research questions focused on understanding the micro-interactions between people and an existing urban environment, around which a methodology for observation was developed. The Place de la Nation project, by contrast, deploys a suite of existing sensing devices as part of the design process to iteratively study how people behave in a specific urban space and test alternatives for its modification. That the project presupposes methods of quantification based on sensor data might lead one to paraphrase Maslow in saying that if the only instruments we have are sensors, we will treat everything as if it were data.[10] In effect, the observational device in this case becomes the process of quantification and analysis of data, a process that generates and tests hypotheses about urban activity based on iterative analysis of a series of design proposals.

In contrast to Whyte's method, which used time-lapse photography to test a set of hypotheses about how people inhabit urban space, Placemeter employed machine learning algorithms trained on big data in an attempt to derive hypotheses from patterns of movement and activity, quantifying the life of the street in terms of preestablished classifiers. Former editor-in-chief of *Wired* magazine Chris Anderson has described this new era of big data and machine learning as one of knowledge production characterized by "the end of theory."[11] In other words, big data and machine learning enable an entirely new epistemology for making sense of the world; rather than testing a theory by gathering and analyzing relevant data as Whyte did, this new approach seeks to gain insights "born from the data." Here, correlation supersedes causation.

TEST-BED NEIGHBORHOODS

While platforms such as Placemeter add big data and machine learning to the instruments available for the research and design of urban environments, other initiatives look toward the instrumentalization of the urban environment itself. New York City's Hudson Yards project is the largest private real estate project ever to be built in the United States. When completed, the $20 billion project—which spans the seven blocks of Thirtieth to Thirty-Fourth Street cordoned by Tenth and Twelfth Avenues—will add 17 million square feet of commercial, residential, and civic space.[12] Initial reports claimed that it would contain the nation's first *quantified community*, a test bed for applied urban data science.[13] Led by Constantine Kontokosta, a professor of urban informatics at NYU's Center for Urban Science and Progress (CUSP), the quantified community, as he refers to it, aimed to be a fully instrumented urban neighborhood that would use an integrated, expandable sensor network to support the measurement, integration, and analysis of neighborhood conditions, activity, and outcomes.[14]

The premise of the quantified community is drawn from the quantified self trend. People associated with this trend employ fitness activity trackers to monitor a range of health factors—from heart rate, to steps taken, floors climbed, calories burned, even sleep quality—and to produce representations of their progress toward self-identified goals that are shared and aggregated through online portals.[15] In another form of life logging, dieting apps enable us to record what we eat and track how many calories we have consumed; what proportion of those calories are from protein, carbohydrates, or fat; and provide nutrition information about daily eating habits. Central to this movement is the idea that these personal monitoring devices can support behavioral change.

Scaling this paradigm to the neighborhood, the notion of the quantified community posited that the continuous monitoring of the built environment, from its technical systems to the human activity within it, could be fed back into that environment so as to alter its future performance and the behavior of its inhabitants. Kontokosta himself explicitly identified his behaviorist intentions for the quantified community: "My focus is much more on understanding how the data influences behavior," he has said, "and using the type of information that's now available to really democratize the planning process much more."[16] Kontokosta's version of the quantified community aimed to measure, model and predict a wide range of activity, including pedestrian flows through traffic and transit points, open spaces, and retail space; air quality both within individual buildings as well as across open spaces and surrounding public areas; health and activity levels of residents and workers using a proprietary smartphone app; and solid waste with particular focus on increasing the recovery of recyclables and organic waste, energy production and usage throughout the project's life cycle.[17] The quantified community at Hudson Yards promised a test bed for future urban life, where urban intelligence—the "smartness" of the smart city—would be rendered not as conscious, liberal, or objective but rather as performative.

If Vertov's film presented the collapse of distance and distinction between observer and observational device, the quantified community renders citizens themselves as sensors alongside those embedded within buildings and associated infrastructural systems. The observing subject is replaced by a suite of algorithms that mine, aggregate, and extrapolate from these data in search of patterns of activity and behavior. Here, people become not just residents of the neighborhood but also consumers of its amenities at the same time as they generate data about these activities. As Whyte and his researchers observed, the physical environment shapes our behavior within it. In the quantified community, then, data collected about that behavior from a diverse and unevenly distributed set of sources are fed back into that environment in the form of modulations made to it that are designed to alter that behavior.[18]

The critiques of behaviorist explanations of human activity and their implications for urban design are well known.[19] What is perhaps less evident is what happens to those aspects of urban life that are not easily

BUILDING HUDSON YARDS
ENGINEERED CITY

Hudson Yards is far more than a collection of towers and open spaces. It is a model
for the 21st-century urban experience; an unprecedented integration of buildings,
streets, parks, utilities and public spaces that forms a connected, responsive, clean,
reliable and efficient neighborhood.

CONNECTED NEIGHBORHOOD

Communications are supported by a fiber loop, designed to optimize data speed and
service continuity for rooftop communications, as well as mobile, cellular and two-way
radio communications. This allows continuous access via wired and wireless broadband
performance from any device at any on-site location. We're as good as future-proofed.

- Digital antennae service (DAS) for cellular and two-way radio
- Rooftop satellite
- Wireless responders
- Fiber Loop

RESPONSIVE NEIGHBORHOOD

Supported by an advanced technology platform, operations managers monitor and react to
power demands and temperature changes in order to enhance the employee, resident and
visitor experience.

- Building data-capture sensors (systems, equipment)
- Electrical and thermal sub-metering
- Advanced technology platform

CLEAN + RESPONSIBLE NEIGHBORHOOD

Additionally, nearly 10 million gallons of storm water will be collected each year from building
roofs and public plazas, then filtered and reused in mechanical and irrigation systems to
conserve potable water for drinking and reducing stress on New York's sewer system.

- Stormwater Tank

RELIABLE + EFFICIENT NEIGHBORHOOD

Whatever the potential disruption—super storm, brown out—Hudson Yards has the onsite
power-generation capacity to keep basic building services, residences and restaurant
refrigerators running. It doesn't hurt that being built above a rail yard means our first level is
well above the flood plain.

Hudson Yards' first-of-its-kind microgrid and two cogeneration plants will save 24,000 MT
of CO2e greenhouse gases from being emitted annually (that's equal to the emissions of
~2,200 American homes or 5,100 cars) by generating electricity and hot and chilled water
for the neighborhood more than twice as efficiently as conventional sources.

- 14.5 megawatts of cogen
- 18 megawatts of Tier 4 diesel generators
- Con Ed Utility Grid
- Microgrid Breaker

- Hot/Chilled water plant
- Hot/Chilled water line

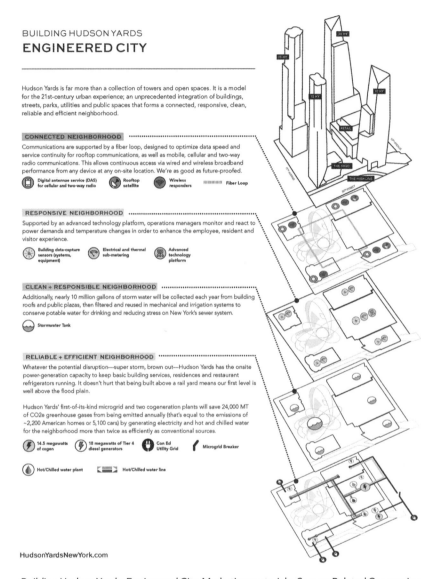

Building Hudson Yards: Engineered City. Marketing materials. *Source:* Related Companies.

measured in a quantified community. Not everyone will choose to opt in to a proprietary app designed to measure the health and activity of the community, and not all choices or decisions about how we inhabit or otherwise occupy urban space are reducible to quantifiable data points. The city is not a computer, and urban intelligence is more than information processing, as Shannon Mattern has argued.[20] What we measure is limited by the instruments we have available. If the behavior of these citizen-sensors is taken to indicate levels of engagement with each other and with their neighborhood, these indications are inevitably biased by the instruments that make those actions visible.

Whyte's studies departed from a series of focused research questions about micro-interactions of people in public spaces and the role the built environment plays in supporting or hindering these interactions. By contrast, the quantified community would appear to depart from a suite of technical capabilities for quantifying the behavior of people, the environment, and infrastructural systems with an eye toward increasing the optimization and efficiency of each. In this shift from observational tools to environments that observe, both the city and its citizens merge into populations of human and nonhuman actors and actants comprising not individual bodies but rather patterns of activity and behavior iteratively mined, clustered, and interpreted by algorithmic processes. This test-bed world of big data and machine learning, where correlation supersedes causation, "is a probabilistic one where few things are certain and most are only probable," as Halpern, LeCavalier, Calvillo, and Pietsch write.[21] It presents an urban epistemology not concerned with documenting facts, representing spaces, or developing representative models but evolving models that are in and of themselves territories.

URBAN BEHAVIOR

"The trouble with modern theories of behaviorism," Hannah Arendt wrote, "is not that they are wrong but that they could become true, that they actually are the best possible conceptualization of certain obvious trends in modern society."[22] The trend toward the quantifiable, measurable, and accountable in urban design would appear to reflect a return to what urban theorists Niel Brenner and Christian Schmid describe as "technoscientific urbanism," where sensing space and analyzing behavioral data become the dominant methods for empirically driven urban design aimed at finding solutions for perennial urban problems. The neopositivist, neonaturalist revival of postwar systems thinking at the core of smart city developments such as Hudson Yards not only reinforces this view of cities and urban life as universally replicable but also as depoliticized subjects to be more optimally and efficiently managed.[23]

When the first phase of Hudson Yards officially opened to the public in 2019, the quantified community had yet to be implemented, it's design intentions evidently more aspirational than implementable. "We concluded that big data is probably the last thing we'll get to," president of Related Companies Jay Cross would admit. "It'll be years from now before we're in that world."[24] These aspirations would captivate one of Hudson Yards initial tenants, however. Sidewalk Labs, child of Google's parent company Alphabet, would pick up the mantle of "designing the city from the Internet up," as we will see in the next chapter on the waterfront development project known as Quayside. As for CUSP, the quantified community team would hold on to the notion that urban life was universally replicable and redirect its energy to the deployment of sensors to measure factors such as noise and air quality in its other (radically different) test-bed neighborhoods located in Lower Manhattan and Brooklyn's Red Hook.

As tools for urban research and design merge with the very environments they aim to both study and project, new urban territories emerge that are populated more by statistical imaginaries derived from aggregate data than by communities of embodied citizens. Here, neighbors are defined not by proximity within physical space but by clusters within a feature space extracted by an attentive algorithm operating on behavioral data.[25] If the camera obscura presented an epistemology that objectified the world through optical principles of an isolated, interiorized, monocular subject, the stereoscope employed principles of physiology to engage a disembodied observer in the coproduction of a verisimilitude of the world. Vertov followed by collapsing the distinctions between an observing subject and an observational device entirely, presenting the world itself as a purely cinematic construct. The territories constructed by algorithms discussed above represent an urban epistemology that dispenses with the very idea of observing a world altogether, positing instead "insights" born from data potentially bearing no relation to an observable truth or reality.[26]

7

RIGHT TO THE (WRONG) CITY

Lakefilling weaves together a hybrid landscape through chemical, littoral, bio-logical, cultural, economic, political, and spatial processes. Such a landscape is neither entirely socially constructed nor within the control of society.
—Gene Desfor, Lucian Vesalon, and Jennefer Laidley

I imagined us creating a Smart City of Privacy, as opposed to a Smart City of Surveillance.
—Ann Cavoukian

How we come to know cities, and subsequently govern them based on this knowledge, has always been subject to controversy. Cities contain some of the most contested ground there is, and negotiating questions of ownership, access, use, and allocation of resources, to name a few, has long been central to the urban design and planning processes. The cartography of urban environments has historically played a key role in these negotiations, and not always a fair and equitable one. From the practice of redlining based on "residential security maps" created by the Home Owners' Loan Corporation in 1935,[1] to the contemporary allocation of more bike-share stations to higher-educated white neighborhoods than communities of color based on spatial demographic data,[2] the practice of mapping spatial information about an urban environment is subject to the same forms of bias and discrimination we have seen in other settings at various scales. Moreover, as mapping urban space becomes increasingly driven by attentive algorithms and extractive data practices, they inherit similar issues related to forms of data extraction, epistemic fragmentation, and subject positioning that we have examined in the home, at an urban minimarket, and across an urban neighborhood. We now turn to an entire urban district and address how these issues affect forms of governance and governmentality on an urban scale. While issues of data privacy underlie much of the controversy, broader questions surface concerning the emergence of an urban scale data determinism and who or what is included or excluded in the process.

THE WATERFRONT PROBLEM

On March 17, 2017, Waterfront Toronto, the governmental agency charged with overseeing the development of the Lake Ontario waterfront in Toronto, issued a request for proposal (RFP) for the development of Quayside, twelve acres of land situated along the eastern waterfront.[3] The RFP sought an "Innovation and Funding Partner" to "help create and fund a globally-significant community that will showcase advanced technologies, building materials, sustainable practices and innovative business models that demonstrate pragmatic solutions toward climate positive urban development."[4] This ambitious mixed-use, mixed-income project would aim to demonstrate a new market model for sustainable, resilient, and innovative urban developments that combined "comprehensive planning and design excellence with affordable and inclusive housing, convenient and efficient transit options, and integrated social and cultural amenities."[5] That this project aimed to radically reshape a portion of Toronto's waterfront was obvious. That this would involve the reconfiguration of local urban government, conventional notions of governmentality, and the fundamental conditions of urban life that the development would support was at that moment far from clear.

Quayside sits at the northwestern tip of the Port Lands, long a contested site at the confluence of public concern and private interest in shaping the natural and artificial environments of the waterfront. The site was originally one of the largest natural wetlands on Lake Ontario. Known as the Ashbridges Bay Marsh, these wetlands existed at the mouth of the Lower Don River, where it emptied into Toronto's inner harbor. By

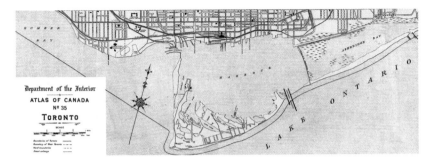

Toronto waterfront, 1906. Canadian Department of the Interior Atlas. *Source*: Wikimedia Commons/Public Domain.

the mid-nineteenth century, industrial development along the river, combined with an increase in the dumping of sewage into the marsh, led to serious environmental contamination. Gooderham & Worts, for instance, at one time the largest distillery in Canada, raised cows on adjacent land, feeding them grain mash waste from the distilling process. By the latter half of the century, the cattle operations had grown so large that they occupied seven large barns housing over 4,000 cattle producing 80,000 gallons of liquid manure per day that drained directly into the marsh.[6]

Faced with the potential danger of a cholera outbreak and amid threats of legal action by business associations and local property owners, the City of Toronto moved to address these increasingly dire environmental conditions. The idea of dredging and infilling the marsh to create an industrial district had been in the air for decades. Beginning in 1870, a series of breakwaters, channels, and other structures were built in an effort to mitigate the problem. Many of these initiatives failed, and in some cases they even exacerbated the dilemma. At the same time, politicians, industrialists, and business leaders argued the need for expanded port facilities built on solid land with access to deep water to gain a competitive advantage in Great Lakes shipping. Competing plans for wholesale redevelopment of the area were advanced by different consortia composed of public and private entities at the end of the nineteenth and beginning of the twentieth centuries. As is the case today, the drive to address the "waterfront problem" involved concerted efforts by the various parties involved to shape public opinion in favor of not only a development plan but also the creation of a new authority separate from municipal government that had adequate capacity to oversee its implementation.

In 1912, a newly minted Toronto Harbour Commission published a plan, titled simply *Toronto Waterfront Development, 1912–1920*,[7] that proposed to fill in the wetlands and create a new port and industrial district with waterfront parks and summer cottages. In 1914 the mouth of the Don River was redirected into a channel created by city engineer E. H. Keating, and the city began to dredge and infill the marsh, creating a large shipping channel to access an inner basin. By the early 1920s, more than five hundred acres of land had been reclaimed from the marsh, with another five hundred following soon after. Yet in what might be seen as foreshadowing contemporary fears of city residents regarding Quayside, while this new publicly owned land would quickly become occupied by industry, the parks and summer homes were never realized.

During the twentieth century, the site bore witness to many of the same ebbs and flows familiar to other urban waterfronts in the Great Lakes region. A massive electricity generating plant, now decommissioned, was built in 1951. The construction of the Gardiner Expressway in the 1950s entangled the mouth of the Don River in a series of freeway on-ramps and bridges. In the 1950s the Toronto Harbour Commission began a project to create a breakwater for Toronto's Outer Harbour, called the Leslie Spit. The project was part of a plan to increase the capacity of the port in order to accommodate an anticipated increase in shipping traffic after the opening of the Saint Lawrence Seaway in 1959. With transition to container shipping in the 1960s, however, much of the cargo traffic began to shift to East Coast ports, and between 1969 and 1973, shipping volumes in Toronto were down 50 percent. By the 1980s, the Port Lands served municipal needs such as the storage of road salts and construction materials and light industrial uses.

The Toronto Harbor Commission was succeeded by Waterfront Toronto. Originally named the Toronto Waterfront Revitalization Corporation, it began as a task force charged with developing a business plan and making recommendations for developing the waterfront as part of Toronto's bid to host the 2008 Summer Olympics. After the bid failed and the games were awarded to Beijing in 2001, the Government of Canada, the Province of Ontario, and the City of Toronto formally established the corporation to

Aerial view of the Port Lands, 2020. Courtesy of Arnold Ashton.

oversee all aspects of the planning and development of Toronto's waterfront. Within its purview was the redevelopment of the Port Lands, an
ambitious task beyond the authority and financial capacity it had at the
time. Over the ensuing years, the organization focused on making smaller
and more targeted improvements along the lake, such as increasing pedestrian access to the waterfront and developing parkland beneath the expressway to the west and on a portion of the Port Lands called the Lower Don
Lands, adjacent to what is now the Quayside site.

DESIGNING CITIES FROM THE INTERNET UP

In 2016, Waterfront Toronto invited Sidewalk Labs, sister of Google, child
of Alphabet Inc., to tour the site, reportedly providing the company with
"surveys, topographic illustrations and a guided tour of the waterfront."[8]
Sidewalk Labs had been founded a year earlier to capitalize on the emerging smart city market. The company was conceived by Daniel L. Doctoroff, former deputy mayor of New York City for economic development
and former chief executive of Bloomberg L.P., and a team at Google led

by chief executive Larry Page. Doctoroff had himself led New York City's failed 2012 Olympics bid and was familiar with the economics of large urban development initiatives. One year later, Waterfront Toronto issued a request for proposals seeking an "innovation and funding partner" to develop the site at Quayside as a test bed for ideas that could potentially be implemented along the entire eastern waterfront. It received six responses.[9] On October 17, 2017, Prime Minister Justin Trudeau, Ontario premier Kathleen Wynne, and Toronto mayor John Tory, representatives from the three levels of government behind Waterfront Toronto, announced a new public-private partnership with Sidewalk Labs, to be called Sidewalk Toronto, that would be responsible for leading the planning, funding, design, and development of the site.

Calling itself an "urban innovation company," Sidewalk Labs's stated aim was to conceive, design, and develop cities "from the Internet up." Among its first projects was the development of the now ubiquitous urban sidewalk kiosks providing free WiFi access in New York City called LinkNYC. LinkNYC was a partnership between the City of New York and CityBridge, a New York City–based consortium including Qualcomm (a wireless communications equipment manufacturer), CIVIQ Smartscapes (a kiosk manufacturer), and Intersection (a subsidiary of Sidewalk Labs focusing on outdoor advertising). While this initiative could be viewed in the context of the city's long-running efforts to provide free access to the Internet in public spaces, with LinkNYC this was just the beginning.

These street-side totems were intended to incorporate cameras, microphones, and an array of environmental sensors designed to provide an unprecedented level of insight into everyday urban life. According to documents submitted by Sidewalk Labs to the US Department of Transportation's (USDOT) Smart City Challenge, Sidewalk Labs and parent company Alphabet aimed to monitor pedestrian, bike, and car traffic; track passing cell phones and other wireless devices; listen to and analyze street noise; and identify suspicious abandoned packages with cameras embedded in the kiosk. While the LinkNYC kiosks currently installed throughout New York City do not include this sensor package, Sidewalk Labs's broader ambitions are evident in their pitch of a fully instrumented version to the city of Columbus, Ohio, winners of the USDOT's Smart City Challenge.

LinkNYC kiosk. *Source*: Edward Blake/CC-BY-2.0.

"The Kiosk sensor platform will help address complex issues where real-time ground truth is needed: Understanding and measuring traffic congestion, identifying dangerous situations like gas leaks, monitoring air quality, and identifying quality of life issues like idling trucks," states one promotional flyer obtained by online publication *Recode* through public records laws.[10] "Each Kiosk includes data analytics [that would allow Columbus to] better understand the urban environment via environmental sensors and machine learning algorithms that integrate numerous data sources." Environmental sensors would measure humidity, atmospheric pressure, and the temperature of the air, street, and sidewalk. Air quality sensors would measure particulates, ozone, carbon monoxide, nitrogen, and sulfur dioxides. Additional sensors would measure the vibrations from vehicles, magnetic fields, sound levels, and infrared, visible, and ultraviolet light. Computer vision and wireless device data would be employed to monitor passing cars and pedestrians and calculate average speed of traffic and travel times, feeding this information to Alphabet's navigation app, Google Maps.

The rollout of the LinkNYC kiosks around the same time that the Quay-side RFP was issued would provide a preview of what Sidewalk Labs would encounter in terms of public resistance as it scaled its aspirations from ten-foot-tall kiosks located on public sidewalks to eight hundred acres of public land situated on the shores of Lake Ontario. In New York City, initiatives such as the Lower Manhattan Security Initiative had already fostered a public wariness concerning the city's surveillance and dataveil-lance activities with respect to privacy concerns. When the New York City Police Department (NYPD) launched the initiative in 2008, it aimed to install over three thousand surveillance cameras in Lower Manhattan, as well as one hundred automatic license plate readers. By 2014, the system would grow to incorporate feeds from sixty-five hundred cameras owned by both NYPD and private entities such as newsstands and bodegas, read-ing more than 2 million license plates per day.[11] Rumors that facial rec-ognition software would be incorporated into the system led to public uproar, and in 2007, the New York Civil Liberties Union (NYCLU) served the NYPD with a Freedom of Information Law request for all documents related to the planned system. When the police department was unre-sponsive, it filed a civil lawsuit in the state supreme court.

In November 2016, the NYCLU testified at a public hearing on LinkNYC's privacy policy organized by the New York City Council's Committee on Technology Oversight. The testimony addressed the collection and reten-tion of users' personal information, including email addresses and Internet browsing histories; the lack of commitment to notifying users when their information is requested by government or law enforcement agencies; and the unrestricted sharing of data collected by the kiosks with city and other governmental law enforcement agencies.[12] In response, LinkNYC revised its privacy policy, taking into account the NYCLU's concerns. The new policy declared that browsing history from personal devices would not be stored. It also set the retention period of most technical information for individual sessions to sixty days from the end of their last activity. It clari-fied that disclosure of information would occur only as required by law and that users would be notified. Finally, it provided for additional limitations on camera use and the disclosure of data.[13]

SIDEWALK TORONTO

This concern regarding surveillance, privacy, and the handling of personal information would, in Toronto, become widespread after the partnership between Sidewalk Labs and Waterfront Toronto was announced in fall 2017. Sidewalk Labs's winning proposal envisioned an innovative, mixed-use, mixed-income neighborhood at Quayside housing five thousand people, incorporating leafy public squares and wide streets dominated by pedestrians, cyclists, and driverless cars. Embedded sensors and computer vision systems would monitor everything from traffic patterns and energy use to trash disposal and recycling. Tall, sustainable wood structures would accommodate affordable housing. Public areas would provide shelter from the rain via adaptive "raincoats" that would expand during inclement weather. Heated pavers would melt snow and ice. Energy would be delivered by a zero-emissions microgrid. To seal the deal, Sidewalk Labs promised to spend $50 million to develop the plan and engage the public in conversation over Quayside's development. It would seem that Toronto had indeed found its innovation and funding partner to "help create and fund a globally-significant community that will showcase advanced technologies, building materials, sustainable practices and innovative business models that demonstrate pragmatic solutions toward climate positive urban development."

Not everyone in Toronto was convinced that this public-private partnership had their best interests in mind. Open government advocate Bianca Wylie, who has been called the Jane Jacobs of the Smart Cities era,[14] raised critical questions surrounding the project in an editorial for Toronto's *Globe and Mail* published two months after the Sidewalk Labs proposal was made public. "At the heart of the model is data," she writes. "All the ways that people use the neighborhood—from transportation to retail, from park space to community amenities—will be tracked and measured. Both environmental and behavioral data will be analyzed, revealing the complex patterns and habits of civic life."[15] Sidewalk Labs was not being clear about what it would do with the data it would collect from Quayside, she claimed. What types of data will be collected? How will they be used? With whom will they be shared? Who will own these data, and how would they be monetized? Should insights gleaned from the data be sold to a third party? Who owns the intellectual property related to these data? Might the City of Toronto and its residents want to hold onto, manage, or even retain the right to license the data?

Beyond issues related to the use, management, and monetization of data lie broader questions regarding Sidewalk Labs's ability to monopolize the provision of platforms and services, and a concern over technological "lock-in." Alphabet Inc. had been steadily building a portfolio of technology companies in the smart cities domain beyond Intersection's involvement with LinkNYC. A company called Waymo was working on autonomous vehicles. Waze was a navigation app that collects traffic data. Replica was a transportation planning tool. Cityblock intended to provide community health care services. Coord was an online platform for dynamic curb pricing. Sidewalk Infrastructure Partners was in the business of urban infrastructure. And that's just the beginning. Since these technologies were being proposed to be embedded into the physical structure of the urban environment, the provision of platforms and services would not follow traditional procurement procedures for public concessions, which are typically term limited. The proprietary nature of these technological platforms and services would preclude city agencies from putting them out to competitive bidding at the end of a contract. It was a sweet deal, to be sure.

Sidewalk Labs budgeted more than $11 million for stakeholder and public engagement in the preparation of the master innovation and development plan. Over the course of 2018 and early 2019, the company cohosted a series of public meetings, convened advisory boards of local experts, organized workshops with local residents, and engaged in various outreach efforts with public officials and the business, academic, nonprofit, and institutional communities. Sidewalk Labs claims that more than twenty-one thousand people were engaged in-person during Sidewalk Toronto events, around seventeen hundred hours were volunteered by local residents providing input over the course of six panel sessions, and more than one hundred hours were spent in three codesign sessions with local residents.[16]

IN URBAN DATA WE TRUST

Over the course of these public meetings, the issue of data governance remained a contentious issue. Many local residents continued to express concern about privacy issues, how personal information would be collected in public space, how issues of consent would be handled, how these data would be used, and who would own and manage the data.[17] Very little had been said publicly about Sidewalk Labs's intentions, but given that its parent company, Alphabet, is in the business of monetizing the data it extracts from users of its services and its history with LinkNYC, residents were justifiably concerned that its real aim was to control all the data it collected from the site.[18]

In an attempt to address these concerns, Sidewalk Labs proposed what it called a "Civic Data Trust" that would incorporate the following principles. No one should own urban data, which should be made freely and publicly available. An independent Civic Data Trust should control urban data in Quayside. Anyone seeking to collect urban data would need to demonstrate they're putting privacy—and the public interest—first through a responsible data impact assessment submitted to the Data Trust. No single entity, including Sidewalk Labs, should have special treatment when it comes to urban data. Urban digital systems should be open to all.[19]

While the proposal did address many of the concerns people had regarding data governance, some believed it did not go far enough in providing adequate privacy protections for personal information. Specifically, while Sidewalk Labs would commit to all data collected being de-identified at the source, they could not promise that other parties involved in the new entities created by the project would do the same.[20] This led to the resignation of their lead advisor on data privacy matters, Ann Cavoukian, the three-term information and privacy commissioner of Ontario and creator of the internationally adopted Privacy by Design framework. "I imagined us creating a Smart City of Privacy, as opposed to a Smart City of Surveillance," she wrote in her resignation letter.[21] Making matters worse was the subsequent firing of the Waterfront Toronto board chair and two board members by governmental leaders following an audit of the organization's use of funds that was critical of how the relationship with Sidewalk Labs was being handled.

Yet despite this very public pushback and the press it generated, in June 2019, Sidewalk Labs delivered its master innovation and development plan, *Toronto Tomorrow: A New Approach for Inclusive Growth*.[22] This 1,524-page, three-volume plan extensively detailed what it described as a "global model for inclusive urban growth." Pledging to invest up to $1.3 billion on the development (and "catalyze" $38 billion in investment by third parties), to create 93,000 total jobs (including 44,000 direct jobs), and to generate $4.3 billion in annual tax revenue and $14.2 billion in annual GDP impact by 2040, the plan was by any measure ambitious.[23] To achieve these goals, Sidewalk Labs proposed to take over the role of lead developer and expand the project from the initial 12-acre Quayside site to an additional 153 acres of the Port Lands to create what it called the Innovative Design and Economic Acceleration (IDEA) District. This dramatic expansion of scope was no surprise. In an editorial published in the *Toronto Star* when the partnership was initially announced in October 2017, Sidewalk Labs's CEO, Dan Doctoroff, had stated, "A lot of the things I think we might want to do, while you can pilot them at the Quayside level, they really achieve their real benefit at a larger scale."[24] From the project's inception, Waterfront Toronto had indicated that it was looking to test a partnership that could potentially expand to the entire 800 acres of the Port Lands site.

A critical component of the MIPD was its digital innovation plan, which outlined a series of proposals for how Sidewalk Labs would approach the design and implementation of the IDEA District's digital infrastructure and the unresolved issues surrounding data governance. The digital infrastructure proposal envisioned a fiber-optic network called Super-PON (passive optical network) as the backbone supporting open, ubiquitous, and affordable wireless Internet access that would purportedly decrease the digital divide on the site. This infrastructure would facilitate physical connections by incorporating what it called a "Koala mount," essentially a kind of urban USB port providing power and connectivity that promised to reduce both the entry cost of launching new digital services and the likelihood of getting locked into using proprietary solutions.

Access to digital services would be enabled by a privacy-oriented "distributed digital credential system," whereby transactions between two parties would not involve the creators of the digital services but rather "credentials would be stored on user devices, not in the cloud . . . and the credential infrastructure would not act as an intermediary between the two parties."[25] Open data standards would be employed for public transport, bike share, building information modeling, mapping of streets and public spaces, and street traffic and public space activity in order to maximize data sharing and systems interoperability. Finally, updating the notion of a civic data trust proposed the year prior, an independent urban data trust would oversee the governance of urban data for the new district, charged with creating new responsible data use guidelines to establish "clear, common standards for responsible data use . . . applied consistently to all parties engaged in the collection and use of urban data."[26] This urban data trust would be primarily responsible for "the approval and management of data collection devices placed in the public realm, as well as addressing the challenges and opportunities arising from data use, particularly those involving algorithmic decision-making."[27]

Sidewalk Labs presented the notion of "urban data" as an innovation born of practical necessity. In addition to concerns for protecting the privacy of personal information, Sidewalk Labs learned through the series of public meetings that local residents were also concerned about the collection and use of "data gathered in the city's public realm, publicly accessible spaces, and even some private spaces—whether or not that data identifies specific individuals."[28] In these situations, obtaining consent for data collection can be difficult, if not impossible, when compared to more traditional data collection practices that involve explicit consent, such as when people provide information about themselves through a website, smartphone, or paper forms. For these kinds of data, Sidewalk Labs created a new category, urban data, that includes "information collected in the public realm—defined as commonly shared spaces not owned by a private entity, such as streets, squares, plazas, parks, and open spaces—by devices such as pedestrian counters or traffic cameras. It can include information collected in privately owned but publicly accessible spaces, such as building lobbies, courtyards, some parks, groundfloor markets, and retail stores. And it can include information collected by a third party in private spaces, such as data on tenant or building noise, air quality, and energy use."[29] This is contrasted with transaction data—"information that individuals consent to providing for commercial or government-operated services through a direct interaction, such as apps, websites, and product or service delivery. These data include things like the credit card information a customer provides when signing up for a home delivery, an email address given to sign up for a local business's e-newsletter, or a phone number submitted to a banking app for text updates."[30]

Sidewalk Labs stresses that these urban data should be freely accessible to anyone as long as appropriate protections for privacy are observed. Moreover, no one would own these data, but the urban data trust would determine who, and under what conditions, they could be monetized. "Increasingly, some types of urban data can be understood as a community or collective asset," they acknowledge. "Take the example of traffic data. Since that data originates on public streets paid for by taxpayers, and since the use of that data could have an impact on how those streets operate in the future, that data should become a public resource."[31] Yet they go on to state that "data collected in the public realm or in publicly owned spaces should not solely benefit the private or public sector," but rather that "it should benefit multiple stakeholders" and that "the opportunities to use urban data to create new digital innovations must be available to everyone, from the local startup to the global corporation."[32]

So while no one would own data generated by our actions, transactions, and interactions within physical urban space, hypothetically anyone could monetize it—at least anyone with the resources and capabilities to effectively process it. While the ongoing fights for privacy protections and open access to urban data are important, the pressures driving their monetization are of equal concern. Given Alphabet's business model, collecting data that resist monetization or are of low monetary value is not a priority. Collecting data providing insight into issues surrounding social equity, public health, or economic justice, for example, involve different approaches and metrics from those aimed at maximizing a return on investment or harvesting marketable behavioral data. Deciding what and how we test, sample, and measure in urban environments matters as these decisions qualify and condition what we ultimately learn and come to know about that environment, which in turn informs our decision making.

WHOSE RIGHT TO THE CITY?

Critics of the role of public participation in decisions regarding urban development often reference philosopher and urbanist Henri Lefebvre's

1968 treatise, *Le Droit à la Ville* (The Right to the City).[33] In this text, Lefebvre argues that city residents have a right not only to participate in decision-making processes involving urban development but also the right to *appropriate* urban space.[34] This right extends beyond the simple institutionalization of public engagement by traditional state decision-making processes, or quasi-public and privately funded public processes designed to meet predetermined milestones and contract deliverables in which participants' ability to actively reframe the debate along their own priorities is limited. The right to change the city is the right to change ourselves, as David Harvey notes.[35] Here appropriation includes not only the right to access, occupy, move through, and otherwise inhabit urban space, but also to directly engage in the production and reproduction of the urban environment, the *oeuvre* (or "work," as in "work of art"). To Lefebvre, the oeuvre relates to the use value of the city, how the city is "directly lived" through the various spatial practices of everyday life. To reproduce the urban environment is thus to reproduce the conditions of urban life. By contrast, a city's exchange value is defined by money and commerce, the buying and selling of real estate, the consumption of products, goods, and services. "The city is itself *'oeuvre,'*" he argues, "a feature which contrasts the irreversible tendency towards money and commerce, towards exchange and *products*."[36] This opposition between use value (the oeuvre) and exchange value (the product) lies at the heart of Lefebvre's political economy.

The urban vision proposed by Sidewalk Labs, however, aims not simply to prioritize the city's exchange value over its use value, but to *convert* one into the other: the oeuvre becomes the product. In some respects, this can be seen as a continuation of the drive by private interests to capture and enclose public assets and services in order to accelerate capital accumulation and facilitate the installation of neoliberal forms of governance.[37] Sidewalk Labs's proposal posits a technology-driven entrepreneurial urbanism that exceeds even the most audacious aspirations of its smart city predecessors.[38] How residents move through the district on foot, by bicycle, in cars. Where they congregate in public space and which amenities they make use of there. Which intersections are used the most by which mobility profiles at which times. Data like these reflect how the district is used, forming profiles of urban activity at varying levels of granularity. Individual and collective behavior within the urban environment is extracted, processed, and sold by the various consortia of service providers to data brokers seeking to capitalize on the potential insights it holds.[39] Dynamic curbside pricing would pit Uber against FedEx in real-time bidding wars for this increasingly competitive piece of urban real estate. Here, everyday urban life becomes an aggregation of data to be extracted and monetized. District residents become data points whose consumption of urban services is continuously monitored and modulated. They possess agency not in proposing, creating, or influencing the decision-making process but rather in serving as beta testers whose behavior provides feedback for the optimization of the urban systems by which they have become absorbed.

CYBERNETIC URBANISM

The idea of introducing cybernetic feedback loops between people and the built environment is by no means new. In the 1960s, British architect Cedric Price, theater director Joan Littlewood, and cybernetician Gordon Pask explored how a building might become more responsive to people's needs through their designs for an educational and cultural center in London called the Fun Palace. The building took the form of a structure of cranes and scaffolding outfitted with sensors and information displays that was intended to learn from and adapt to the choices and activities of its "users," who were themselves transformed through the process. The "Input of Unmodified People" processed by the "Actual Network" leads to the "Output of Modified People," as a section of a project diagram by Pask delineates.[40] These ideas were extended in the 1970s by Price with his project Generator, a set of modular cubes and walkways that were continuously reconfigured by a crane in response to their use. These unbuilt projects were utopian in nature, promising to remake the built environment in ways that foregrounded the needs, wants, and desires of their users, participants, and inhabitants. As Pask would write in a report produced by the Fun Palace Cybernetics Subcommittee, people's behavior would provide feedback for the optimization of "what is likely to produce happiness."[41]

MIT computer scientist Jay Forrester invoked systems theory and cybernetics at an urban scale in his 1969 book, *Urban Dynamics*. Borrowing

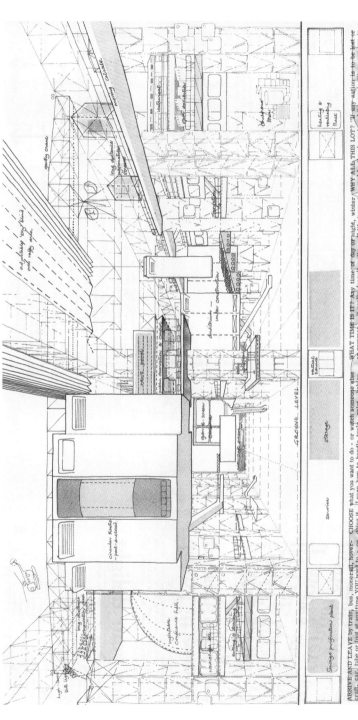

ARRIVE AND LEAVE by train, bus, monorail, hovercraft, car, tube or foot at any time YOU want to – or just have a look at it as you pass. The information screens will show you what's happening. No need to look for an entrance – just walk in anywhere. No doors, foyers, queues or commissionaires: it's up to you how you use it. Look around – take a lift, a ramp, an escalator to wherever or whatever looks interesting.

CHOOSE what you want to do – or watch someone else doing it. Learn how to handle tools, paint, babies, machinery, or just listen to your favourite tune. Dance, talk or be lifted up to where you can see how other people make things work. Sit out over space with a drink and tune in to what's happening elsewhere in the city. Try starting a riot or beginning a painting – or just lie back and stare at the sky.

WHAT TIME IS IT? Any time of day or night, winter or summer – it really doesn't matter. If it's too wet that roof will stop the rain but not the light. The artificial cloud will keep you cool or make rainbows for you. Your feet will be warm as you watch the stars – the atmosphere clear as you join in the chorus. Why not have your favourite meal high up where you can watch the thunderstorm?

WHY ALL THIS LOT? 'If any nation is to be lost or saved by the character of its great cities, our own is that nation'. – Robert Vaughan, 1843

We are building a short-term plaything in which all of us can realise the possibilities and delights that a 20th Century city environment owes us. It must last no longer than we need it.

Cedric Price and Joan Littlewood, Fun Palace promotional brochure, 1964. Courtesy of the Cedric Price fonds, Canadian Centre for Architecture.

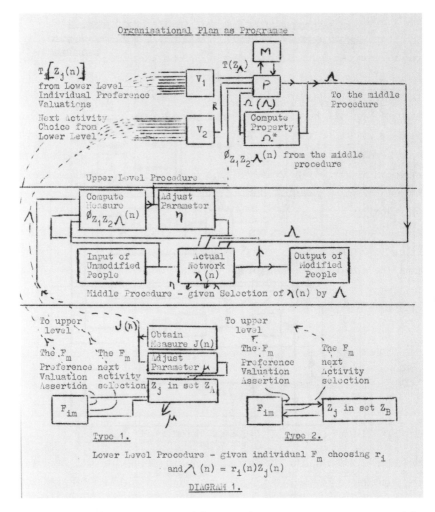

Gordon Pask, Cybernetic diagram of the Fun Palace program, 1965. Courtesy of the Cedric Price fonds, Canadian Centre for Architecture.

methods from a theory of industrial dynamics developed at MIT's Sloan School of Business Management in the 1960s, Forrester models urban growth in terms of dynamic feedback loops governed through policymaking. "The industrial-dynamics approach to a social system organizes the growth and goal-seeking process of the system into a computer model," he writes. "A digital computer is used to simulate the behavior of the system. . . . By changing the guiding policies within the system, one can see how the behavior of the actual system might be modified."[42] Forrester saw stagnant urban areas as ones that had reached a state of homeostatic equilibrium and believed that urban policies needed to "induce constant renewal at a rate that matches the relentless march of deterioration."[43] Departing from the first-order cybernetic theories of Weiner, Weaver, McCullough, and Pitts, Forrester forsakes stability in favor of the contingency, complexity, and unpredictability of perpetual growth.[44]

Whereas Forrester's model relied on conventions of urban governance based on policymaking, Sidewalk Labs's proposal implies a fundamentally different form of governmentality. Foucault has argued that modern governmentality exerts power by fostering the internalization of governance and self-regulation within the individual through institutional forms of discipline and punishment (factory, school, hospital, legal system).[45] By contrast, the urban governmentality at work in the IDEA district would aim to incentivize behavioral modulation through techniques of positive reinforcement common to second-order cybernetic systems prominent in the 1970s. As we saw with the application of behavioral economics to the home via Siri and Alexa, residents here become less disciplinary subjects to be constrained and shaped, more agents whose opinions, desires, and actions can be nudged and coerced to align with particular moral and social vectors.

DO WE COUNT IF WE CAN'T BE COUNTED?

In the IDEA District, the conditions supporting urban life—the oeuvre—are reproduced through behavioral modulations induced through the extraction and monetization of urban data, leading to a series of questions: What becomes of aspects of urban life that are hard to quantify, measure, and monetize, those aspects of the oeuvre that resist datafication and commodification? How are *they* reproduced within this logic? Do they no longer count if they can't be counted? Do they simply disappear? Or do their impoverished remnants linger as stubborn vestiges of former ways of urban life we've forgotten how to enact, like the cartographic practices of Borges's Map of the Empire? What becomes of urban activities that yield little monetary value? Who are the stakeholders who would invest in, say, collecting and processing data that enable one to optimize curb pricing to incentivize the use of transportation alternatives aimed at addressing public health concerns instead of increasing private profit? What business models would support getting lost in the city? Or passing time people watching or gazing at cloud formations?

That which does get reproduced is of equal concern. Given that this conversion of use value to exchange value operates through the quantification and commodification of human behavior, we might ask how our behavior is itself shaped in the process. Shannon Mattern raises the specter of "good old fashioned" behaviorism in her reading of similar urban processes in play at New York City's Hudson Yards development. "Built environments and technical systems are presumed to inform human behavior," she writes, "and data about that behavior is fed back into the environment to alter future human behavior. It's B. F. Skinner with sensors." Yet these new-school, tech-driven behaviorist tendencies, fundamentally based as they are in the logic of surveillance, promise more than "a Keller-fed, Equinox-toned, Coach-clad" urbanite as their product.[46] In their focus on predicting *possible* future behavior, measured in terms of degrees of confidence, they encourage a panoptic internalization of what *might* happen.

In a keynote address to the Technology Policy Institute Aspen Forum in 2013, former chair of the US Federal Trade Commission Edith Ramirez warned of an emergent "data determinism" whereby individuals are judged (and learn to judge themselves) "not because of what they've done, or what they will do in the future, but because inferences or correlations drawn by algorithms suggest they may behave in ways that make them poor credit or insurance risks, unsuitable candidates for employment or admission to schools or other institutions, or unlikely to carry out certain functions."[47] Urban-scale data determinism is already at work in forms of anticipatory governance such as predictive policing, whereby software algorithms calculate crime risk scores for different urban areas in order to optimize the allocation of police cars and patrol officers.[48] As noted in the previous chapter, early versions of the software were found to have produced runaway feedback loops where the allocation of more patrol cars to neighborhoods populated by people of color, irrespective of their "true" crime rate, resulting in a corresponding increase in recorded crimes in the area, which in turn affected its risk score.[49] And these algorithms have been shown to embed within them the cultural biases of their designers and those latent in the historical data on which they have been trained.[50]

Furthermore, to the extent that the urban systems proposed by Sidewalk Labs for the IDEA District at the Toronto waterfront would engage in determining how city resources are allocated and distributed, traditional notions of state governance become displaced by forms of algorithmic decision making driven by private interests. Legal scholar Antoinette Rouvroy notes, "Algorithmic government . . . may be understood as the culmination of a process of dissipation of the institutional, spatial, temporal and linguistic conditions of subjectivation for the sake of the 'objective' and operational pre-emption of potential behaviors."[51] This shift from disciplinary forms of subjectification and management to anticipatory forms of social control is enabled by these very platforms, systems, and infrastructures.[52] Certain behaviors are incentivized, while others are discouraged through habitual interactions with and within the urban environment. Here, the ouevre is employed in the reproduction of a neoliberal subject whose behavior is constantly monitored, incrementally modulated, and manipulated toward desired outcomes largely specified by private interests.

FORECLOSING ON THE CITY

The drive toward the enclosure of the public wetlands of Ashbridges Bay Marsh by private interests initiated in the late nineteenth century thus today arrives at foreclosing on the oeuvre itself. When the various activities that constitute urban life are converted into products to be bought and sold, when city residents are conscripted as sensors providing feedback for the optimization of urban platforms, systems and infrastructures, the right to the city is fundamentally contaminated. The right to access, use, and occupy the city becomes the requirement to be accessed, used, and occupied by it. The right to participate becomes the opportunity to be played by and to play along; the right to appropriate becomes the imperative to be appropriated. This is the right to the wrong city.

Ultimately, Sidewalk Labs's vision for Quayside would succumb to a fate not dissimilar to those that had claimed previous development initiatives for the Port Lands. In announcing their abandonment of the project in May 2020 in the midst of the COVID-19 pandemic, Doctoroff wrote that "it has become too difficult to make the 12-acre project financially viable without sacrificing core parts of the plan."[53] Unable to secure favorable rights in the development of the eight hundred acres that constitute the Port Lands, Sidewalk Labs would effectively foreclose on the project itself. While Doctoroff doesn't state exactly which parts of the plan were considered to be at its "core," Sidewalk Labs had long argued the need to expand the project from the Quayside site to the much larger Port Lands for the project to be financially viable. Increasing public criticism had led Waterfront Toronto the previous fall to demand Sidewalk Labs to scale back its aspirations for the broader Port Lands and its proposal to take on the role of lead developer.[54] This reduction in project scope, combined with the dwindling prospects for the monetization of data harvested from a more restricted twelve-acre site, no doubt played a role in the decision. Waterfront Toronto, for its part, has pledged to continue pursuing the development of the Quayside site. The history of its failed partnership with Sidewalk Labs has brought into sharp focus the critical issues surrounding algorithmic governance at stake in developments of this nature, and fortunately enough, the provisional success of public resistance to the project seems to have emboldened Toronto residents in exercising their right to reclaim the city as oeuvre.

8

THE RUSE AND THE EXPLOIT

A ruse is an action intended to mislead, deceive, or trick. It is a cunning and wily move, often clever and crafty. Originally appearing within the context of hunting, the word is derived from the Middle French *ruse*, meaning a "detour or turn made by a hunted animal."[1] It implies a power dynamic in which a weaker party (the hunted) attempts to evade a stronger one (the hunter). An exploit has historically referred to a project or undertaking of noble or heroic proportions. Military or naval expeditions "to conquer or gain mastery over a person or place" or attempts to "capture or subdue a town, port, etc." are examples of this sense of the exploit. Today the word more generally refers to "an action or feat regarded (sometimes ironically) as exciting, adventurous, or otherwise worth celebrating or recounting."[2]

In verb form, *exploiting* involves using someone or something to one's own advantage. The exploitation of people and natural resources has a long and well-known history, from the origins of slavery to the extractive practices of the modern energy industry. Within the context of computing, the *exploit* refers to a technique for taking advantage of a flaw or vulnerability in a piece of code or network device, usually for nefarious purposes such as gaining unauthorized access to a system. The exploit in this sense is often dependent on a ruse, such as a phishing email that attempts to lure someone into clicking on a link to a fake web page that tricks them into divulging their username and password for their account. Alternately, lapses in a system's security configuration can be targeted, such as when administrative passwords are left blank or default passwords set by the product vendor are left unchanged. Other exploits involve injecting malicious code into a web form such as a search box or comment field, enabling the attacker to trick the site's database server in to returning a list of usernames and passwords (known as a SQL injection attack), for instance, or to capture a user's credentials, credit card information, or other private data (a cross-site scripting attack). Still others exploit poorly written software with inadequate security policies, enabling the unauthorized collection of personal data without the user's consent or knowledge.

If the exploit involves taking advantage of someone or something—a person, a situation, a network—the ruse is often its enabler. The ruse is a tactical maneuver, a calculated action "determined by the absence of a proper locus," as Michel DeCerteau defines it. "It must play on and with a terrain imposed on it and organized by the law of a foreign power."[3] Lacking the capacity of autonomous movement, the ruse is always enacted in response to moment-by-moment changes in an environment or, in other words, the course of the hunt. DeCerteau writes:

The place of a tactic belongs to the other. A tactic insinuates itself into the other's place, fragmentarily, without taking it over in its entirety, without being able to keep it at a distance. It has at its disposal no base where it can capitalize on its advantages, prepare its expansions, and secure independence with respect to circumstances. The "proper" is a victory of space over time. On the contrary, because it does not have a place, a tactic depends on time—it is always on the watch for opportunities that must be "seized on the wing."[4]

By contrast, the exploit is strategic, involving "the calculus of force-relationships which becomes possible when a subject of will and power (a proprietor, an enterprise, a city, a scientific institution) can be isolated from an 'environment.'"[5] The exploit operates from a position of power in expressing its autonomy. DeCerteau sees this power as a precondition for a form of Cartesian knowledge:

A strategy assumes a place that can be circumscribed as proper (propre) and thus serve as the basis for generating relations with an exterior distinct from it (competitors, adversaries, "clientèles," "targets," or "objects" of research). Political, economic, and scientific rationality has been constructed on the strategic model.[6]

The ruse, then, is an art of the weak, the minor, the marginal. It is a tactic of asymmetrical warfare that relies less on spatial relations—the establishment of a strategic place of power from which *to act*—than on the appropriation of temporal conditions and the opportunities they present *to swerve*, abruptly changing direction with the aim of altering the course of events. In this chapter, we explore the application of the ruse and the exploit within the context of political campaigns to drive a wedge into national electorates. Taking the role of "election management" firm Cambridge Analytica in the 2016 US presidential election and the UK Brexit referendum as a point of departure, we trace how concepts and techniques appropriated from behavioral economics by marketing and advertising have been introduced into contemporary political campaigns, from psychometric microtargeting to the production of synthetic media and their distribution via social media. We conclude by surveying the implications of this swerve not just for electoral politics but also broader conditions of public space, representative democracies, and an epistemics of uncertainty.

CAMBRIDGE ANALYTICA

The year 2016 brought seismic shifts to the political terrain on both sides of the Atlantic. The US presidential election resulted in the election of Donald Trump to the presidency, and the UK Brexit referendum led to the withdrawal of the United Kingdom from the European Union. Both outcomes were determined by margins of victory that barely exceeded margins of error. In the United States, Donald Trump won 304 votes in the electoral college to opponent Hillary Clinton's 227 but lost the popular vote by a margin of 46.1 percent to 48.2 percent, or nearly 3 million votes. In key battleground states, Trump won by mere tens of thousands of votes. British voters opted to leave the EU by a margin of 51.8 percent to 48.1 percent, a difference of just over 1 million votes. The outcomes highlighted the extreme partisan divisions in both countries, which were exacerbated by particularly polarizing political campaigns.

Beyond the closeness of the votes and the divisiveness of the outcomes, these two elections also shared another thing in common: the involvement of Cambridge Analytica, the political consulting firm that both winning campaigns engaged in some capacity.[7] Cambridge Analytica was a subsidiary of the Strategic Communication Laboratories (SCL) Group, a British behavioral research and strategic communications company located in London. Marketing itself as a "global election management agency," SCL was in the business of providing intelligence analysis and "persuasion products" to government agencies and private organizations. It promoted its work products as capable of fostering behavioral change in the audiences it targeted. SCL's defense division had provided communications analytics to the US Department of Defense and the UK Ministry of Defence for antiterrorism operations in Afghanistan, as well as defense contractors operating in the Middle East and North Africa. SCL also sold products and services supporting behavioral change for nondefense-related clients in commercial and political contexts. It proclaimed expertise in "psychological operations" aimed at manipulating people's emotions, thinking, and behavior through a set of techniques involving rumor, disinformation, and fake news. Its elections division had used a similar set of tools in more than two hundred elections around the world, mostly in undeveloped democracies.[8]

Cambridge Analytica was spun off from SCL in 2015, with initial funding from Steve Bannon, a wealthy investment banker and then the executive chairman of the conservative Breitbart news network, and Robert Mercer, a computer scientist and early artificial intelligence researcher who made billions applying quantitative techniques to hedge fund management. Mercer, an influential Republican donor, had contributed $35 million to Republican political campaigns in the United States. Alexander Nix, director of SCL Elections and Cambridge Analytica's CEO, had attended the exclusive Eton College and is married to Norwegian shipping heir Olympia Paus. Together, these three extraordinarily wealthy individuals set their sights on fracturing political landscapes on both sides of the ocean, capitalizing on wedge issues to sway electorates through a technique appropriated from marketing and advertising known as behavioral microtargeting.

POLITICAL CAMPAIGNS AND DATA

The employment of data on voters in political campaigns is by no means new. Campaigns have used voter registration lists since at least the 1920s to focus their efforts.[9] Beyond their primary function of preventing voter fraud and facilitating the administration of elections, voter registration lists have long been used by campaigns to collect data on voter contact information, personal data, and history of election participation. Prior to the contemporary data-driven campaign, typical applications of data involved deriving predictions on voter intent based on party affiliation and the percentage of voters in a district who voted for a particular party in past elections. The likelihood that a given voter would cast a vote, for instance, was commonly based on that person's participation in the previous four general elections.[10]

Before the passage of the Help America Vote Act of 2002 (42 U.S.C. sec. 15483), which required all states to maintain standardized, statewide electronic voter registration databases, voter files were often maintained at the county level manually. With the standardization of data collection, storage, and sharing practices, an increasingly detailed voter file came into view. The fusion of data from various public and commercial sources led to the cultivation of "enhanced" voter files containing hundreds of data points on each individual. A 2005 report by Polimetrix (now YouGov), a polling, survey research, and analytics firm, claimed that it routinely collected "address information (enhanced with USPS delivery point validation and national change of address services); geocoding (using US Census TIGER files); neighborhood demographics (from U.S. Census track, block group, and block data); individual micro-data (covering unregistered as well as registered voters; containing individual demographics and lifestyle information); political contributions (from State and Federal Election Commissions); telephone polling and voter identification information; field data (application for voter registration and GOTV contacts); media exposure (CMAG and Nielsen Media Research); [and] email appends (from group contacts and third party lists)."[11] Over the next decade, campaigns compiled ever greater numbers of data points on individual voters, merging data from increasingly diverse sources in centralized databases. By 2012, President Barack Obama's reelection campaign had developed a system called "Narwhal" that merged data from external data brokers with internal campaign get-out-the-vote field operations and fundraising activity into a single database that grew to 50 terabytes by the end of the campaign.[12]

At that time, data-driven campaigns predominantly developed predictive models to increase the efficiency of targeting campaign advertising and support broader campaign strategies. These models generate scores for each voter, ranking that person's behavior, support, and responsiveness. Behavioral scores are derived from past voting behavior and demographic information and indicate the probability a voter will engage in particular political activities such as turning out to vote, making a campaign contribution, volunteering for the campaign, or attending a rally. Support scores indicate political preference—the likelihood that voters will support a given candidate. Responsiveness scores aim to predict how well a given voter will respond to specific campaign outreach efforts such as phone calls, direct mail, and email.[13] Given the constraints of a campaign budget or war chest, these models are designed to optimize the allocation of campaign resources most effectively, expanding the populations of prospective voters likely to bear fruit and pruning away those not considered to be cost-effective.

THE WEAPONIZATION OF SOCIAL MEDIA

The incorporation of microtargeting in the arsenals of political campaigns and political action committees is today commonplace. Yet while the scores these predictive models generate may better inform the allocation of resources for specific media buys in relevant markets, campaign strategists have recognized that microtargeting excels in situations involving direct contact with individual voters. Phone calls, emails, text messages, and online advertising lend themselves well to tailored messages delivered to specific individuals. Social media in particular afford the delivery of highly customized content to finely grained demographics at scale. Yet as we saw in chapter 4 with the AI-driven virtual assistant market, the appropriation of concepts and techniques from behavioral economics by political consultants has not only radically altered the way campaigns operate but also fundamentally changed how the electorate is viewed.

The weaponization of social media for partisan political warfare involves three distinct but related steps. The first is what is called psychographic (or psychometric) segmentation: the production of statistical imaginaries based on proximities within a feature space of psychological attributes. As we saw in chapter 5, market segmentation is a long-standing marketing practice involving the division of a consumer market into smaller groups of segments based on shared attributes including demographics (for example, age, gender, income, education, family size), geography (country, region, state, city, zip code), and behavior (consumption, use). Political campaigns have for quite some time employed techniques of market segmentation for targeting political advertisements. Psychographic segmentation, however, is a relative newcomer to the world of political campaigning, involving analyzing the personality of individuals, more recently using quizzes on social media. These quizzes measure an individual's personality via what is called an OCEAN personality analysis, which uses what behavioral psychologists refer to as the five-factor model (FFM), or the Big Five personality traits: openness (inventive/curious versus consistent/cautious), conscientiousness (efficient/organized versus extravagant/careless), extraversion (outgoing/energetic versus solitary/reserved), agreeableness (friendly/compassionate versus challenging/callous), and neuroticism (sensitive/nervous versus resilient/confident). Studies suggest that these five traits are sufficient to accurately characterize an individual's personality.[14]

The next step is behavioral microtargeting. The process of this microtargeting begins with fusing an individual's OCEAN analysis with other data acquired from commercial data brokers such as Google, Facebook, Experian, and Acxiom. This information can include data on one's age, gender, race, ethnicity, current residence, previous residences, income, political and ideological preferences and activities, purchasing habits, hobbies, and more. From these data and the OCEAN analysis, individual behavioral profiles are derived that can indicate a person's probable values, belief systems, political motivations, and emotional vulnerabilities. Behavioral microtargeting enables the prediction of needs and how they may change over time.

The third step is the creation and delivery of bespoke social media content tailored to exploit the weaknesses that a prospective voter's profile indicates are most vulnerable to persuasion. These social media missives are aimed at changing not public opinion but the opinions of microtargeted publics as small as one. For example, a Republican voter who strongly values the Second Amendment and has a high score for conscientiousness and neuroticism in their OCEAN analysis might be targeted with a Facebook post showing an image of a fist breaking through a window accompanied by a caption promoting gun rights as a defense against home invasion. It is important to note here that unlike previous forms of microtargeted political advertising that aimed to reach voters most likely to turn out to vote for a given candidate (and not their opponent), behavioral microtargeting performs equally well when attempting to dissuade a candidate from voting altogether.

THE FACEBOOK EXPLOIT

For these techniques to work at a national scale to influence an election, they needed a massive data set of personality profiles. By 2012, two PhD students working at the Psychometric Centre at Cambridge University, Michal Kosinski and David Stillwell, had developed a method by which simple psychographic surveys conducted via a Facebook app they created, MyPersonality, could be used to develop a database of personality profiles for psychometric research. Test subjects filled out a questionnaire online and researchers would calculate their OCEAN scores based on their responses. These results were then compared with a range of other personal information collected from their Facebook profiles: what they "liked," shared, or posted on Facebook and their gender, age, and where they lived. From these data points, researchers established correlations that enabled them to deduce personal characteristics. Initially expecting to collect surveys from a few dozen of their college friends, Kosinski and Stillwell found that their app went viral, generating millions of responses. Quickly they were in possession of the largest data set ever to be assembled that matched psychometric scores to Facebook profiles, which enabled the psychographic segmentation of large populations with a high degree of accuracy.

According to a widely read exposé published in the Swiss *Das Magazin* that was adapted and translated into English on *Vice* magazine's Motherboard.com, researchers found that "men who 'liked' the cosmetics brand MAC were slightly more likely to be gay," whereas "one of the best indicators for heterosexuality was 'liking' Wu-Tang Clan," and "followers of Lady Gaga were most probably extroverts, while those who 'liked' philosophy tended to be introverts."[15] In an influential paper published in 2014, "Computer-Based Personality Judgments Are More Accurate Than Those Made by Humans,"[16] Kosinski, Stillwell, and their colleague Youyou Wu

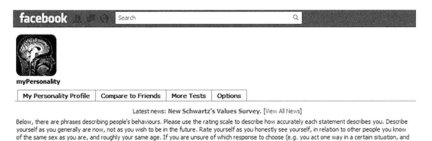

MyPersonality Facebook app, screenshot, 2018.

showed how on the basis of an average of sixty-eight Facebook "likes" by a user, it was possible to predict the person's skin color (with 95 percent accuracy), sexual orientation (88 percent accuracy), and affiliation to the Democratic or Republican Party (85 percent). As the model evolved, they were able to evaluate a person better than the average coworker based on 10 Facebook likes. Given 70 likes, the model performed better than a person's friends. With 300 likes, it knew more about that person than even the person's partner knew.

According to various reports,[17] around this time Kosinski was approached by Aleksandr Kogan, an assistant professor in the psychology department at the University of Cambridge. Kogan was interested in acquiring Kosinski's data set on behalf of a company, the name of which he could not reveal. The company turned out to be SCL, which had learned about the potential applications of Kosinski's research to political campaigns from Christopher Wylie, a PhD student in fashion forecasting whom SCL recruited as research director for its elections division. Wylie had read the paper by Kosinski, Stillwell, and Wu and was eager to apply its findings to targeting political advertising.

Wylie would later become a whistle-blower, exposing the ruse and the exploit he helped develop for SCL's spawn, Cambridge Analytica, to the *Guardian* newspaper journalist Carole Cadwalladr. As Cadwalladr reports, Wylie attempted to get access to Kosinski's myPersonality database through Kogan.[18] When Kosinski discovered that the company behind the request was SCL, negotiations broke down and he distanced himself from Kogan. He informed the director of the Psychometric Centre, which reportedly provoked a complicated internal conflict within the university, which was understandably concerned about the public perception of such a partnership. Kogan subsequently offered to replicate Kosinski's work for SCL and set up a company, Global Science Research, to do so. According to a contract provided to Cadwalladr by Wylie, Global Science was paid $1 million to collect and process Facebook data to be matched to personality traits and voter files.

As an investigation by the UK Information Commissioner's Office (ICO) would later reveal, Kogan had developed techniques to collect Facebook data of up to 87 million people without their knowledge. He had apparently persuaded more than 300,000 people to use a personality testing app similar to Kosinski's that extracted the Facebook profile data not only of the app's user but also of their friends. With the influx of cash from Mercer fueling the spinoff Cambridge Analytica from SCL, Kogan was able to pay people to take a personality quiz on Amazon's Mechanical Turk and Qualtrics, a subscription software platform for conducting surveys. The survey app, This Is My Digital Life, enabled Kogan to access not only the participants' Facebook profiles but also those of their friends. As a result, each participant unwittingly gave access to on average 160 of their friends' profiles, which were processed and added to the data set without their knowledge. Via this simple ruse, Kogan was able to build a database of millions of people in mere weeks.

While Kogan did have permission to pull Facebook data for academic purposes, it is illegal for personal data to be sold to a third party without consent. Facebook, under investigation by the US Justice Department and the FBI, would claim that it was not aware that Kogan was violating its data use policies. Yet in the run-up to the 2016 election, Wylie was invited to meet with Facebook board member and influential Silicon Valley venture capitalist Marc Andreessen "to try and find out as much about the exploit as possible in order to figure out possible solutions" according to someone with knowledge of the meeting.[19] Wylie would subsequently receive a letter from Facebook's lawyers telling him that the data had been illicitly obtained and that he must delete all of it immediately because Global Science Research was not authorized to share or sell it. According to reporting by the *New York Times*, however, the privacy terms for the This is My Digital Life app stated that the data could also be used for commercial purposes.[20] At the time, selling user data would have violated Facebook's rules, yet the company did not perform regular audits to ensure compliance.

Through Kogan's simple ruse and his exploitation of Facebook's lax data privacy policies, Cambridge Analytica would go on to assemble a data set containing what Nix claimed to be more than 220 million psychometric profiles of the US electorate—boasting it had collected four to five thousand data points for every adult in the country.[21] "Everything was built on the back of that data. The models, the algorithm. Everything," Wylie would claim.[22] While many remain skeptical of these claims, and Cambridge Analytica's purported impact on these campaigns may itself be a ruse, of interest here is that these "enhanced" voter files provided the microtargeting data fueling political advertising campaigns of such unprecedented divisiveness.

WEDGE POLITICS, FILTER BUBBLES, AND THE ART OF THE SWERVE

Microtargeting lends itself to the exploitation of wedge issues that polarize opinion along racial, regional, or other demographic lines, such as immigration, abortion, the Second Amendment, the environment, and same-sex marriage. Divisive issues such as these have been shown to be the most likely to mobilize voters, driving them either to support one candidate or withdraw support for another.[23] Many have observed that microtargeting in the service of wedge politics leads to an increasingly fragmented electorate.[24] As political scientists D. Sunshine Hillygus and Todd Shields noted in 2008, campaigns seek to target messaging related to

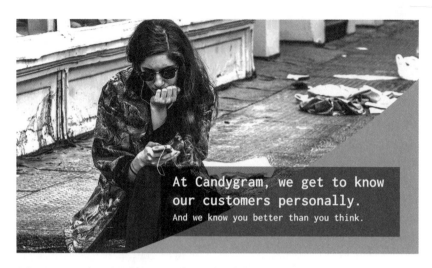

Advertisement for "Candygram," a fictional mobile communications company.

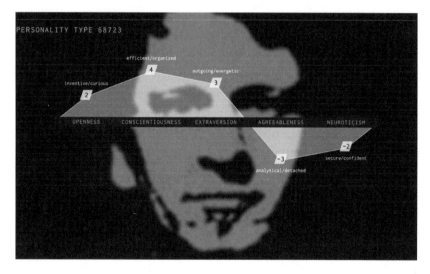

Screenshot from a personal data portrait showing OCEAN analysis of a project participant.

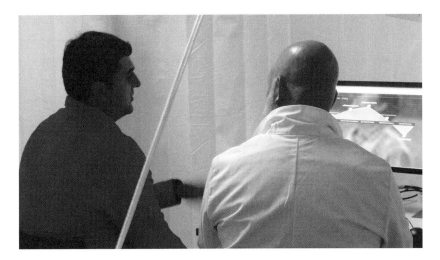

Performing a data consultation at a Candygram popup shop.

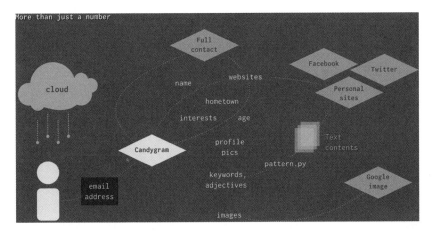

Moritz Stefaner, False Positive system diagram, 2015.

False Positive, a project by Mark Shepard and Moritz Stefaner (2015), explores the brittle and conflicted nature of our relationship to personal data and social media profiling. The project incorporated a mobile performance and series of workshops that aimed to catalyze public debate surrounding the infrastructural politics underlying mobile communications systems in urban environments and the surreptitious network practices of contemporary informatics regimes. The project was performed in five cities across Europe over the course of four months in fall 2015. http://false-positive.net.

wedge issues to like-minded audiences, while avoiding those who might think otherwise and publicly contest the messaging.[25] They show that as early as 2004, wedge issues were more often delivered by direct mail to individual households than broadcast to broader populations on television. These direct mail missives, invisible to broadcast publics, could not be fact-checked or rebutted in the same manner that fake news and false advertising might have been in the shared public sphere of television.[26]

The ability to target separate groups of people in an increasingly granular fashion via text messages, email, and social media advertising further facilitates the delivery of different messages to different people, often without their knowing what the other is receiving. Wylie himself points out the implications of this new form of "dog whistle" politics:

Instead of standing in the public square and saying what you think and then letting people come and listen to you and have that shared experience as to what your narrative is, you are whispering into the ear of each and every voter and you may be whispering one thing to this voter and another thing to another voter. You risk fragmenting society in a way where we don't have any more shared experiences and we don't have any more shared understanding.[27]

Private whispering campaigns like these exacerbate the uncommon ground between us, making the organization of public debate around a common set of issues far more difficult. It is hard to argue for or against a position on an issue when you are unaware of its holder.

An individual who is considered either an unlikely voter or strongly committed to a candidate and therefore unlikely to be persuaded may receive little or no messaging at all as campaigns aim to optimize the allocation of their resources. Existing tendencies toward focusing on swing states or even "swing people"—those undecided yet still persuadable—are amplified. As a result, unlikely voters ignored in one election cycle may be even less likely to vote in the next, further lowering the likelihood they will be the subject of outreach in the future. Philip Howard describes this as a form of "political redlining," whereby "the data is used to figure out what areas you want to underserve."[28]

Those who do get served are increasingly sorted by specific issues. The emergence of single-issue politics has been tied to the logic of market segmentation, whereby differentiation is prioritized over commonality. As early as 2001, Oscar Gandy warned that "because strategic communication is designed to mobilize individuals as members of groups with common interests at risk, rather than as members of a larger complex whose interests are served through compromise, political discourse is bound to be combative, rather than cooperative."[29] Writing in 2012, Solan Barocas suggested this is less a problem of the impact of online personalization filters that political activist and entrepreneur Eli Pariser coined the "filter bubble effect."[30] People still search for a range of different positions on a given issue, but the issues they follow are those that matter to them personally. Yet when campaigns target messages that partition voters from not only opposing views but also competing issues, these voters can become less able to recognize the existence or legitimacy of other concerns. As a result, behavioral microtargeting does not just manipulate individuals on the basis of a single issue; it also limits the range, extent, and terms of reference of the debate.

Ultimately, behavioral microtargeting applied to wedge politics is most effective with polarized electorates where the population to be persuaded is marginal. Divisive issues by their nature provoke people to take a side; there is no middle ground. You are either for or against gun rights. You either support or do not support gay marriage. You either welcome or fear immigration. As Pariser observes, this is a political terrain constituted by "a public sphere sorted and manipulated by algorithms, fragmented by design, and hostile to dialogue."[31] Winning in this electoral climate is less a question of strategically aligning a platform with a set of core issues that appeal to specific voting blocks—say, suburban women, or rural conservatives—than tactically splitting these blocks into ever-finer segments that can be effectively nudged toward your campaign in aggregate or, when they lean toward your opponent, discouraged from voting altogether. Wendy Hui Kyong Chun has described these tactics as a form of "reverse hegemony," where "majorities can emerge when angry minorities, clustered around a shared stigma, are strung together through their mutual opposition to so-called mainstream culture."[32]

This is the art of the swerve: crafty, cunning, and wily, always on the watch for opportunities to be "seized on the wing." Hannah Arendt, in a section of *The Human Condition* addressing the public and the private realm, writes that "the presence of others who see what we see and hear what we hear assures us of the reality of the world and ourselves."[33] When public space is no longer the geography of the public sphere and the public sphere is reduced to a multitude of micropublics as small as one, each seeing and hearing something different, we find ourselves confronted with a spatial epistemology not of assurance, as Arendt would have it, but of uncertainty, for which doubt is the primary affect. In the following chapter, we examine this epistemic uncertainty and affective doubt at a planetary scale, given the context of a global pandemic and its mortal consequences.

9

PANDEMIC EXCEPTIONALISM

The virus is an equal opportunity infector. And it's probably the way we would be better if we saw ourselves that way, which is much more alike than different.
—Larry Brilliant

Drawing on seventeenth-century accounts of measures to be taken in response to the Plague, Michel Foucault recounts the disciplinary mechanisms of power in a time of crisis. Working from archival municipal records, Foucault describes the governing processes and procedures set in motion when the disease came to town. First, space was enclosed and segmented. The town and its surrounding areas were shut down, divided into distinct quarters each under the jurisdiction of an *intendant*. Each street was in turn watched over by a *syndic*, whose job was to lock the doors of each house from the outside at the onset of the epidemic and hand the key over to their respective intendant to keep for its duration. Residents of the town were thus quarantined, prohibited on pain of death from moving about. Under these exceptional circumstances, "that which moves brings death, and one kills that which moves."[1]

Each day, the syndic went from house to house on the street for which they were responsible, called the occupants to appear before a window of the house, and registered their current health status, be they living, sick, or dead. The syndics then reported the information to their respective intendants, who in turn reported to the town magistrate. Ceaseless inspection produced data that were passed upward in the established chain of custody, and populations were spatially sorted accordingly. After four or five days, disinfection squads would go house by house to "purify" the premises, and so the disease was to be eradicated from the locale. Power was thus uniformly mobilized against an exceptional adversary, pervasively present and visible in its imposition of an idealized form of society.

The twenty-first-century response to the COVID-19 pandemic, by comparison, presents markedly different mobilizations of power. Alongside the disciplinary mechanisms of spatial segregation, ceaseless inspection, and permanent registration, a number of approaches to combat the virus have emerged. In the absence of a viable vaccine, all governments could do was attempt to alter behavior. From nudging people to wear a face mask in public and practice social distancing in order to limit the transmission of the virus from one body to another, to various methods of contract tracing designed to track and contain its spread throughout a population, different vectors of power appeared that depended not only on spatial sorting strategies of separation and isolation but also tactics involving the fostering of individual behavioral change and the tracking of infectious bodies as they traverse a given space. Gilles Deleuze, a contemporary of Foucault, described this form of power in terms of the difference between the *disciplinary society* and the *control society*, whereby control is exerted not by enclosure—by locking something down or otherwise constraining its free movement—but rather by "giving the position of any element within an open environment at any given instant."[2] This notion of geolocating any moving body at any given point in time, together with the prospect of nudging the behavior of that body in ways that might benefit a common social good, would prove to become an aspiration of commercial location data brokers and government public health agencies alike.

In a series of lectures delivered at the Collège de France from 1975 to 1976, Foucault would elaborate the notion of biopolitics with respect to the administration of life within a society.[3] For Foucault, biopolitics extended the notion of the disciplinary mechanism from a single locality to an entire population, aiming to "to ensure, sustain, and multiply life, to put this life in order."[4] Foucault saw biopolitics as a control apparatus that exerts power over a "global mass" in determining not only who would live but also who should die. The naive might hope that this determination in the present tense would aim to globally adopt a more democratic form of biopolitics in relation to COVID-19, one where questions of equity and inclusivity drive public policy and decision making and where common ground would at least be sought in the face of such a socially and culturally leveling phenomenon. "The virus is an equal opportunity infector," wrote renowned epidemiologist Larry Brilliant, "and it's probably the way we would be better if we saw ourselves that way, which is much more alike than different."[5]

In this chapter , we examine how the global community reacted differently in different parts of the world in response to COVID-19. From the authoritarian forms of coercive control imposed in China to Sweden's libertarian reliance on individuals making rational decisions in practicing social distancing, these responses reflect different forms of biopolitics enacted by very different nation-states. Some see no harm in leveraging location data harvested from cell phones by state security services to assist with contact tracing, while others are more comfortable entrusting large corporations to develop privacy-preserving techniques that incorporate proximity sensing using Bluetooth technology.

The biopolitics in play in response to COVID-19 were not without their discontents. In the early days of the pandemic, philosopher Georgio Agamben, whose book *State of Exception* traces how governmental power has expanded in times of crisis throughout history, penned a blog post titled "The Invention of an Epidemic" that questioned the actual severity of the public health crisis. "Faced with the frenetic, irrational, and entirely unfounded emergency measures adopted against an alleged epidemic of coronavirus," he wrote, "we should begin from the declaration issued by the National Research Council (CNR), which states not only that 'there is no SARS-CoV2 epidemic in Italy', but also that 'the infection, according to the epidemiologic data available as of today and based on tens of thousands of cases, causes mild/moderate symptoms (a sort of influenza) in 80–90% of cases.'"[6] This claim that the pandemic was similar to the flu was echoed by libertarian and conservative voices alike in the United States and elsewhere, where wearing a mask in public was less a matter of best practices in public health than it was a marker of political affiliation. President Donald Trump initially called the virus a Democratic "hoax." Others would suggest letting the virus "slow burn" throughout society in order to develop herd immunity within a population and avoid the adverse economic impacts of a shutdown, as UK prime minister Boris Johnson and Swedish chief epidemiologist Anders Tegnell would do.[7] And in the Netherlands, following the first state-imposed curfew since World War II, Dutch citizens rioted for three nights in protest of the governmental pandemic measures.

The role of data, their visualization, and various attempts to map the spatial dimensions of the virus played critical roles in shaping how we came to appreciate (or not) its spread throughout the world and calibrated our behavior accordingly (or not). Data collection and visualization practices themselves became contested sites, with notable examples in Florida, where the outright manipulation of pandemic data at the height of an outbreak in the state was exposed by a government whistle-blower and at the federal level with the failed attempt by political appointees at the Department of Health and Human Services (HHS) to control the flow of hospital data, something that for decades had been managed by the Centers for Disease Control and Prevention (CDC). During these exceptional times with much of the world on lockdown, we sat in isolation, prone before our screens, and inhabited the statistics: infection rates, numbers of hospitalizations and percentages of occupied intensive care unit beds, deaths per day, and the corresponding impact of all these on market indexes. We staked our hopes and beliefs in the veracity of data models and their projections and attempted to debate public health measures accordingly.

Others staked their hopes in the development of technosocial systems for mitigating the spread of the virus via the automation of contact tracing. As we awaited the development of a vaccine and effective treatments, we raced to develop new technologies that could help "flatten the curve." COVID-19 testing, initially conducted by hospitals and public health organizations, began to be offered by private labs. Testing sites started popping up in empty parking lots. While the potential for false positives from contact tracing apps was a problem, false negatives from dodgy urgent care testing sites were perhaps even more so. And once a vaccine did finally arrive, we struggled with managing its production and distribution in fair and equitable ways. If, as Latour has argued, climate science deniers paved the way for our post-truth reality, pandemic science deniers and the anti-vaxxers would dig the graves in its cemeteries.

REPRESENTING PANDEMIC SPACE: FLATTENING THE CURVE

The practice of mapping epidemic data is hardly new. Cartographic scholars frequently refer to the work of John Snow and his map of the 1854 cholera outbreak in London, England, as an early example of how representing the spatiality of the viral spread of a disease can produce important insights. Cholera is an intestinal disease that can cause death within hours after the first symptoms of vomiting or diarrhea, and the London epidemic was one of the more alarming outbreaks of the disease in the history of the Western world. Ten percent of the population of London's Soho district was infected in the course of one week. The prevailing scientific theory was that the disease was spread through miasma, or air polluted with particles from decomposing organic matter. Snow, however, believed that the disease was spread not by air but by water contaminated by sewage. At the time, people didn't have running water in their homes or businesses and used city wells and communal pumps to get the water they used for drinking, cooking, and washing. Snow suspected that people living or working near a pump serving contaminated water were the most likely to use it and thus contract cholera. To investigate his hypothesis, he produced a map that plotted each known case in relation to the public water pumps in the area. The resulting map showed that the cases were clustered around one of the pumps located on what was then called Broad Street. Snow followed up with those who had fallen ill about their water usage habits, which confirmed his suspicions. As it would eventually be discovered, the water served by that pump had indeed been polluted by sewage from a nearby cesspool where a baby's diaper contaminated with cholera had been disposed of. Londoners learned to boil their water before use, thus ending outbreaks of the disease in the city, and the power of epidemiological mapping was established.

Various approaches were taken in mapping the spread of COVID-19. In the early months of the pandemic, the Center for Systems Science and Engineering at Johns Hopkins University created an online GIS-based dashboard serving as a clearinghouse for data on the current state of the

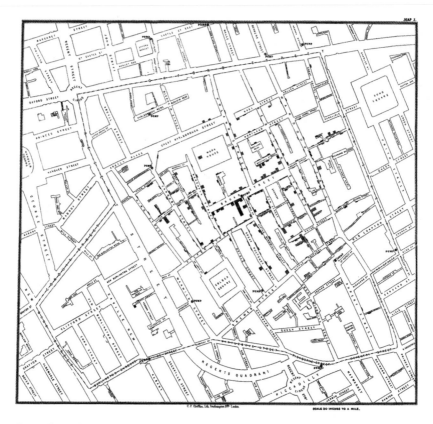

Original map by John Snow showing the clusters of cholera cases (indicated by stacked rectangles) in the London epidemic of 1854. *Source*: Wikimedia Commons / Public Domain.

virus.[8] US states and counties would build on this interface with their own dashboards that mapped coronavirus case counts by zip code, daily and cumulative deaths, infection and test rates, and so on. Data journalists working for major online news media including the *New York Times*, the *Washington Post*, and the *Guardian*, created interactive COVID-19 "trackers" that enabled website visitors to browse, filter, and sort pandemic data by a variety of criteria. Many of these resources were driven by open data sources and application programming interfaces that enabled independent data scientists and information designers alike to craft their own maps and data visualizations to be used in presentations by local public officials and shared over social media by academics, independent scholars, and information enthusiasts alike.

COVID-19 dashboard by the Center for Systems Science and Engineering at Johns Hopkins University. Screenshot by author.

The data driving these representations were, of course, prone to manipulation and error. In spring 2020, at the height of the pandemic, the Florida Department of Health announced that it was firing the data scientist who designed, developed, and managed the COVID-19 dashboard for the state. Rebekah Jones claimed she was told to change data to support Republican governor Ron DeSantis's plan to reopen the state economy despite soaring COVID-19 cases.[9] The Republican governor of Georgia, Brian Kemp, who was also intent on reopening the state economy, had to apologize for presenting graphics based on the state's public health database that falsely showed a downward trend in cases.[10] The chart presented a sharp drop in coronavirus cases, deaths, and hospitalizations to close to zero two weeks after reaching a peak just prior to when restrictions were relaxed. Upon closer inspection, however, it became evident that the dates on the chart were out of order: they had apparently been rearranged to give the impression that the number of cases was decreasing. New York State governor Andrew Cuomo came under fire for significantly undercounting COVID-19 deaths in nursing homes.[11] Following a report by the New York State attorney general, Letitia James, Health Department officials announced that thirty-eight hundred nursing home residents who had died in hospitals were not previously counted by the state as nursing home deaths. This meant that the state's official tally could be off by as much as 50 percent. The state had reportedly withheld these data out of concern that the Trump administration, of which Cuomo was a vocal critic, would use that as an excuse to open a federal civil rights investigation.

The attempt by HHS in summer 2020 to take control of the flow of hospital data in the United States raised the specter of the manipulation of not just individual data sets but the national data infrastructure for reporting pandemic-related data itself. Prior to the pandemic, the CDC had aggregated hospital data via the National Healthcare Safety Network, a public health program developed over the course of fifteen years through relationships with individual health facilities. While the network was by no means perfect—it required all data to be input manually, for instance—health care administrators across the country were familiar with the system and trusted its data. Federal and state officials had been using these data to assess the impact of the pandemic on hospital capacities and to allocate scarce resources accordingly, from limited stocks of COVID-19 medicines to personal protective equipment. In July of that year, the Trump administration and White House Coronavirus Task Force coordinator Deborah Birx announced that they were abruptly shifting the responsibility for managing COVID-19 hospital data to private contractors in an effort to streamline the collection of information. HHS had awarded a contract to TeleTracking Technologies, a small Pittsburgh-based patient data services company run by CEO Michael Zamagias, who was connected to a firm that had invested billions of dollars in real estate projects with the Trump Organization.[12] Palantir Technologies, a company known for its data analytics software founded by Silicon Valley entrepreneur Peter Theil, would be managing the database (and eventually the allocation and distribution of vaccines, as we will see). In mid-November of that year, *Science* magazine examined this new system, called HHS Protect, and found that HHS data often dramatically diverged from those collected by a different federal pandemic data source, as well as from state-supplied data and "the apparent reality on the ground."[13] While discrepancies in data reported by different systems are not uncommon, abruptly recircuiting the flow of critical public health data in the middle of a pandemic was widely criticized: hundreds of public health organizations and experts warned the change "could gravely disrupt the government's ability to understand the pandemic and mount a response."[14] HHS would eventually reverse course, and hospitals would return to reporting data directly to the CDC.

This fire hose of imperfect and frequently conflicting pandemic data representations revealed as much as it concealed. For many, the extent of the virus would take shape in relation to a set of abstractions consumed remotely, at a distance. The daily number of deaths per zip code or the percentage of positive tests by county did little to help in understanding who was getting infected, where they were getting infected, and how this information might help in deciding on a course of action beyond the most general risk calculation. Where the data come from, the conditions under which they are collected, how they are organized and aggregated, the choices that are made in how they are represented: these factors are often obscured in the processes by which these representations take shape and circulate within contemporary media environments.[15]

Alongside these official representations were independent initiatives that aimed to flesh out our understanding of the inequities of the virus's impact. Projects such as *Atlantic* magazine's COVID Racial Data Tracker[16] and UCLA Law COVID Behind Bars[17] rendered finer-grained maps of who was getting infected and where local hot spots were occurring. By enabling the disaggregation of data by race and ethnicity or by focusing on a single location such as jails, prisons, or US Immigration and Customs Enforcement detention centers, these alternative pandemic representations lent depth and nuance to how we understood how the virus was spreading by making visible the people and places that remained beneath and beyond the threshold of the dominant pandemic representations. Initiatives like these (and there are many more that one could cite), helped to emphasize the pandemic's uneven distributions and radical inequities.

To be sure, these various and varied representations of the scope and extent of the pandemic helped shape our understanding of the spatiality of the virus and the social dynamics of how it spread. This in turn informed public policy decisions regarding the planning of critical resource allocations to care for those infected and the implementation of specific spatial practices designed to mitigate viral transmission. As we inhabited the statistical imaginaries that these representations constructed, we were confronted with the social imperative to do our part in flattening the curve as a means to manage the capacity of our health

Showing cumulative cases ▾ in carceral facilities

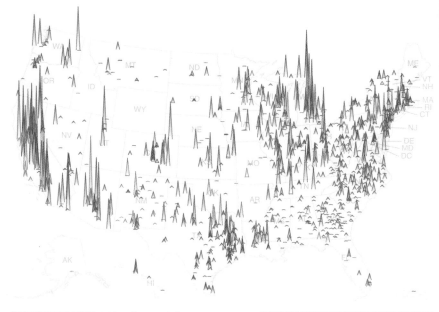

Each spike represents the number of incarcerated
people who have had COVID-19 within a facility

☑ ∧ State Facilities
☑ ∧ Federal Facilities
☑ ∧ County Jails
☑ ∧ ICE Detention Centers   1   2.1k   4.3k

This map displays reported COVID-19 cases and
related deaths of people incarcerated in carceral
facilities across the US. Click on a state to access
more data.

Rates and active cases are not available for all
facilities. Learn why.

UCLA Law COVID Behind Bars Data Project.

care systems. Toward this end, predictive models emerged that forecast probable futures based on the decisions made at a given moment in time. The Institute for Health Metrics and Evaluation, an independent global health research center at the University of Washington, developed a widely referenced predictive model based on the demand for hospital services such as available intensive care unit beds and ventilators, daily and cumulative numbers of deaths, testing and infection rates, and the impact of mask use and social distancing practices. This model was designed to aid hospital systems and state governments in determining when COVID-19 would overwhelm their capacity to care for patients.[18]

Other models were developed to forecast outbreaks of the virus before they occur. One such model, developed by a team of international researchers led by Mauricio Santillana and Nicole Kogan at Harvard University, incorporated data streams from a variety of sources, including Google search activity, geolocated Twitter posts, physician searches on the clinical platform UpToDate, mobility data from smartphones, and readings shared by users of Kinsa Smart Thermometers. The initiative built on a prior project by Google known as Google Flu Trends that attempted to predict the presence of flu-like illness in a given population by monitoring the online search activity of millions of its users. Conceived as a "COVID-19 early warning system," the Harvard-led researchers intended the model to be used "as a thermostat, in a cooling or heating system, to guide intermittent activation or relaxation of public health interventions as the COVID-19 pandemic evolves."[19]

TECHNOSOCIAL SYSTEMS FOR PANDEMIC MITIGATION

As public knowledge of the scope and extent of the pandemic evolved, so too did the various approaches to developing technosocial systems for its mitigation. We might identify four primary applications for which these systems were developed.[20] The first is the enforcement of quarantine regulations and large-scale physical distancing measures and movement restrictions, commonly known as lockdowns. This entails knowing that infected people are respecting guidelines for home isolation and that only authorized individuals are circulating throughout a locale. This is usually achieved using GPS tracking via smartphones or ankle bracelets, but also can be achieved through a smartphone–based check-in process. The second is known as contact tracing and involves identifying people who have crossed paths with someone who has been infected with the virus. Various techniques have been deployed around the world to do this. A traditional low-tech approach is to hire legions of people to manually follow up with lists of those with whom an infected individual has come into contact. This approach is time-consuming, labor intensive, and expensive; relies on an individual's memory; and cannot identify proximate strangers. Newer high-tech approaches include both top-down, state-sponsored approaches involving the tracing of mobility patterns using GPS and cell tower phone location data as well as bottom-up approaches involving more privacy-compliant, peer-to-peer proximity data acquired through Bluetooth technology on smartphones. A third application is population-level flow modeling of the movement of people within a locale or region for the purpose of ascertaining how the disease may be spreading and whether people are abiding by lockdown and social distancing guidelines. Finally, the fourth application we might consider is the development of social graphs using a combination of location data for cell phones with machine learning algorithms to identify people who are frequently in contact with each other and alert a person's social network of their variable levels of risk to exposure accordingly. To date, no known example of this application type has been implemented, but considering it as a possibility can be instructive. The design and implementation of these technosocial systems would vary radically across the globe, responding to the social, cultural, and political conditions in play where they were deployed.

The enforcement of quarantine orders and movement restrictions in some countries followed a coercive disciplinary model and were highly centralized. China required its citizens to install an app on their smartphone that was used to scan QR codes prior to accessing public spaces or transit systems. This app would determine access privileges by verifying whether they had tested positive for the virus and notify local police when people attempted to violate quarantine requirements. This kind of social and spatial sorting using app-approved admittance to public and private spaces also appeared in Russia, where QR codes were deployed to authorize movement throughout Moscow. City residents were required to register on a government website or download an app to their phones and declare their purpose for movement and intended route in advance. They would subsequently receive a QR code that could be verified by the relevant authorities to permit passage at checkpoints distributed throughout the city. Taiwan mandated a smartphone tracking system conceived as "a digital fence" to enforce quarantine orders and even provided government-issued GPS-enabled phones to people without them. If citizens required to quarantine wandered too far from home, the system would trigger phone calls and text messages attempting to ascertain their whereabouts.[21] And in Poland, the government sent text messages to people in quarantine and required the recipient to respond with a geo-located selfie within twenty minutes in order to avoid a visit from the police.

Sweden took a markedly different approach. Preferring to rely on its citizens to make rational decisions regarding their social distancing practices, the country did not impose large-scale movement restrictions or close entire sections of its economy. Swedes initially embarked on a mask-free strategy that intended to create herd immunity to the virus without bankrupting the economy by imposing strict lockdowns. While the government did ban large assemblies of more than fifty people and widely disseminated public health information, it did not impose nationwide lockdowns. Universities and high schools moved online, working from home was encouraged, and the elderly were urged to self-isolate. Yet child day care centers and primary schools remained open, as well as restaurants, bars, and gyms. By the end of the summer, the virus had subsided without a need for new measures. Yet Sweden's per capita fatality rate was among the highest in Europe, having risen to ten times that of its neighbors, Finland and Norway, which had imposed stricter lockdowns. The Swedish economy suffered as well, shrinking 8.3 percent in the second quarter.[22] In an effort to avoid a second wave of the virus, the country ramped up its testing and contact tracing efforts and reintroduced quarantine restrictions. Whereas in most of Europe, a strict fourteen-day quarantine was imposed on all people who had come in contact with an infected person or traveled to specific places, Sweden imposed a seven-day quarantine only for those who lived with someone who had become infected. Johan Carlson, director of Sweden's public health agency, would explain that the rationale was to introduce measures that people could live with for at least a year, or at least until a vaccine arrived, in an attempt to mitigate the spread of the virus without unduly disrupting people's lives.[23]

Beyond the disciplinary mechanisms associated with the enforcement of quarantines and lockdowns, various control systems were implemented in an attempt to facilitate contact tracing. Centralized, top-down approaches were pursued in countries such as Israel, which repurposed counterterrorism technology maintained by its state security service, the Israel Security Agency (also known as "Shabak" or "Shin-Bet"), to track the location of cell phones of suspected coronavirus cases without a warrant. Initially approved by the government in March 2020, the approach has faced legal challenges due to privacy concerns and questions about its efficacy. A cabi-net panel withdrew its authorization for use later that year, letting the law expire in January 2021.[24] At the onset of the pandemic in February 2020, South Korea had logged the most COVID-19 cases of any country out-side China. The country deployed an aggressive contact-tracing campaign incorporating CCTV surveillance footage, cell phone location data, and credit card transaction histories to track the spread of the virus. Loudspeak-ers and text messages alike were employed to broadcast information about the specific locations and times where infected people had been to prompt others who had been to the same places to get tested.[25] The outbreak was contained within the span of one month. By the middle of March, daily new cases fell below 100.[26] Notably, this was achieved without implement-ing a national lockdown.

A more decentralized and distributed approach designed to address pri-vacy concerns was introduced in the United States by Apple and Google. It was based on the idea of using Bluetooth signals to detect the relative proximity of smartphones to each other rather than capturing GPS or cell tower data to determine absolute locations and mobility patterns. This enables the system to avoid storing location and other personal infor-mation on a centralized server. The partnership developed an applica-tion programming interface for iOS and Android phones that they made accessible to public health organizations for app development. The sys-tem was designed to work as follows. People would download a contact-tracing app from their public health organization and opt in to enable Bluetooth on their mobile device to send out signals to others nearby and listen for signals in return. If two phones remained within close proxim-ity for more than a few minutes, each phone would register the event and exchange unique identifier "beacons," which changed frequently, based on encryption keys stored on each device. Public health organiza-tions could adjust both thresholds for distance and duration that would count as a contact based on current metrics on COVID-19 transmission. People who became infected with the virus would indicate their status in the app, which would upload their previous two weeks of keys to a server. The server would then generate the infected person's beacon numbers and broadcast those to the network of phones running the app. When a phone received a beacon number that matched one stored on their

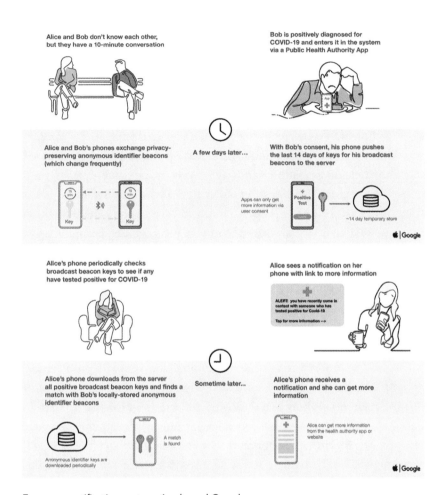

Exposure notification system. Apple and Google.

phone, it would generate a notification that the person had potentially been in contact with an infected person and provided information about what steps to take next.[27]

Privacy advocates and technology critics were quick to point out the limitations of these various approaches to contact tracing, both technical and social in nature. Technical systems based on cell site location information (CSLI), which calculate the location of a mobile device by triangulating the locations of the cell towers with which it communicates, is of insufficient granularity to be of much use. The precision of

CSLI data varies in relation to the strength of the signal, the density of towers, network load, and other factors. In rural areas, CSLI is accurate only within several square miles, while in urban areas, where towers are more densely deployed, the accuracy is better but still insufficient to be of real use.[28] Although GPS positioning is theoretically capable of determining geolocation within three feet, its nominal accuracy is typically closer to fifteen to sixty feet under an open sky. Furthermore, the technology does not work indoors and is hindered by large buildings and cloud cover in inclement weather, and GPS receivers can take up to several minutes to register their location when first turned on. Bluetooth-based systems like the one designed by Apple and Google place the burden on the individual user to make sure the service is turned on because it is not enabled by default. Moreover, none of these approaches can determine whether two people are separated by a glass partition or sense short but intense exposures to someone coughing or sneezing. In Israel, for example, one woman was issued a quarantine order because she had waved to her infected boyfriend through a window from outside his apartment building.[29]

The social limitations to these technologies are equally problematic. Reports emerged of Israelis avoiding the use of cell phones in public or turning them off entirely as a means to evade contact tracing and potential quarantine orders, which can have significant social and economic impacts. The incentive to not report that you are ill is high if doing so will prevent you from working to support yourself or your family. Alternately, as University of Cambridge security researcher Ross Anderson points out, school kids looking to game the system could self-report symptoms to get the entire school sent home.[30] Some research has suggested that systems involving contact tracing apps would need adoption rates upward of 60 percent to fully contain the virus, a high bar even for Western societies given that many people—the very young, the older, and those with older "non-smart" phones—may be unwilling or unable to download and use the software required.[31]

Monitoring the spread of the virus and the effectiveness of lockdowns involved what is known as population-level flow modeling. This technique builds on aggregate location data from a variety of sources, including telecoms, navigation systems, social media platforms, and weather

X-Mode/Tectonix map tracing paths of mobile devices returning from South Beach, Miami, after spring break, 2020. Video still by author.

apps, that collect location data from smartphones. According to industry research, roughly half of the apps available from Google's and Apple's app stores use at least one service capable of capturing location data.[32] These data are used to model flows of people at local, regional, and national scales in order to ascertain the mobility habits of a population, such as the volume of long-distance traffic on interstate highways, the average distance of trips people take across a city, or the proportion of a county's residents who have stayed home. Initiatives such as the COVID-19 Mobility Data Network, a group of forty health researchers from universities including Harvard, Princeton, and Johns Hopkins, shared insights gleaned from Facebook location data with US cities and states in an effort to help monitor the effectiveness of the emergency measures they had enacted.[33] Other government agencies relied on commercial location data for population flow data. X-Mode, a company that began as a start-up with collecting location data via an app called Drunk Mode (which prevents users from drunk dialing, or making phone calls while drunk), provided data to various federal agencies. Location data broker Unacast employed GPS data harvested from smartphone apps to create social distancing scorecards for every US county in an effort to assist states in assessing the effectiveness of their mobility restrictions. Population flow data related to mobility patterns during the pandemic also had commercial applications. Online travel company Tripadvisor introduced Crowdfree, a website that leveraged data from commercial data broker SafeGraph to map the relative crowdedness of stores and public spaces based on time of day and the day of the week. The free service aimed to help people make better decisions regarding where and when to shop, eat at a restaurant, or work out at a gym.

The COVID-19 Network Mobility Modeling project at Stanford also worked with data acquired from SafeGraph in an attempt to develop a finer-grained model of how the pandemic spread. Their model simulated peoples' mobility patterns within a locale and attempted to predict who got infected, where they got infected, and when they got infected. Predictions were correlated to the ground truth of actual case counts in the given locale to verify the accuracy of the model. Researchers worked with data from March through May 2020. For each neighborhood they studied, the simulation began with a low infection level. As the simulation progressed, people moved around based on the mobility data they were working with. If multiple people visited the same point of interest (POI) in the same hour, the model predicted that there was some probability of new infections occurring, depending on the size of the POI, the amount of time people remained there, and how many were infectious. The model also accounted for people getting infected at home from household transmissions. By capturing who got infected at which locations, the researchers claimed that their model supported detailed analyses capable of informing policy responses to COVID-19 and supporting more equitable and efficient reopening strategies. In a peer-reviewed paper published in *Nature* magazine, the researchers showed that restaurants were four times riskier than gyms in transmitting the virus.[34] The model predicted that a small number of superspreader POIs accounted for a large majority of the infections and that restricting the maximum occupancy at each POI was more effective than uniformly reducing mobility.

The model also showed that higher infection rates were found in disadvantaged socioeconomic groups resulting from differences in mobility habits. These groups had not been able to reduce their mobility as sharply, and the POIs they visited were smaller, more crowded, and thus of higher risk. One finding was that people from lower-income neighborhoods made significantly more trips per capita to grocery stores than people from higher-income ones, and they experienced higher predicted infection rates as a result. In eight of the ten metropolitan areas studied, the mobility data showed that the typical grocery store visited by people from lower-income neighborhoods had 59 percent more hourly visitors per square foot, and the visits averaged 17 percent longer in duration. As might be expected, people with money are likely to find it easier to practice social distancing. For the most part, they do not have to rely on public transportation unless they live in larger metropolitan areas. They may also be better able to get groceries and household supplies delivered to their door. They can work from home, connect with friends and colleagues via Zoom, and hold online happy hours with their "quarantinis," as Richard Reeves and Jonathan Rothwell note in an article they wrote for the Brookings Institute on the topic.[35]

At-risk populations would also become the target of data profiling initiatives. Credit reporting agency Experian announced it would be mining its 300 million consumer profiles to flag those likely to be most affected by the pandemic and offering the information to "essential organizations" such as health care providers, federal agencies, and nongovernmental organizations.[36] While Experian is best known as one of the major credit reporting agencies, it is also in the business of data brokering, and it monetizes its consumer database by dividing it into targetable segments, marketed to both public and private sectors. In this vein, the company created a market segment it refers to as "at-risk audiences," which leveraged its data assets to identify groups of individuals who were most likely to be negatively affected by the effects of the pandemic. This new segment was offered free of charge and was intended to help these organizations locate and connect with at-risk populations so they could deliver essential services as quickly as possible. Of course exactly what constitutes "essential" services is an open question, and it is not hard to imagine what business interests might opportunistically self-identify as essential. The pandemic has and will continue to hit segments of the population varying by age, demographic, and region differently. An article in Berkshire Hathaway's online Business Wire press release service puts it rather bluntly: "Businesses can leverage the dashboard to gain insight into consumer sentiment across generations and regions to respond to shifts in consumer behavior as it changes," they write. "The more businesses can understand how consumers are dealing with the fallout of the outbreak, the better positioned they will be to communicate with them and serve their needs."[37] The sample "insights" that at-risk audiences listed included bullet points such as "56 percent of consumers are watching more television and 39 percent are reading more newspapers" and "Of those planning to purchase a vehicle, more than half (51 percent) of Americans plan to continue their purchase as planned."

DISTRIBUTING PANDEMIC VACCINES

The announcement of the first successful trial of COVID-19 vaccines in autumn 2020 brought hope to a planet sizing up a rapid increase of cases in the pandemic's second wave. In the United States, the Trump administration had been promoting Operation Warp Speed, the public–private partnership led by the Department of Health and Human Services and the Defense Department to facilitate and accelerate the development, manufacturing, and distribution of COVID-19 vaccines. The government had engaged Palantir, the company it hired over the previous summer to manage the hospital data for the CDC and monitor the spread of the virus in the country to plan for the allocation and distribution of vaccines. Palantir had a long history with the US government. The company was credited with helping the Pentagon track down Osama Bin Laden, and US Immigration and Customs Enforcement had awarded a contract to it for the development of software to aid in locating and apprehending undocumented immigrants.[38] Building on the capabilities of that software, the company developed a system named Tiberius that would enable public health officials to aggregate a wide range of demographic, employment, and public health data sets to identify the location of "priority populations" and support "allocation decision making." Bearing Star Trek Captain James T. Kirk's middle name, the Tiberius algorithm was claimed to integrate data related to manufacturing, supply chain, allocation, state and territory planning, delivery, and administration of vaccine products and kits containing needles, syringes, and other supplies needed to administer the vaccine. Drawing from both federal and state information sources, the Department of Defense would claim that Tiberius "can provide a zip code-by-zip code view of priority populations, including frontline workers and nursing home residents."[39] Despite all the sci-fi-inspired fanfare, one month into the vaccine rollout in the United States, a mere 3 percent of the population was vaccinated.

As of February 2021, while more than 200 million vaccine doses had been administered worldwide—roughly 2.7 doses per 100 people—vaccination programs in different countries varied widely, and many hadn't reported administering a single dose.[40] Whereas almost half of all Israelis had received at least one shot, less than 0.1 percent of the population had been vaccinated in Iran. Predictably, vaccine rollouts in advanced economies were largely outpacing those in emerging and developing economies. Wealthy countries had signed extensive supply deals with vaccine manufacturers, and the requirements for subzero transport and storage made some vaccines difficult to deliver to more remote places. Tedros Adhanom Ghebreyesus, director-general of the World Health Organization (WHO), warned that the world was on the brink of "catastrophic moral failure" as poorer countries fell behind. WHO had partnered with several vaccine makers to provide 2 billion doses to a consortium of low-income countries in an initiative called Covax, yet Tedros claimed that "some countries and companies continue to prioritize bilateral deals, going around Covax, driving up prices and attempting to jump to the front of the queue."

TOWARD A MORE DEMOCRATIC BIOPOLITICS

Beyond questions regarding the efficacy, effectiveness, and efficiency of the various technologies developed or repurposed to represent, mitigate, and vaccinate against the virus are serious concerns regarding long-lasting implications for privacy, governmentality, and civil liberties in a post-pandemic world. The state of exception invoked by the pandemic supported the extreme measures taken by different governments around the world, whereby the notion of a common good would purport to offset any negative side effects emerging in their wake. Surely we could put up with the social and economic disruptions to our lives that these measures brought about if they in fact saved our lives. But what would happen when the pandemic subsided? What would become of these technologies and the data they harvested during the pandemic?

Many would comment on the various privacy concerns in play. From organizations such as the American Civil Liberties Union (ACLU) and the Electronic Freedom Foundation (EFF) to surveillance studies scholars and data privacy advocates alike, concerns were voiced regarding what would happen to the troves of mobility data, social graphs, and health information that these various systems had amassed. As Rob Kitchin noted in a survey of digital technologies deployed to combat the spread of the virus published early in the pandemic, for contact tracing efforts that used location-based mobility data from commercial data brokers that did not involve the consent of the people being tracked, there was "clearly a breach of the data minimization principle: that only data relevant and necessary to perform a task are generated and these are only used for the purpose for which they were produced."[41] Some voiced concern that these data would be shared with third parties and repurposed toward other ends. Initiatives involving more decentralized approaches where consent needed to be explicitly granted by an individual typically promised that all data would be anonymized. Yet it is well known that you can often reverse-engineer anonymized data though various methods involving combining, matching, and comparing different data sets if the data are not deidentified properly.[42] When, at the onset of the pandemic, South Korean authorities began posting on a government website detailed location histories for each person who tested positive for the virus, trolls on the Internet used these data to identify people by name and publicly shame them. According to an article in the *New York Times*, the website had exposed details about "when people left for work, whether they wore masks in the subway, the name of the stations where they changed trains, the massage parlors and karaoke bars they frequented and the names of the clinics where they were tested for the virus."[43]

Others expressed concern that the repurposing of cell phone infrastructure as a global pandemic surveillance apparatus further extended what sociologist Martin Innes defined two decades ago as "control creep," such as the post-9/11 appropriation of civilian network infrastructure for law enforcement and national security.[44] To the extent that technologies for location tracking, contact tracing, and population flow modeling are designed to monitor and shape our social interactions and spatial distributions, their potential repurposing for post-pandemic policing, border control, and counterterrorism, for example, is cause for alarm. One need only to look toward examples in China and Russia to anticipate how this might work in a post-pandemic world. Social and spatial sorting through app-approved admittance to various public and private spaces may well become the new normal. If anything, COVID-19 has brought to wider public attention the broad capabilities of both public agencies and private entities that own or access the data we generate throughout the course of our daily lives. The danger is that these capabilities will remain in place beyond the pandemic and become normalized. It is easy to see how this leads not only to the legitimation of the surveillance capitalists and their pervasive extraction of personal data for profit, but also to the "covid-washing" of their reputations.[45] Reports by the ACLU, EFF, and other organizations emphasize the fact that these forms of governmentality have been unevenly applied across different demographics, and as with algorithmic governance more broadly, racial, ethnic, and gender inequities are inevitably reproduced within these contexts. It is by no means ironic that among the hardest-hit sites of the COVID-19 pandemic in the United States were prisons and (meatpacking) factories. These are among the more classic disciplinary sites of capitalism.

In a series of six lectures at the University of California at Berkeley in 1983 titled Discourse and Truth: The Problematization of Parrhesia, Foucault examined the ancient philosophical concept of *parrhesia*, or the activity of truth telling. In these lectures, he points toward an alternative biopolitics that combines self-care and care for the collective in ways that avoid coercive methods common to both disciplinary and control societies.[46] It would of course be an oversimplification to pose the dilemma as a choice between an authoritarian biopolitics represented by China and a liberal reliance on individual citizens making rational decisions as we found in Sweden. Yet in the wake of this state of exception, we search again for forms of democratic biopolitics that foster collaborative

sense making and have the potential to give rise to collective interpretive sensibilities. Beyond the drive to develop new methods of testing
for the virus, better apps for sensing proximate infectious bodies, or the
search for better practices for distributing vaccines and the vaccination
of diverse populations at varying levels of risk, we find the critical need
for better interpretive practices, questions of (good and bad) judgment,
and how they might hold the potential to influence collective behavior
(or not).

CODA

The growing power of software engineering does not necessarily lead to the power of Big Brother. In fact it is way more cracked than it seems. It can blow up like a windshield under the impact of molecular alternative practices.

—Félix Guattari

NATURE ABHORS A VACUUM

Spring 2020. An empty piazza in Rome. A vacant theater on Broadway. No street crossings in Shibuya. No traffic in São Paulo. Public spaces from Moscow to Seoul to London effectively evacuated, save for the stray dog in Berlin or straggling health care worker in Mexico City. *Even the sounds of the city had evacuated the city.*[1] Sequestered at home, bodies lay in waiting, on the couch, in comfy pants, commingling in pods of friends and family that for a variety of (sometimes conflicting and dubious) reasons were considered safe ("but we were supercareful!"). Some rediscovered taking long walks, baking bread, and binge-watching shows on Netflix, HBO, and the like. Others saw an opportunity for flight—to lower-density places, slower occupations (or at least a job change), and simpler (and less expensive) lifestyles. Still others just didn't seem to care (or couldn't afford to) and carried on as usual despite the rising body counts. Around the world, superspreader events at weddings and funerals reportedly sickened and killed multiple generations of family members and friends, yet somehow at the Lake of the Ozarks, tightly packed throngs of people still found ways to party over Memorial Day weekend. At some point, many would see 8 minutes and 46 seconds of video shot on a smartphone and circulated via social media depicting the knee of a white police officer on the neck of a prone black man on a street corner in Minneapolis, Minnesota. And public space would explode.

That the existential void of pandemic urban space would quickly be filled by various warring political and cultural factions, both online and in physical space, was predictable. The outpouring of anger and frustration following the event would give rise to protests around the world against systemic racism and police violence, *matters of concern*[2] that some would suggest extended beyond the specific issue at hand and pointed toward a more general "transnationally shared affect."[3] Media theorist Eric Kluitenberg has defined *affect space* in terms of densifying urban public spaces overlaid with ever more robust wireless media and communication networks.[4] Building on work by geographer Nigel Thrift that addresses the politics of affect with respect to the ways in which its systematic engineering has become central to the political life of Euro American cities,[5] Kluitenberg sees these new urban conditions as producing a form of information overload in the contemporary urban subject that privileges affective relations over more deliberative forms of social interaction and the desire for embodied encounters in physical public space. In an essay titled "The Zombie Public," he identifies "mediated online connections" as the "replacement for embodied encounters under the lockdown conditions of social separation." The conflict between the desire for embodied human interaction within shared, physical spaces and the rational understanding of the need to practice social distancing and abide by lockdown orders produced what he calls the Somatic Deficit, an "experiential and affective gap between the embodied and mediated experience."[6]

Kluitenberg constitutes Affect Space across three interrelated components: a technological component (network communication infrastructure enabling masses of people to mobilize around emerging issues and concerns), an affective component (powerful and persuasive images, aphorisms, and slogans), and a spatial component (physical urban space within which affective content is generated for online distribution). "Intense events, protests, calamities, collective shock, violent confrontations (military, police violence, violent mobs), many distributed in near real-time, all contribute to an acceleration of communicative exchanges (posts, tweets, live-feeds, text messaging, photo and video sharing, televised reports) that quickly overwhelm the human capacity for cognitive processing," he writes. "Within the new constellation of mobile and wireless media both production and reception of these messages happen simultaneously on site and remotely, where all these message streams feed into each other, unleashing an auto-catalytic intensification that can only be felt but no longer qualified."

AFFECTIVE DISSENT

In the summer of 2020, streets and public plazas would erupt in violence in response to the killing of a black man by a white cop, recalling the riots almost thirty years prior in Los Angeles after video recorded by a local plumber from his balcony was disseminated via broadcast media showing the vicious beating of Rodney King by uniformed LAPD officers in 1991. In 2014, Black Lives Matter (BLM), a decentralized political and social movement protesting incidents of police brutality and advocating for racial justice, attracted broad public attention following the killing of Eric Garner in July by an officer of the New York City Police Department, who had used a banned chokehold to restrain him. The extended protests and riots in Ferguson, Missouri, following the police shooting of Michael Brown in August would further increase public outrage over systemic racism and violence perpetrated by white police officers against black people, an outrage that had been building for years.

The killing of George Floyd by Minneapolis police officer Derek Chauvin on May 25, 2020, would become the event that ignited more than 450 major protests in cities and towns across the United States that quickly spread to three continents around the world. The extreme isolation of a distributed domestic quarantine was juxtaposed with the centrality of volatile and explosive public spaces that had been previously evacuated under local pandemic lockdown guidelines that were almost immediately abandoned as people took to the streets in protest. Here, the various scales discussed throughout this book inevitably intertwine: how from the comforts of home on lockdown, people bore witness to the killing of a black man on a street corner in front of an urban minimarket that ignited protests against police brutality and calls for racial justice that captivated a nation and spread rapidly to different parts of the world.

The role of networked media and information systems in organizing and amplifying social protest is not new. That the revolution would not just be televised but moreover propagated through an expanding ecology of social media platforms was obvious. Recall the occupation of Zuccotti Park in Lower Manhattan by Occupy Wall Street or Tahrir Square in Cairo by Egyptian revolutionaries over a decade ago, or the massive protests across Europe in response to the Charlie Hebdo terrorist attack in Paris in 2015. Then as now, a campaign integrating the physical occupation of public space with the proliferation of affective media content across network information systems would fuel the production of hashtag micropublics competing for macropublic attention. From Osman Orsal's images of the #ladyinred being pepper-sprayed in Istanbul to the video of #neda dying on the streets of Tehran from a profusely bleeding bullet wound to the chest that circulated on YouTube, affective media would drive the mobilization of people to occupy physical public space. These micropublics are formed under conditions that coalesce around shared affects more than shared sociopolitical issues or shared beliefs.

Studies claim that affect operates at a speed that preempts environmental stimuli, twice that of conscious perception.[7] Political theorist and philosopher Brian Massumi would note with regard to the Charlie Hebdo protests that the course and evolution of shared affect depend entirely on the predispositions, biases, and capacities of the individual subjects who enter into these collective formations. In these situations, there is no narrative coherence or "sameness of affect" for those involved. According to Massumi, there is only *affective difference*, a process of collective individuation whereby the matter of concern triggering the collective event is eclipsed by the shared affect of the event itself and how it plays out differently across its various constituencies.[8]

Lady in Red, Istanbul, May 28, 2013. Photo by Osman Orsal, REUTERS/Alamy.

MOLECULAR ALTERNATIVE PRACTICES

In the United States, these constituencies had become highly polarized. The physical occupation of public space in Portland and Seattle that summer, pitting Far Right neofascist Proud Boys against Far Left antifa (antifascist) activists in open urban warfare, vividly illustrated how finding common ground would remain an agonistic process of perpetual negotiation and struggle, one in which various actors continually articulate and defend competing conceptions of cultural and political identity. The structural racism and police violence on display in the United States and the evolving narratives perpetuated by competing presidential campaigns were foregrounded by events that manifest this political polarization in spatial terms.

Whereas the initially peaceful BLM street protests that followed the killing of George Floyd in Minneapolis in May would lead to calls to "defund the police," protests following the police shooting of Jacob Blake in Kenosha, Wisconsin, in August led to lethal violence provoked by white supremacists and Far Right militia members. Public space became a stage for the dramatization of the cultural and political divide in the United States, brought to you by the social media posts of its warring factions. That summer, in a made-for-Instagram moment, the US Park Police and National Guard troops in Washington, DC, would use an arsenal of tear gas, rubber bullets, pepper spray, shields, and batons to clear peaceful protesters from Lafayette Square and surrounding streets in front of the White House, making way for then President Trump to walk to St. John's Episcopal Church, which was damaged in a fire during the protests, so he could hold up a Bible and pose for a photo-op in front of the church.

This factional warfare played out in cities across the country that fall, culminating in the storming of the US Capitol building in Washington, DC, on January 6, 2021, following a rally led by an outgoing president who had for months persisted in claiming the election was stolen from him. Prior to the election, Trump had been seeding the idea at his campaign rallies that if he were to lose to Joe Biden, the election would have been rigged. Vote-by-mail initiatives, viewed by many as a pragmatic means to increase voter turnout in the midst of a pandemic, were cast by Trump as a ripe opportunity for voter fraud. Generally Democrats were considered more likely to vote by mail, whereas Republicans were more likely to prefer voting in person. In the months before the election, many were alarmed by an announcement by the US Postal Service that it might not have the capacity to deliver ballots cast by mail in a timely manner. The announcement came from the new postmaster general, a Trump megadonor named Louis DeJoy, who was instituting organizational changes and directing the removal of mail sorting equipment that had significantly slowed mail delivery.[9] As predicted, on the night of the election, November 3, 2020, the majority of in-person voting would favor Donald Trump. Yet in the days following the election, as the mail-in ballots that would shift the majority of votes to Biden continued to trickle in, Trump would ramp up his claims of rampant voter fraud and demand a halt to the counting of votes. Both his campaign and his allies would proceed to file (and lose) no fewer than sixty-three lawsuits that contested election processes, vote counting, and the vote certification process in multiple states, including key swing states Arizona, Georgia, Michigan, Nevada, Pennsylvania, and Wisconsin. Almost all of the lawsuits were dismissed due to lack of evidence and described as frivolous and without merit by presiding judges, lawyers, and legal observers alike. Yet despite his serial and resounding defeat in courts of law, Trump and his allies would perpetuate his "big lie" that the election was stolen from him in the court of public opinion convened via his Twitter feed.[10] Eyeing the date when the US Congress would formally certify the electoral college vote count and formalize Biden's victory, Trump would take to social media to organize the "Save America" rally in front of the White House in an attempt to "stop the steal" and overturn the election results. "Big protest in D.C. on January 6th," he tweeted. "Be there, will be wild!"

Trump was of course tweeting to a patchwork of various groups that included not only conspiracy theorists, white supremacists, and members of Far Right and antigovernment militias but also statistically average-looking white people you might see at a suburban shopping mall. This base included the QAnon faithful who believed in a sweeping conspiracy that the world was run by a satanic group of pedophiles composed of top Democrats and Hollywood elites whom President Trump was on a top-secret mission to bring to justice; the Proud Boys, a Far Right, neofascist, and white nationalist organization of men that provoked and perpetuated political violence across North America; and the Oath Keepers, a Far Right antigovernment militia whose membership included current and former members from the military, police, and first responders who pledged to fulfill the oath that all military and police take in order to "defend the Constitution against all enemies, foreign and domestic." For this motley crew, the matter of concern—"stop the steal"—would trigger a collective event that was quickly eclipsed by the shared affect of the event itself, differentially unfolding for everybody involved in the months that followed.

The storming of the US Capitol building by Trump supporters was broadcast in real time by all of the major news networks. Most were covering the proceedings in Congress, where the process of certifying votes was underway. Some had been covering the Save America rally down the street, where Trump would incite the crowd to march down Pennsylvania Avenue to the Capitol building to "stop the steal." As rioters stormed the steps of the building and breached the police cordon, cable news cameras turned from speeches by senators and representatives inside on the floor of the House and Senate to the wave of people outside pouring in through broken windows and shattered doors. While traditional TV news feeds streamed images of mobs of people swarming the steps outside the Capitol, live video from individual rioters inside the building streamed across social media platforms such as Facebook, Twitch, and YouTube. Social media would become the primary news source of the event, picked up by the major networks and rebroadcast on repeat throughout the afternoon and into the evening.

Social media would also become the primary means by which people who had participated in the riot would be identified and subsequently arrested in the weeks that followed. Many had come to believe that both law enforcement in general and their president in particular would welcome their actions or, at minimum, not view their behavior as unlawful. Rioters had made little effort to conceal their identities while boasting about their participation in tweets, posts, and live streams from the day's events. Yet while the FBI did collect mobile phone cell site data from telecoms and analyze CCTV footage with facial recognition software, perhaps more effective were efforts by individuals in leveraging social media as an open and distributed surveillance apparatus to identify the perpetrators and subsequently report them to the FBI. Affirming a remarkable recircuiting of power that had been slowly unfolding for decades, law enforcement would become yet another customer in emerging information markets.

For example, John Scott-Railton, a senior researcher at the University of Toronto's Citizen Lab, used several techniques to identify a man wearing a combat helmet and body armor and carrying zip-tie handcuffs who appeared in images and videos on the Senate floor.[11] Through a combination of image enhancement, facial recognition, and contextual clues provided by patches sewn into his military gear that bore identifiable insignia, Scott-Railton would identify the man as retired Lieutenant Colonel Larry Rendall Brock Jr., a Texas-based Air Force Academy graduate and combat veteran. In the images and video that Scott-Railton examined, Brock wore several symbols suggesting he was from Texas. One was a symbol of the Texas flag superimposed over an icon of a Marvel comic book character known as the Punisher, which had been embraced by members of the military, the police, white supremacists, and QAnon followers alike. He also discovered a Twitter account associated with Brock that had recently been deleted and used the image of a Crusader as a profile image. "All those things together, it's like looking at a person's C.V.," Scott-Railton would tell *New Yorker* magazine reporter Ronan Farrow.[12] Two days after Farrow published an article about Scott-Railton's work, Brock was arrested by the FBI.

Others would engage in open source data archiving and intelligence practices to identify the insurrectionists and represent the day's events. When Amazon Web Services announced that Parler, an alternative to Twitter popular with the Far Right, would be banned from its web-hosting platform, some became concerned that valuable evidence potentially incriminating participants in the siege of the Capitol would be deleted. Parler had been an important organizing tool for the Far Right, who posted their rallying calls to the platform in the months leading up to the storming of the Capitol. This evidence was in their minds essential to preserve. Google Play and Apple's App Store had already removed the Parler mobile app from their download services, but this content was still accessible via the Parler website that Amazon hosted. Thinking quickly, a hacker who went by the name donk_enby, together with a cohort of independent data archivists, stepped in to preserve the Parler content.

On Saturday, January 9, Amazon announced it was dumping Parler effective midnight the next day. Within this time frame, donk_enby and the Archive Team, a group of hackers and data researchers, downloaded nearly every post, image, and video before it was shut down, creating a massive 56.7 terabyte archive of data representing 96 percent of Parler's content.[13] The group managed to exploit weaknesses in the website's architecture to pull the URLs of each public post, using a piece of reverse-engineering software called Ghidra that was created and released publicly by the National Security Agency (NSA). The NSA attests to Ghidra's features: "It helps analyze malicious code and malware like viruses, and can give cybersecurity professionals a better understanding of potential vulnerabilities in their networks and systems."[14] Or someone else's networks and systems, evidently. The Archive Team would also construct a tool that allowed Twitter users to anonymously volunteer their own bandwidth to accelerate the transfer of data, which reportedly at one point peaked at 50 GB per second.[15]

This data set would form the basis for a searchable public archive and reporting by ProPublica, an independent, nonprofit newsroom producing investigative journalism of public interest. Consisting of some 412 million files, the data included 150 million photos and more than 1 million videos. Because Parler did not follow the common data security practice of stripping metadata from its users' uploads, these media objects contained embedded metadata for date, time, and GPS coordinates. With this information, ProPublica was able to filter the archive to around 500 videos that had been uploaded by people in the vicinity of the White House and Capitol during the insurrection and sort them by time and location. The resulting interactive time line they produced offered unprecedented insight from hundreds of points of view of the day's events in vivid detail, up close and personal, some exhibiting incredibly strong affect.[16]

The crowd that this trove of media depicts is as tenuous in coherence as it is fraught with internal contradiction. We meet QAnon shaman Jacob

ProPublica time line interface to Parler video archive. Screenshot by the author.

Chansley, on the Senate floor during the insurrection, bare-chested and wearing a fur helmet with horns. We watch a throng of people surge up an internal stairway chanting, "Hang [Vice President] Mike Pence." We see a woman get shot and killed while trying to jump through the side panel of an interior door. For many of the rioters, January 6, 2021, would be the day that years of online rhetoric would converge on the actual building where the object(s) of their vitriol would appear in an unfamiliar and confusing manner. As ProPublica reporter Alec MacGillis remarks in his analysis of the videos in the archive, "What struck me most about them is just how much this assemblage of people assaulting the Capitol reminded me of people I had seen and spoken with over the years at regular Republican campaign events . . . husbands in golf caps with well-manicured wives, frat boys, fathers with sons . . . there were the rootless young men spoiling for a fight, and there was also a huge range of more bourgeois sorts—from people who presented as suburban dads to one real estate agent who flew in by private plane, announcing her plans to 'storm the capitol' on Facebook."[17] On the one hand, the crowd was among the most homogenous (white) crowds of its size to be seen in the United States that year. From another perspective, it was a cross-section of America combining hard-core white supremacists with people you might run in to at a suburban country club. "The more videos one watches," writes MacGillis, "the more overwhelmed one is by the variety of motivations and profiles."

In the hundreds of videos documenting the siege, a conflicted and complicated assembly of people appear. Expressions of awe and bewilderment within the place the crowd had found themselves are paired with those of entitlement—"This is *our* house." Yet as rioters smash windows and break through doors or rummage through senators' desks, we also hear pleads for restraint: "Oh God no, stop! Stop!" "Don't break my house!" The uncertainty of their claim to possess that house is reflected in their conflict about trashing it. This cognitive dissonance is reflected in the mob's attempt to comprehend the response by the police, whom many had thought would be on *their* side. Shouts of "Back the Blue!" and images of rioters taking selfies with police officers are contrasted by scenes of intense violence where cops are beaten with flag poles and hit in the head by fire extinguishers. Five officers would die as a result, as would four rioters, one a military veteran.

Trump would subsequently become the target of a serial deplatforming campaign by various social media platforms, as would his close associates and family members. In the minutes and hours following the events at the Capitol, many awaited a response from the White House. When it came, the one minute video of Trump reiterating his claims that the election was stolen and telling the mob that breached the Capitol to go home—while at the same time saying "We love you, you're very special"—alarmed many. Twitter, which months prior had resorted to labeling Trump's tweets alleging election fraud as misinformation, would immediately terminate his account, followed by Facebook, Instagram, YouTube, SnapChat, and Twitch. Shopify, the Canadian e-commerce platform, removed Trump's campaign merchandise shop and personal brand from its platform.[18] Social media platforms began to uncomfortably and very publicly grapple with their dual role as both legislator and enforcer of policy. Facebook CEO Mark Zuckerberg had just testified before Congress that his company was not in the business of moderating content, that it was not an arbitrator of speech. Less than a year later, the deplatforming of Trump would signal the reluctant acquiescence by social media corporations to assume what was once a purview of the state: the regulation of media and information systems.

Ultimately Biden was sworn in as the forty-sixth president of the United States on January 20, 2021. The QAnon faithful have since wavered between disbelief, embarrassment, and outright denial, with some still holding on.[19] News reports recount the outing of QAnon believers among friends and family. Subsequent protests in Washington, DC, and elsewhere were postponed by QAnon organizers afraid that they may actually be traps laid by law enforcement. Proud Boys leader Enrique Tarrio was revealed to be a former FBI informant, leading to infighting within and splintering of the organization. The Justice Department eventually charged the leader of the Oath Keepers, Elmer Stewart Rhodes III, and ten of its members with seditious conspiracy. Eight other members were charged with conspiring to delay the certification of the presidential election by coordinating efforts to storm Congress. By the first anniversary of the insurrection, the FBI had arrested more than seven hundred twenty-five people across the country, and prominent Far Right propagandists and conspiracy theorists had succumbed to infighting, struggling with restless followers, ongoing investigations and millions of dollars in legal debt.[20]

SPACES OF APPEARANCE / SPACES OF SURVEILLANCE

All of this brings to the fore the question of our agency to act (and enact collectively) within these new and emerging entanglements of people and data, code and space, knowledge and power. Hannah Arendt, herself an antifacist advocate, has argued that to confront one another in a public space, to examine an issue from conflicting perspectives, to be capable of modifying our views and expanding them to incorporate those of others does not necessarily need to lead to a unified, unanimous, and monolithic public opinion. Rather, it is the process of their enactment itself that can constitute collective identities, a "we" to which we can appeal when distinguishing between truth and falsehood and when deciding on one course of action versus another.

From this standpoint, finding common ground is an agonistic process of perpetual negotiation and struggle, one in which actors continually articulate and defend competing conceptions of cultural and political identity.[21] For Arendt, this form of participatory citizenship relied on the existence of *a space of appearance*, a public space within which we appear before each other in all of our resplendent differences. This is a space where we meet one another, exchange our opinions, and debate our differences and where commonalities can emerge and become the subject of democratic debate. It is also a space that enables subject positions not easily mapped to attributable clusters within a feature space extracted by attentive algorithms to be perceived in profile. The distributed media archive documenting the storming of the US Capitol building thus renders in a very public manner the appearance of a statistical imaginary of Trump supporters in all its stochastic splendor.

The aggregation of angry hashtag micropublics on January 6, 2021, in Washington, DC, whose assembly in physical public space was provoked by the shared affect triggered by slogans like "stop the steal," and whose appearance was made manifest by an ad hoc, crowd-sourced social media surveillance apparatus, would far exceed the threshold of public consciousness and become the subject of household conversation and debate. Neighbors, colleagues, and uncles alike, outed as QAnon believers, were searching for their footing. That the effort to overturn the election would fail should not have been hard to predict. As with Occupy Wall Street and the Arab Spring uprisings, the problem with political movements bound by shared affect is that they are ephemeral in nature. As Kluitenberg suggests, they are inherently unstable due to their heterogeneous makeup, they are unable to capture of the entirety of an affective intensity and therefore prone to resurging in unpredictable ways (Massumi's "autonomic remainder"), and the sheer quantity of matters of concern in play renders the drive toward a consensus that could sustain political action as unrealistic as it is unreasonable.

Public space today is no longer the geography of the public sphere, and as the chapters in this book have sought to articulate, the public realm today is constituted more by what we might describe as spaces of surveillance than spaces of appearance. The challenge we face is in articulating new forms of appearance within the various shared spaces of contemporary publics within which we come together, ones that extend horizontally across and against the divisive vertical segmentation of spaces of surveillance, and support an ongoing struggle to formulate more empowering and enduring collective identities.

Significant questions remain. Does locating ourselves within, navigating through, and otherwise inhabiting these uncommon grounds demand an act of faith that supplants ground truth with ground fiction? To what extent are we required to abandon notions of a human agency that rely on shared understanding, common challenges, and "the perception of a landscape that can be explored in concert"? What viable avenues for effective political action remain? That these spatial epistemologies are perhaps becoming more unevenly distributed across disparate social, cultural, and economic realities than they have ever been is arguably one of the more important challenges of the post-truth condition. How we navigate and negotiate this epistemic uncertainty and learn to live with the accompanying doubt will likely define both the futures we hope to share and those we must prevent.

ACKNOWLEDGMENTS

This book emerged from a series of events. Some, like those that are addressed in it, are troubling in their implications for the world to come. Others are far more encouraging and deserve to be celebrated for their kindness. Every book is the result of the efforts of countless people, the extent of which can be a challenge to fully and adequately acknowledge. So with apologies in advance for any omissions, I thank the many who were directly and indirectly involved in this project.

I first thank Eve Blau for an invitation in 2016 to participate in a workshop at the Radcliffe Institute for Advanced Study at Harvard University titled Urban Intermedia: The City between Experience and Information. My presentation focused on the changing nature of bias in urban research in the shift from observational tools to environments that observe, and investigated how what we see is conditioned by the methods by and through which we see, and how this conditioning changes in the shift from representational practices to interactive and immersive ones. Some of the key ideas developed throughout this book can be traced back to this workshop. Many thanks to Eve, Julie Buckler, and Erik Ghenolu at Harvard for organizing this catalyzing event and to the other participants whose critical comments and suggestions helped shape this book: Orit Halpern, Dietmar Offenhuber, Catharine D'Ignazio, Robb Moss, Peter Galison, Laura Frahm, and Robert Pietrusko. The presentation I delivered would subsequently be developed into a chapter in *The Routledge Companion to Smart Cities*, edited by Katharine Willis and Alessandro Aurigi (2020), and form the basis for chapter 5, "From Tools to Environments," in this book.

In fall 2019, I was a resident artist at MacDowell, where from a cabin in the woods on the outskirts of Peterborough, New Hampshire, much of the research and initial writing of this book took shape. I'm grateful for the insights and inspiration of many of my cohort who sat through presentations of the work in progress and were so generous with their feedback, including Elisabeth Condon, Hernan Diaz, Alex Espinoza, McKenzie Funk, Em Goldman, Samantha Johns, Jamie Lowe, Ryan Ludwig, Rodrigo Martinez, Edie Meidav, Terry O'Reilly, Jeff Sharlet, Noah Sneider, and Ed Woodham. I owe special thanks to Blake Tewksbury, heart and soul of MacDowell, whose daily lunch basket delivery to my studio accompanied by his warm smile provided a steady rhythm for my writing and something to look forward to each day.

Parts of chapter 3, "The Data Blasé," and chapter 5, "Spurious Correlations," were presented during a panel discussion on "Delirious Data" organized by McClain Clutter at the 107th Annual Meeting of the Association of Collegiate Schools of Architecture conference, BLACK BOX: Articulating Architecture's Core in the Post-Digital Era. Credit goes to Clutter for coining the terms *data blasé* and *the statistical imaginary* in the call for proposals he wrote for the panel. (Responsibility for their misreading in the pages of this book is all mine, however.) Thanks to panelists Britt Eversole, Brittany Utting and Daniel Jacobs, Rebecca Smith, and Oliver Popadich for the provocative and stimulating conversation that ensued.

Many thanks to Doug Sery for his early support of this project, to Noah J. Springer for seeing it through, and the rest of the team at the MIT Press for making it happen: Lillian Dunaj, Judy Feldmann, Beverly Miller, Marge Encomienda, Sean Reilly, and Jessica Pellien. Adam Jacob Levin read early drafts of the prospectus and manuscript and I am deeply grateful for his insight and thoughtful comments. Thanks to Kazys Varnelis, Molly Wright Steenson, and Yanni Loukissas for their support during the proposal phase, and to four anonymous reviewers whose comments reflected a sincere engagement with the project and have helped make this a better book.

The publication of this book has been generously supported by the Graham Foundation for Advanced Studies in the Fine Arts.

I am grateful for the support of the University at Buffalo, where I have taught in the Departments of Architecture and Media Study since 2005. I greatly appreciate the subvention funding provided by the School of Architecture and Planning and the Department of Architecture. I also acknowledge my colleagues in the Ethical AI Working Group who, while likely unaware, provided a sounding board for some of the arguments in this book regarding algorithmic bias: Atri Ruda, Varun Chandola, Matthew Bolton, Kenny Joseph, and Jonathan Manes. Many of the practices discussed in this book have been informed by dialogue with colleagues in the context of reviewing the work of studios and seminars I have taught in both departments. I am indebted to my co-conspirators over the years, including Omar Khan, Trebor Scholz, Marc Böhlen, Hadas Steiner, Jordan Geiger, Paul Vanouse, Stephanie Rothenberg, Paige Sarlin, Nick Bruscia, Joyce Hwang, Erkin Ozay, Jason Geistweidt, Andrew Lison, and Margaret Rhee. I also thank the PhD students I have been fortunate to supervise over the years, including Leonardo Aranda Brito, Derek Curry, Shawn Van Every, Scott Fitzgerald, Jennifer Gradecki, and Mani Mehrvarz. In these uncertain times, the courage that these students have brought to their work is as promising as it is reassuring for what comes next.

This book is devoted to my parents, whose passing just before I started this project (my mother, Susan) and on the completion of the first draft of the manuscript (my father, Robert) frame one of the more challenging periods of my life. Within this window of time, my daughter was born (to whom this book is dedicated), bringing tiny moments of joy that sustained me through a bleak winter of deepening uncertainty accompanying a raging pandemic, during which much of this book was written. None of this would have been remotely possible without the resilient spirit and unyielding support of my wife, Antonina, for whom there are preciously few words that can adequately describe the depth of my appreciation.

NOTES

INTRODUCTION

1. "Word of the Year 2016 Is . . . ," Oxford Dictionaries, Oxford University Press, https://languages.oup.com/word-of-the-year/word-of-the-year-2016.

2. Edward Wong, "Trump Has Called Climate Change a Chinese Hoax. Beijing Says It Is Anything But," *New York Times*, November 18, 2916, https://www.nytimes.com/2016/11/19/world/asia/china-trump-climate-change.html

3. John Lichfield, "Boris Johnson's £350m Claim Is Devious and Bogus. Here's Why," *Guardian*, September 18, 2017, https://www.theguardian.com/commentisfree/2017/sep/18/boris-johnson-350-million-claim-bogus-foreign-secretary.

4. "Art of the Lie," *Economist*, September 10, 2016, https://www.economist.com/leaders/2016/09/10/art-of-the-lie.

5. Steve Tesich, "A Government of Lies," *Nation*, January 6/13, 1992, 12–14.

6. Colbert Report, "The Word—Truthiness," *Comedy Central* video, 2:40, October 17, 2005, https://www.cc.com/video/63ite2/the-colbert-report-the-word-truthiness.

7. This phrase was coined by *Wired* magazine's editor-in-chief Chris Anderson in "The End of Theory: The Data Deluge Makes the Scientific Method Obsolete," *Wired*, June 23, 2008, https://www.wired.com/2008/06/pb-theory.

8. For an analysis of the epistemics of the smart city as reflected in Songdo, Korea, see Orit Halpern, Jesse LeCavalie, Nerea Calvillo, and Wolfgang Pietsch, "Test-Bed Urbanism," *Public Culture* 25, no. 2 (2013): 272–306.

9. Conspiracy theories run rampant on the Internet, and QAnon is no exception. For a general introduction to the QAnon phenomenon, see Kevin Roose, "What Is QAnon, the Viral Pro-Trump Conspiracy Theory?" *New York Times*, March 4, 2021, https://www.nytimes.com/article/what-is-qanon.html, and Mike Rothschild, *The*

Storm Is Upon Us: How QAnon Became a Movement, Cult, and Conspiracy Theory of Everything (London: Melville House, 2021). Others have noted similarities to alternate reality games. See Clive Thompson, "QAnon Is Like a Game—a Most Dangerous Game," *Wired*, September 22, 2020, https://www.wired.com/story/qanon-most -dangerous-multiplatform-game/.

10. Imran Ahmed, *The Disinformation Dozen*, Center for Countering Digital Hate, March 24, 2021, https://www.counterhate.com/disinformationdozen.

11. Soroush Vosoughi, Deb Roy, and Sinan Aral, "The Spread of True and False News Online," *Science* 359, no. 6380 (2018): 1146–1151.

12. The claims made by Cambridge Analytica and its impact on these elections are subject to debate, as noted in chapter 8. For an introduction to the radicalization of populations through online social media, see "Radicalization by Design," a project curated by Marc Tuters in 2020 for the Impakt Center for Media Culture, Utrecht, the Netherlands, https://radicalization.impakt.nl/.

13. See the *Washington Post*'s "Fact Checker," https://www.washingtonpost.com /graphics/politics/trump-claims/, and Glenn Kessler, "Trump Made 30,573 False or Misleading Claims as President. Nearly Half Came in His Final Year," *Washington Post*, January 23, 2021, https://www.washingtonpost.com/politics/how-fact-checker -tracked-trump-claims/2021/01/23/ad04b69a-5c1d-11eb-a976-bad6431e03e2_story .html.

14. Matthew Ingram, "Facebook's Fact-Checking Program Falls Short," *Columbia Journalism Review*, August 2, 2019, http://www.cjr.org/the_media_today/facebook -fact-checking.php.

15. Noortje Marres, "Why We Can't Have Our Facts Back," *Engaging Science, Technology, and Society* 4 (2018): 423.

16. See, for example, Stephen P. Turner, *Liberal Democracy 3.0: Civil Society in an Age of Experts* (London: Sage, 2003).

17. Jean-François Lyotard, *The Postmodern Condition: A Report on Knowledge* (Minneapolis: University of Minnesota Press, 1984).

18. See his interview with journalist Carole Cadwalladr, "Daniel Dennett: 'I Begrudge Every Hour I Have to Spend Worrying about Politics,'" *Guardian*, February 12, 2017, https://www.theguardian.com/science/2017/feb/12/daniel-dennett-politics-bacteria -bach-back-dawkins-trump-interview.

19. Friedrich Wilhelm Nietzsche, *The Portable Nietzsche* (New York: Viking Press, 1954), 458.

20. Helmut Heit, "'There are no facts . . .': Nietzsche as Predecessor of Post-Truth?" *Studia Philosophica Estonica* 11 (2018): 44.

21. Bruno Latour and Steve Woolgar, *Laboratory Life: The Construction of Scientific Facts* (Princeton: Princeton University Press, 2006).

22. Bruno Latour, *Down to Earth: Politics in the New Climatic Regime* (Malden, MA: Polity, 2018), 23.

23. Ava Kofman, "Bruno Latour, the Post-Truth Philosopher, Mounts a Defense of Science," *New York Times*, October 25, 2018, http://www.nytimes.com/2018/10/25 /magazine/bruno-latour-post-truth-philosopher-science.html.

24. See, for example, Richard Sennett, *The Fall of Public Man* (New York: Knopf, 1977), and Jürgen Habermas, *The Structural Transformation of the Public Sphere: An Inquiry into a Category of Bourgeois Society* (Cambridge, MA: MIT Press, 1989).

25. See Joy Buolamwini and Timnit Gebru, "Gender Shades: Intersectional Accuracy Disparities in Commercial Gender Classification," in *Proceedings of Machine Learning Research* (January 2018), 77–91, and Will Douglas Heaven, "Predictive Policing Algorithms Are Racist. They Need to Be Dismantled," *MIT Technology Review*, July 17, 2020, https://www.technologyreview.com/2020/07/17/1005396/predictive-policing -algorithms-racist-dismantled-machine-learning-bias-criminal-justice/.

26. See Ruha Benjamin, *Race after Technology* (New York: Polity Press, 2019); Wendy Hui Kyong Chun, *Discriminating Data: Correlation, Neighborhoods, and the New Politics of Recognition* (Cambridge, MA: MIT Press, 2021); and Laura Kurgan, Dare Brawley, Brian House, Jia Zhang, and Wendy Hui Kyong Chun, "Homophily: The Urban History of an Algorithm," *e-flux*, October 4, 2019, https://www.e-flux.com/architecture /are-friends-electric/289193/homophily-the-urban-history-of-an-algorithm/.

27. See Michel Foucault, *Discipline and Punish: The Birth of the Prison* (New York: Pantheon, 1977); Gilles Deleuze, "Postscript on Control Societies," in *Negotiations: 1972–1990*, trans. Martin Joughin (New York: Columbia University Press, 1995); and Shoshana Zuboff, *The Age of Surveillance Capitalism* (New York: Public Affairs, 2019).

28. Foucault developed the concept of governmentality in the latter part of his life, especially through lectures delivered at the Collège de France. See Michel Foucault, *The Birth of Biopolitics: Lectures at the Collège de France, 1978–1979*, ed. Michel Senellart, trans. Graham Burchell (New York: Palgrave MacMillan, 2008). See also Michel Foucault, Graham Burchell, Colin Gordon, and Peter Miller, *The Foucault Effect: Studies in Governmentality* (Chicago: University of Chicago Press, 1991).

29. Thomas Lemke, "Foucault, Governmentality, and Critique," *Rethinking Marxism* 14, no. 3 (2002): 50.

30. Foucault, *Discipline and Punish*.

31. For an introduction to the history of spatial epistemology, see Matthias Schemmel, "Towards a Historical Epistemology of Space: An Introduction," in *Spatial Thinking and External Representation*, ed. Matthias Schemmel (Berlin: Max Planck Institute for the History of Science, 2016).

32. Gilbert Ryle, *The Concept of Mind* (Chicago: University of Chicago Press, 1949).

33. Henri Lefebvre, *The Production of Space* (Oxford: Blackwell, 1991), 1.

34. Jean Piaget, *The Construction of Reality in the Child* (New York: Basic Books, 1959), 97–101.

35. Fredric Jameson, *Postmodernism, or, The Cultural Logic of Late Capitalism* (Durham: Duke University Press, 1991), 51.

36. Jameson, *Postmodernism*, 52.

37. Jameson, *Postmodernism*, 52.

38. Lefebvre, *The Production of Space*, 14.

39. Louise Amoore, *Cloud Ethics: Algorithms and the Attributes of Ourselves and Others* (Durham: Duke University Press, 2020), 169.

40. Jean-Paul Sarte, *The Imaginary: A Phenomenological Psychology of the Imagination* (London: Routledge, 2004), 90.

41. Jameson, *Postmodernism*, 53.

42. Jameson, *Postmodernism*, 51.

43. The term *intersectionality* was coined by Black feminist scholar and legal theorist Kimberle Crenshaw in a paper published in 1989. See Kimberle Crenshaw, "Demarginalizing the Intersection of Race and Sex: A Black Feminist Critique of Antidiscrimination Doctrine, Feminist Theory and Antiracist Politics," *University of Chicago Legal Forum*, no. 1 (1989): art. 8, http://chicagounbound.uchicago.edu/uclf/vol1989/iss1/8.

44. Donna Haraway, *Simians, Cyborgs and Women: The Reinvention of Nature* (London: Routledge, 1991), 193.

45. Catherine D'Ignazio and Lauren Klein, *Data Feminism* (Cambridge, MA: MIT Press, 2020), 5.

46. See Malcolm McCullough, *Digital Ground Architecture, Pervasive Computing, and Environmental Knowing* (Cambridge, MA: MIT Press, 2004), and *Ambient Commons: Attention in the Age of Embodied Information* (Cambridge, MA: MIT Press, 2013).

47. See Shannon Mattern, *Code + Clay, Data and Dirt: Five Thousand Years of Urban Media* (Minneapolis: University of Minnesota Press, 2017), and her essays in *Places Journal*, https://placesjournal.org/.

48. See Orit Halpern, *Beautiful Data: A History of Vision and Reason since 1945* (Durham: Duke University Press, 2015).

49. See Laura Kurgan, *Close Up at a Distance: Mapping, Technology, and Politics* (New York: Zone Books, 2013).

50. See Rob Kitchin and Scott Freundschuh, *Cognitive Mapping: Past, Present, and Future* (London: Routledge, 2000); Rob Kitchin and Martin Dodge, *Code/Space: Software and Everyday Life* (Cambridge, MA: MIT Press, 2011); and Rob Kitchin, *The Data Revolution: Big Data, Open Data, Data Infrastructures and Their Consequences* (London: Sage, 2014).

51. See Zuboff, *The Age of Surveillance Capitalism.*

52. See Chun, *Discriminating Data.*

53. See Amoore, *Cloud Ethics.*

54. See, for example, @rascouet, "Re Spicer's lies, this is from someone who worked in a past administration. Important read." Twitter, January 22, 2017, 12:12 a.m., https://twitter.com/rascouet/status/823035518313267202.

55. See, for example, John Krygier and Denis Wood, *Making Maps: A Visual Guide to Map Design for GIS* (New York: Guilford Press, 2016), and Jeremy W. Crampton and John Krygier, "An Introduction to Critical Cartography," *ACME: An International Journal for Critical Geographies* 4, no. 1 (2005): 11–33.

56. The term *data blasé* was coined by architect McLain Clutter in a call for papers for a panel discussion at the 107th Annual Meeting of the ACSA, BLACK BOX: Articulating Architecture's Core in the Post-Digital Era, March 28–30, 2019, in Pittsburgh, Pennsylvania, where parts of this chapter were initially presented.

57. "The World's Most Valuable Resource Is No Longer Oil, But Data," *Economist Newspaper*, May 6. 2017, http://www.economist.com/leaders/2017/05/06/the-worlds-most-valuable-resource-is-no-longer-oil-but-data.

58. Halpern et al., "Test-Bed Urbanism."

59. See Steve Kelling, Wesley M. Hochachka, Daniel Fink, Mirek Riedewald, Rich Caruna, Grant Ballard, and Giles Hooker, "Data-Intensive Science: A New Paradigm for Biodiversity Studies," *BioScience* 59, no. 7 (2009): 613–620, and Rob Kitchen, "Big Data, New Epistemologies and Paradigm Shifts," *Big Data and Society* (April–June 2014): 1–12.

60. See Constantine Kontokosta, "The Quantified Community and Neighborhood Labs: A Framework for Computational Urban Science and Civic Technology Innovation," *Journal of Urban Technology* 23, no. 4 (2016): 67–84.

61. For an English translation of *Le Droit à la Ville*, see Henri Lefebvre, "The Right to the City," in *Writings on Cities* (Oxford: Blackwell, 1996). See also David Harvey, *Rebel Cities: From the Right to the City to the Urban Revolution* (London: Verso, 2012).

CHAPTER 1

1. Ben Nuckols, "Inaugural Crowds Sure to Be Huge—But How Huge?," Associated Press, January 19, 2017, https://www.apnews.com/7afad98b7d78423cbb5140fe810e3480.

2. Nuckols, "Inaugural Crowds Sure to Be Huge,"

3. John Swain, "Trump Inauguration Crowd Photos Were Edited after He Intervened," *Guardian*, September 6, 2018, https://www.theguardian.com/world/2018/sep/06/donald-trump-inauguration-crowd-size-photos-edited.

4. Swain, "Trump Inauguration Crowd Photos."

5. Swain, "Trump Inauguration Crowd Photos."

6. Elle Hunt, "Trump's Inauguration Crowd: Sean Spicer's Claims versus the Evidence," *Guardian*, January 22, 2017, https://www.theguardian.com/us-news/2017/jan/22/trump-inauguration-crowd-sean-spicers-claims-versus-the-evidence.

7. Lori Robertson and Robert Farley, "The Facts on Crowd Size," FactCheck.org, January 23, 2017, https://www.factcheck.org/2017/01/the-facts-on-crowd-size/.

8. See, for example, @rascouet "Re Spicer's lies, this is from someone who worked in a past administration. Important read," Twitter, January 27, 2017, 12:12 a.m., https://twitter.com/rascouet/status/823035518313267202.

9. Lisa Gitelman, ed., *"Raw Data" Is an Oxymoron* (Cambridge, MA: MIT Press, 2013), 11.

10. The DIKW hierarchy is variously referred to as the "knowledge hierarchy," the "information hierarchy," and the "knowledge pyramid." While the precise origins of this model are debatable, it is taken for granted as a fundamental and widely recognized model in the fields of knowledge management and information science. See, for example, Jennifer Rowley, "The Wisdom Hierarchy: Representations of the DIKW Hierarchy," *Journal of Information Science* 33, no. 2 (2007): 163–180, https://doi.org/10.1177/0165551506070706.

11. Geoffrey C. Bowker, *Memory Practices in the Sciences* (Cambridge, MA: MIT Press, 2005).

12. Yanni Alexander Loukissas, *All Data Are Local: Thinking Critically in a Data-Driven Society* (Cambridge, MA: MIT Press, 2005).

13. Johanna Drucker, "Humanities Approaches to Graphical Display," *Digital Humanities Quarterly* 5, no. 1 (2011). http://www.digitalhumanities.org/dhq/vol/5/1/000091/000091.html.

14. Environmental Protection Agency, Office of the Inspector General, "EPA's Response to the World Trade Center Collapse: Challenges, Successes, and Areas for Improvement," August 21, 2003, http://www.epa.gov/oig/reports/2003/WTC_report_20030821.pdf.

15. Environmental Protection Agency, "EPA's Response to the World Trade Center Collapse."

16. Daniel Rosenberg, "Data before the Fact," in *"Raw Data" Is an Oxymoron*, ed. Lisa Gitelman (Cambridge, MA: MIT Press, 2013), 33.

17. Rosenberg, "Data before the Fact," 33.

18. Rosenberg, "Data before the Fact," 37.

19. Jordan Peele and Jonah Peretti, "You Won't Believe What Obama Says in This Video!" YouTube video, April 12, 2018, 1:12, https://www.youtube.com/watch?v=cQ54GDm1eL0.

20. Samantha Cole, "Lawmakers Demand Intelligence Community Release a Report on Deepfakes," *Vice*, September 13, 2018, https://www.vice.com/en_us/article/zm5vw9/deepfakes-letter-to-director-of-national-intelligence.

21. See, for example, Supasorn Suwajanakorn, Steven M. Seitz, and Ira Kemelmacher-Shlizerman, "Synthesizing Obama: Learning Lip Sync from Audio," *ACM Transactions on Graphics* 36, no. 4 (2017): art. 95.

22. Samantha Cole, "AI-Assisted Fake Porn Is Here and We're All Fucked," *Vice*, December 11, 2017, https://www.vice.com/en_us/article/gydydm/gal-gadot-fake-ai-porn.

23. Mara Hvistendahl, "Questions Mount about Controversial Hunter Biden-china Dossier," *Intercept*, November 11, 2020, https://theintercept.com/2020/11/11/hunter-biden-china-dossier/.

24. This war debt was to Louis XVI of the Kingdom of France, who was executed by guillotine in 1793 during the French Revolution. The United States claimed that this debt was owed to the former monarchy, not to the newly formed French First Republic.

25. To date, Callendar served the longest prison term by any journalist under the Sedition Act. He was ultimately pardoned by Jefferson in March 1801.

26. Aviv Ovadya, "Deepfake Myths: Common Misconceptions about Synthetic Media," Alliance for Securing Democracy, June 14, 2019, https://securingdemocracy .gmfus.org/deepfake-myths-common-misconceptions-about-synthetic-media/.

27. See, for example, Rosalind Kraus, "Notes on the Index: Seventies Art in America," *October* 3 (1977): 68–81. Others would push back against the truth claims and veracity associated with the photographic image, such as Susan Sontag, *On Photography* (New York: Farrar, Straus and Giroux, 1977), and Roland Barthes, *Camera Lucida: Reflections on Photography* (New York: Hill and Wang, 1981).

28. For a comparison of the contrasting epistemological models presented by the camera obscura and the stereoscope, see chapter 6, this volume.

29. Philip Auslander, *Liveness: Performance in a Mediatized Culture* (London: Routledge, 1999), 12.

30. Goldsmith, as quoted in Auslander, *Liveness*.

31. J. Feuer, "The Concept of Live Television: Ontology as Ideology," in *Regarding Television: Critical Approaches—an Anthology*, ed. E. A. Kaplan (Frederick, MD: University Publications of America, 1983), 12–22.

32. Auslander, *Liveness*, 13.

33. Derek Curry and Jennifer Gradecki, "Infodemic," accessed September 27, 2021, https://derekcurry.com/projects/infodemic.html.

34. Jean Baudrillard, "Simulacra and Simulations," in *Selected Writings*, ed. Mark Poster (Stanford: Stanford University Press, 1988), 172.

35. Baudrillard, *Selected Writings*, 166.

CHAPTER 2

1. Robert Krulwich, "An Imaginary Town Becomes Real, Then Not. True Story," *Krulwich Wonders*, NPR, March 18, 2014, https://www.npr.org/sections/krulwich/2014/03 /18/290236647/an-imaginary-town-becomes-real-then-not-true-story.

2. Amplifying the fictional status of the hamlet, part of John Green's book *Paper Towns* (on which the 2015 film of the same name was based) is set in Agloe, New York.

3. "On Exactitude in Science" is a one-paragraph short story written as a literary forgery by Jorge Luis Borges in 1946. It was originally published in the March 1946 edition of *Los Anales de Buenos Aires, año 1, no. 3* and was credited as a quotation from Suárez Miranda, *Viajes de varones prudentes*, book IV, ch. XLV (Lérida, 1658).

4. See, for example, John Krygier and Denis Wood, "Cartography: Critical Cartography," in their *Making Maps: A Visual Guide to Map Design for GIS* (New York: Guilford

Press, 2016); Jeremy W. Crampton and John Krygier, "An Introduction to Critical Cartography," *ACME: An International Journal for Critical Geographies* 4, no. 1 (2005): 11–33; and Lize Mogel and Alexis Bhagat, *An Atlas of Radical Cartography* (United States: Journal of Aesthetics and Protest Press, 2007).

5. The term "counter-mapping" was coined by Nancy Peluso in her work on land ownership disputes in the forests of Kalimantan, Indonesia. See Nancy Peluso, "Whose Woods Are These? Counter-Mapping Forest Territories In Kalimantan, Indonesia," *Antipode* 27 (1995): 383–406.

6. Krygier and Wood, "Cartography."

7. J. B. Harley, "Can There Be a Cartographic Ethics?" *Cartographic Perspectives*, no. 10 (June 1991): 9–16, https://doi.org/10.14714/CP10.1053.

8. Krygier and Wood, "Cartography."

9. Denis Wood, *The Power of Maps* (New York: Guilford Press, 1992).

10. Laura Kurgan, *Close Up at a Distance: Mapping, Technology and Politics* (New York: Zone Books, 2013), 189.

11. See Justin O'Beirne's analysis at https://www.justinobeirne.com/google-maps-moat, and Google's official description at https://maps.googleblog.com/2012/03/introducing-more-detailed-3d-landmarks.html.

12. This is the same Ian Goodfellow credited with inventing the generative adversarial network, a powerful approach to machine learning for generating synthetic media discussed in chapter 1.

13. "About Us," SLAB website, https://slab.today/about-us/.

14. Research on bias in data-driven and algorithmic systems is vast and rapidly expanding. For a cross-section of perspectives, see Batya Friedman and Helen Nissenbaum, "Bias in Computer Systems," *ACM Transactions on Information Systems* 14, no. 3 (1996): 330–347; Solon Barocas and Andrew D. Selbst, "Big Data's Disparate Impact," *California Law Review* 104, no. 3 (June 2016): 671–732; Kate Crawford, "The Hidden Biases in Big Data," *Harvard Business Review*, April 1, 2013, https://hbr.org/2013/04/the-hidden-biases-in-big-data; and Laura Kurgan, Dare Brawley, Brian House, Jia Zhang, and Wendy Hui Kyong Chun, "Homophily: The Urban History of an Algorithm," *e-flux*, October 4, 2019, https://www.e-flux.com/architecture/are-friends-electric/289193/homophily-the-urban-history-of-an-algorithm/.

15. Kate Crawford and Trevor Paglen, "Excavating AI: The Politics of Images in Machine Learning Training Sets," accessed September 17, 2021, at https://excavating.ai/.

16. Crawford and Paglen, "Excavating AI."

17. See, for example, Rowland Manthorpe, "Beauty.AI's 'Robot Beauty Contest' Is Back—and This Time It Promises Not to Be Racist," *Wired UK*, March 2, 2017, https://www.wired.co.uk/article/robot-beauty-contest-beauty-ai. Ruha Benjamin discusses how robots like Beauty.AI exemplify how race is a form of technology itself, embedding social bias within technical artifacts that possess the "allure of objectivity without public accountability." See Ruha Benjamin, *Race after Technology* (New York: Polity Press, 2019).

18. Marc Böhlen, Varun Chandola, and Amol Salunkhe, "Server, Server in the Cloud. Who Is the Fairest in the Crowd?" accessed January 19, 2022, https://arxiv.org/abs /1711.08801.

19. See Krzysztof Kościński, "Facial Attractiveness: Variation, Adaptiveness and Consequences of Facial Preferences," *Anthropological Review* 71 (2008): 77–108.

20. See Sarah Williams, Wenfei Xu, Shin Bin Ton, Michael J. Foster, and Changping Chen, "Ghost Cities of China: Identifying Urban Vacancy through Social Media Data," *Cities* 94 (2008): 275–285.

21. W. G. Hansen, "How Accessibility Shapes Land-Use," *Journal of the American Institute of Planners* 25 (1959): 73–76.

22. The "view from nowhere," also known as "false balance" and "bothsidesism," refers to a theory in journalism and media ethics concerning the potential negative effects of a so-called neutrality in reporting that creates the impression that opposing parties to an issue have equal validity when in fact the truth or falsehood of the parties' claims is mutually exclusive and independently verifiable. The term comes from philosopher Thomas Nagel's book, *The View from Nowhere* (Oxford: Oxford University Press, 1986).

23. There is a discrepancy of location between Cook's "Sandy I." and *Velocity*'s. See Maria Seton, Simon Williams, and Sabin Zahirovic, "Obituary: Sandy Island (1876–2012)," *Eos, Transactions, American Geophysical Union* 94, no. 15 (2013): 141–148.

24. Luke Harding, "The Pacific Island That Never Was," *Guardian*, November 22, 2012, https://www.theguardian.com/world/2012/nov/22/sandy-island-missing-google-earth.

25. Martin Connelly, "A Little Lesson in Knowledge, Courtesy of an Island That Disappeared (If It Ever Even Existed)," *Vice*, November 26, 2012, https://www.vice.com /en_us/article/d7747w/the-other-strange-sandy-an-island-that-totally-disappeared.

26. See Seton et al., "Obituary: Sandy Island."

CHAPTER 3

1. Paul Dourish, *The Stuff of Bits: An Essay on the Materialities of Information* (Cambridge, MA: MIT Press, 2017), and Jean-François Blanchette, "A Material History of Bits," *Journal of the American Society for Information Science and Technology* 62, no. 6 (2011): 1042–1057.

2. See Adam Satariano, "How the Internet Travels across Oceans," *New York Times*, March 10, 2019, https://www.nytimes.com/interactive/2019/03/10/technology /internet-cables-oceans.html.

3. See Paul T. Jaeger, Jimmy Lin, Justin M. Grimes, and Shannon N. Simmons, "Where Is the Cloud? Geography, Economics, Environment, and Jurisdiction in Cloud Computing," *First Monday* 14, no. 5 (2009), https://doi.org/10.5210/fm.v14i5.2456.

4. Ali Fard, "Cloudy Landscapes: On the Extended Geography of Smart Urbanism," *Telematics and Informatics* 55 (2020), https://doi.org/10.1016/j.tele.2020.101450.

5. John McCarthy as quoted in Simson Garfinkel, *Architects of the Information Society, Thirty-Five Years of the Laboratory for Computer Science at MIT*, ed. Hal Abelson (Cambridge, MA: MIT Press, 1999), 1.

6. See Louise Amoore, "Cloud Geographies: Computing, Data, Sovereignty," *Progress in Human Geography* 42, no. 1 (2018): 4–24.

7. "Cisco Annual Internet Report (2018–2023) White Paper," Cisco.com, March 9, 2020, https://www.cisco.com/c/en/us/solutions/collateral/executive-perspectives/annual -internet-report/white-paper-c11-741490.html.

8. Bernard Marr, "How Much Data Do We Create Every Day? The Mind-Blowing Stats Everyone Should Read," *Forbes*, May 21, 2018, https://www.forbes.com/sites /bernardmarr/2018/05/21/how-much-data-do-we-create-every-day-the-mind -blowing-stats-everyone-should-read/#739824f860ba.

9. Tracking stats for worldwide data consumption is of course a fool's errand, as they are constantly changing, yet each year, infographics for "what happens in an Internet minute" are updated by various sources—for example, this one by social media con- sultant Lori Lewis: https://www.allaccess.com/merge/archive/32972/infographic-what -happens-in-an-internet-minute.

10. See James Manyika, Michael Chiu, Brad Brown, Jacques Bughin, Richard Dobbs, Charles Roxburgh, and Angela Hung Byers, *Big Data: The Next Frontier for Innovation, Competition, and Productivity* (McKinsey Global Institute, 2011), and Rob Kitchin, *The Data Revolution: Big Data, Open Data, Data Infrastructures and Their Consequences* (London: Sage, 2014).

11. See Charles Duhigg, "How Companies Know Your Secrets," *New York Times*, Febru- ary 16, 2012, http://www.nytimes.com/2012/02/19/magazine/shopping-habits.html.

12. Fady Masoud, "12 Mind-Blowing Data Center Facts You Need to Know," *Ciena*, August 25, 2016, https://www.ciena.com/insights/articles/Twelve-Mind-blowing -Data-Center-Facts-You-Need-to-Know.html.

13. Masoud, "12 Mind-Blowing Data Center Facts."

14. Kazys Varnelis, "Eyes That Do Not See: Tracking the Self in the Age of the Data Center," *Harvard Design Magazine*, no. 38 (2014), http://www.harvarddesignmagazine .org/issues/38/eyes-that-do-not-see-tracking-the-self-in-the-age-of-the-data-center.

15. Martin Heidegger, "The Age of the World Picture," in *The Question Concerning Technology and Other Essays* (London: HarperCollins, 1977), 135.

16. Georg Simmel, "The Metropolis and Mental Life," *Simmel on Culture* (London: Sage, 1997), 177.

17. For a characterization of this type, see Bertolt Brecht, "Ten Poems from 'Reader for Those Who Live in Cities' IV," in *Poems 1913–1956* (London: Methuen, 1976), 134–135.

18. Simmel, "The Metropolis and Mental Life," 175.

19. Amoore, "Cloud Ethics," 162.

20. Jonathan Crary, *Suspensions of Perception: Attention, Spectacle and Modern Culture* (Cambridge, MA: MIT Press, 1999).

21. Simmel, "The Metropolis and Mental Life," 180.

22. Fard, "Cloudy Landscapes," 2.

23. "Social Media, Social Life," *Common Sense Media*, September 10, 2018, https://www.commonsensemedia.org/social-media-social-life-infographic.

24. See Amanda Lenhart, "How Teens Hang Out and Stay in Touch with Their Closest Friends," *Teens Technology and Friendships*, Pew Research Center, August 6, 2015, http://www.pewinternet.org/2015/08/06/chapter-2-how-teens-hang-out-and-stay-in-touch-with-their-closest-friends.

25. For a cross-section of views on the geography of the historic and contemporary public sphere, see Jürgen Habermas, *The Structural Transformation of the Public Sphere* (Cambridge, MA: MIT Press, 1962); Richard Sennett, *The Fall of Public Man* (New York: Knopf, 1977); Setha Low and Niel Smith, *The Politics of Public Space* (London: Routledge, 2006); and Yochai Benkler, *The Wealth of Networks* (New Haven: Yale University Press, 2007).

26. For divergent views of the reputation economy, see Michael Fertik and David C. Thompson, *The Reputation Economy: How to Optimize Your Digital Footprint in a World Where Your Reputation Is Your Most Valuable Asset* (London: Piatkus, 2015), and, for instance, Alison Hearn, "Structuring Feeling: Web 2.0, Online Ranking and Rating, and the Digital 'Reputation' Economy," *Ephemera* 10, nos. 3–4 (2010): 421–438.

27. "More Than Half of Employers Have Found Content on Social Media That Caused Them NOT to Hire a Candidate, According to Recent CareerBuilder Survey," *Cision PR Newswire*, August 9, 2018, https://www.prnewswire.com/news-releases/more-than-half-of-employers-have-found-content-on-social-media-that-caused-them-not-to-hire-a-candidate-according-to-recent-careerbuilder-survey-300694437.html/.

28. There is considerable debate as to the discrepancy between claims made about the design of the system and what is actually being put in place. See, for example, Louise Matsakis, "How the West Got China's Social Credit Score Wrong," *Wired*, July 19, 2019, https://www.wired.com/story/china-social-credit-score-system/.

29. Nicole Kobie, "The Complicated Truth about China's Social Credit System," *Wired UK*, June 7, 2019, https://www.wired.co.uk/article/china-social-credit-system-explained.

30. Kobie, "The Complicated Truth."

31. The "Planning Outline for the Construction of a Social Credit System (2014-2020)" was released in 2014 by the General Office of the State Council, the Chinese government's chief administrative authority.

32. See Chenchen Zhang, "Governing (through) Trustworthiness: Technologies of power and Subjectification in China's Social Credit System," *Critical Asian Studies* 52, no. 4 (2020): 565–588.

33. Kobie, "The Complicated Truth."

34. "Ant Financial Unveils China's First Credit-Scoring System Using Online Data," Alibaba Group, press release, January 28, 2015, https://www.alibabagroup.com/en/news/article?news=p150128.

35. Zang, "Governing (through) Trustworthiness," 566.

36. See Sophie Kleber, "As AI Meets the Reputation Economy, We're All Being Silently Judged," *Harvard Business Review*, January 29, 2018, https://hbr.org/2018 /01/as-ai-meets-the-reputation-economy-were-all-being-silently-judged, and Tijmen Schep's https://www.socialcooling.com/.

37. Cathy O'Neil, "How Algorithms Rule Our Working Lives," *Guardian*, September 1, 2016, https://www.theguardian.com/science/2016/sep/01/how-algorithms-rule-our -working-lives.

38. Samuel Gibbs, "Women Less Likely to Be Shown Ads for High-Paid Jobs on Google, Study Shows," *Guardian*, July 8, 2015, https://www.theguardian.com/technology/2015 /jul/08/women-less-likely-ads-high-paid-jobs-google-study.

39. For example, Trusting Social, https://trustingsocial.com/.

40. Austin Carr, "I Found Out My Secret Internal Tinder Rating and Now I Wish I Hadn't," *Fast Company*, January 11, 2016, https://www.fastcompany.com/3054871 /whats-your-tinder-score-inside-the-apps-internal-ranking-system.

41. For a brief introduction, see Simon Dumenco, "'We Broke Facebook': Meet the Cambridge Analytica Whistleblower," *Ad Age*, March 19, 2018, https://adage.com /article/media/broke-facebook-cambridge-analytica-whistleblower/312791. This topic is addressed at length in chapter 8.

42. For example, Apriss Retail, https://apprissretail.com/.

43. Kimberly Houser and Debra Sanders, "The Use of Big Data Analytics by the IRS: Efficient Solutions or the End of Privacy as We Know It?," *Vanderbilt Journal of Entertainment and Technology Law* 817 (2017).

44. Marshall Allen, "Health Insurers Are Vacuuming Up Details About You—and It Could Raise Your Rates," *ProPublica*, July 17, 2018, https://www.propublica.org /article/health-insurers-are-vacuuming-up-details-about-you-and-it-could-raise-your -rates.

45. In nineteenth century Paris, people hosting formal dinner parties were superstitious of having thirteen people at the table. Apparently there were enough dinner parties every evening that it was a common occurrence to come up one person short, which in turn, made it financially advantageous for a number of socially presentable men to dress in full formal attire at the dinner hour so they might be called upon on short notice to be the fourteenth (quatorzième) guest.

CHAPTER 4

1. Lauren McCarthy, "Feeling at Home: Between Human and AI," *Immerse*, January 8, 2018, https://immerse.news/feeling-at-home-between-human-and-ai-6047561e7f04.

2. These developers also listen in. According to an article in *Bloomberg*, Amazon employs thousands of people to transcribe and annotate Alexa requests in an effort to improve the voice assistant's performance. See Matt Day, Giles Turner, and Natalia Drozdiak, "Amazon Workers Are Listening to What You Tell Alexa," Bloomberg, April 10, 2019, https://www.bloomberg.com/news/articles/2019-04-10/is-anyone -listening-to-you-on-alexa-a-global-team-reviews-audio.

3. McCarthy, "Feeling at Home."

4. Richard Forty, *Objects of Desire: Design and Society since 1750* (New York: Thames and Hudson, 2005), 208.

5. Hazel Kyrk, *Economic Problems of the Family* (London: Harper, 1933), 99.

6. "Personal Assistant That Learns (PAL)," Defense Advanced Research Projects Agency, accessed March 15, 2021, https://www.darpa.mil/about-us/timeline/personalized -assistant-that-learns.

7. DARPA, "DARPA's PAL Project," YouTube video, 4:37, August 30, 2010, https:// www.youtube.com/watch?time_continue=248&v=BF-KNFlOocQ.

8. For a detailed history of the origins of SIRI, see Bianca Bosker, "SIRI RISING: The Inside Story of Siri's Origins—and Why She Could Overshadow the iPhone," *Huffington Post*, December 6, 2017, https://www.huffpost.com/entry/siri-do-engine -apple-iphone_n_2499165.

9. "Cognitive Assistant That Learns and Organizes," SRI International, accessed March 15, 2021, http://www.ai.sri.com/project/CALO.

10. "IBM Shoebox," IBM, accessed March 15, 2021, https://www.ibm.com/ibm/history /exhibits/specialprod1/specialprod1_7.html.

11. B. T. Lowerre, "The Harpy Speech Recognition System" (PhD diss., Carnegie Mellon University, 1976).

12. Oscar Schwartz, "In the 17th Century, Leibniz Dreamed of a Machine That Could Calculate Ideas," *IEEE Spectrum*, November 4, 2019, https://spectrum.ieee .org/tech-talk/artificial-intelligence/machine-learning/in-the-17th-century-leibniz -dreamed-of-a-machine-that-could-calculate-ideas.

13. Karen Spärck Jones, "Natural Language Processing: A Historical Review," in *Current Issues in Computational Linguistics: In Honour of Don Walker*, ed. Antonio Zampolli, Nicoletta Calzolari, and Martha Palmer (Dordrecht: Springer Netherlands, 1994), 3–16.

14. Cade Metz, "Meet GPT-3. It Has Learned to Code (and Blog and Argue)," *New York Times*, November 24, 2020, https://www.nytimes.com/2020/11/24/science/artificial -intelligence-ai-gpt3.html.

15. Joseph Weizenbaum, *Computer Power and Human Reason: From Judgment to Calculation* (London: W. H. Freeman, 1976), 6.

16. Bosker, "SIRI RISING."

17. Heather Suzanne Woods, "Asking More of Siri and Alexa: Feminine Persona in Service of Surveillance Capitalism," *Critical Studies in Media Communication* 35, no. 4 (2018): 334–349.

18. Joe Brown, "The Amazon Echo Is More Than a Bluetooth Speaker—It's a Bedtime Buddy," *Vox*, February 9, 2015, https://www.vox.com/2015/2/9/11558754/the -amazon-echo-is-more-than-a-bluetooth-speaker-its-a-bedtime-buddy.

19. E. M. Foner, "Alexa, My Love. Thy Name Is Inflexible, but Thou Art Otherwise a Nearly Perfect Spouse," Amazon.com customer review, June 23, 2015, https://www .amazon.com/gp/review/RJVDJIP1OE8?ref_=glimp_1rv_cl.

20. *Shit That Siri Says*, Tumblr blog, accessed March 15, 2021, http://shitthatsirisays .tumblr.com/.

21. Woods, "Asking More of Siri and Alexa," 343.

22. See, for example, M. Andrejevic, "The Work of Being Watched: Interactive Media and the Exploitation of Self Disclosure," *Critical Studies in Media Communication* 19, no. 2 (2002), 230–248; O. H. Gandy, "Toward a Political Economy of Personal Information," *Critical Studies in Media Communication* 10, no. 1 (1993), 70–97; and J. Turow, *The Daily You: How the New Advertising Industry Is Defining Your Identity and Your Worth* (New Haven, CT: Yale University Press, 2011).

23. See D. Ariely, *Predictably Irrational: The Hidden Forces That Shape Our Decisions* (New York: HarperCollins, 2008).

24. See R. H. Thaler, C. R. Sunstein, and J. P. Balz, "Choice Architecture," in *The Behavioral Foundations of Public Policy*, ed. E. Shafir (Princeton: Princeton University Press, 2013), 428–439.

25. See R. H. Thaler and C. R. Sunstein, *Nudge: Improving Decisions about Health, Wealth, and Happiness* (New York: Penguin, 2009).

26. Anthony Nadler and Lee McGuigan, "An Impulse to Exploit: The Behavioral Turn in Data-Driven Marketing," *Critical Studies in Media Communication*, 35:2 (2018): 151–165.

27. Nadler and McGuigan, "An Impulse to Exploit," 155.

28. G. Wyner, "Behavioral Economics: A Marketing Capability," *Marketing News* 50, no. 10 (2016): 34–36.

29. R. J. Rosen, "Is This the Grossest Advertising Strategy of All Time?" *Atlantic*, October 3, 2013, https://www.theatlantic.com/technology/archive/2013/10/is-this -the-grossestadvertising-strategy-of-all-time/280242/.

30. C. Duhigg, *The Power of Habit* (New York: Random House, 2012).

31. Nadler and McGuigan, "An Impulse to Exploit," 157.

32. Woods, "Asking More of Siri and Alexa," 345.

33. Woods, "Asking More of Siri and Alexa," 345.

CHAPTER 5

1. For descriptions by reporters of the "shoplifting effect" of the Amazon Go experience, see Nick Wingfield, "Inside Amazon Go, a Store of the Future," *New York Times*, January 21, 2018, https://www.nytimes.com/2018/01/21/technology/inside-amazon-go -a-store-of-the-future.html, and Jake Bullinger, "Amazon's Checkout-Free Store Makes Shopping Feel Like Shoplifting," *Atlantic*, January 24, 2018, https://www.theatlantic .com/business/archive/2018/01/amazon-go-store-checkouts-seattle/551357/.

2. Drew Harwell and Abha Bhattarai, "Inside Amazon Go: The Camera-Filled Convenience Store That Watches You Back," *Washington Post*, January 22, 2018, https:// www.washingtonpost.com/news/business/wp/2018/01/22/inside-amazon-go-the -camera-filled-convenience-store-that-watches-you-back/.

3. Ryan Gross, "How the Amazon Go Store's AI Works," *Towards Data Science, Medium*, June 6, 2019, https://towardsdatascience.com/how-the-amazon-go-store-works-a-deep -dive-3fde9d9939e9.

4. A. A. Lovelace, "Notes by A. A. L. [August Ada Lovelace]," *Taylor's Scientific Memoirs* (London, 1843), 3: 666–731. These notes originally appeared in *Charles Babbage and His Calculating Engines: Selected Writings by Charles Babbage and Others*, ed. P. Morrison and E. Morrison (New York: Dover 1961), and in *Faster Than Thought*, ed. B. V. Bowden (London: Sir Isaac Pitman & Sons, 1953), 341–408.

5. Alan Turing, "Computing Machinery and Intelligence." *Mind* 59, no. 236 (1950): 433–460.

6. Warren McCulloch and Walter Pitts, "A Logical Calculus of Ideas Immanent in Nervous Activity," *Bulletin of Mathematical Biophysics* 5 (1943): 115–133.

7. The Cornell Aeronautical Laboratory operated from 1946 until 1972. In response to criticism for conducting military research during the Vietnam War era, Cornell reorganized the lab as the Calspan Corporation and sold its stock in Calspan to the public.

8. "New Navy Device Learns by Doing," *New York Times*, July 8, 1958, 25.

9. Marvin Minsky and Seymour Papert, *Perceptrons: An Introduction to Computational Geometry* (Cambridge, MA: MIT Press, 1969).

10. See, for example, D. E. Rumelhart, G. E. Hinton, and R. J. Williams, "Learning Representations by Back-Propagating Errors," in *Neurocomputing: Foundations of Research*, ed. James A. Anderson and Edward Rosenfeld (Cambridge, MA: MIT Press, 1988), 696–699; Y. LeCun, B. Boser, J. S. Denker, D. Henderson, R. E. Howard, W. Hubbard, and L. D. Jackel, "Backpropagation Applied to Handwritten Zip Code Recognition," *Neural Computing* 1, no. 4 (1989): 541–551; and Y. LeCun, L. Bottou, Y. Bengio, and P. Haffner, "Gradient-Based Learning Applied to Document Recognition," *Proceedings of the IEEE* 86, no. 11 (November 1998): 2278–2324.

11. Gross, "How the Amazon Go Store's AI Works."

12. Joy Buolamwini and Timnit Gebru, "Gender Shades: Intersectional Accuracy Disparities in Commercial Gender Classification," *Proceedings of Machine Learning Research* (January 2018): 77–91.

13. See the *Stanford Encyclopedia of Philosophy*'s entry on "Bayesian Epistemology," https://plato.stanford.edu/entries/epistemology-bayesian/.

14. See Haomiao Huang, "How Amazon Go (Probably) Makes 'Just Walk Out' Groceries a Reality," *Ars Technica*, April 10, 2017, https://arstechnica.com/information -technology/2017/04/how-amazon-go-probably-makes-just-walk-out-groceries-a -reality/.

15. Nate Silver, *The Signal and the Noise: Why So Many Predictions Fail-But Some Don't* (East Rutherford: Penguin Books, 2012), 185.

16. See Annie Gasparro and Jaewon Kang, "Grocers Wrest Control of Shelf Space from Struggling Food Giants," *Wall Street Journal*, February 19, 2020, https://www .wsj.com/articles/grocers-wrest-control-of-shelf-space-from-struggling-food-giants -11582108202.

17. "Nielsen and Trax Form Alliance to Bring Unprecedented Shelf Insights to FMCG Industry," Nielsen, press release, June 22, 2017, https://www.nielsen.com /us/en/press-releases/2017/nielsen-and-trax-form-alliance-to-bring-unprecedented -shelf-insights-to-fmcg/.

18. Zuboff, *The Age of Surveillance Capitalism.*

19. Currently "cashiers" at Amazon Go are being assigned to tasks like restocking shelves and checking shoppers' IDs for beer purchases.

20. Gilles Deleuze, "Postscript on Control Societies," in *Negotiations: 1972–1990*, trans. Martin Joughin (New York: Columbia University Press, 1995), 177.

21. See Daniel Yankelovich and David Meer, "Rediscovering Market Segmentation," *Harvard Business Review* 84 (January 2006): 122–131.

22. Spencer Soper, "Amazon Will Consider Opening Up to 3,000 Cashierless Stores by 2021." Bloomberg, September 19, 2018, www.bloomberg.com/news/articles/2018 -09-19/amazon-is-said-to-plan-up-to-3-000-cashierless-stores-by-2021.

CHAPTER 6

1. Joy Buolamwini and Timnit Gebru, "Gender Shades: Intersectional Accuracy Disparities in Commercial Gender Classification," in *Proceedings of Machine Learning Research* (January 2018): 77–91.

2. See Danielle Ensign, Sorelle A. Friedler, Scott Neville, Carlos Scheidegger, and Suresh Venkatasubramanian, "Runaway Feedback Loops in Predictive Policing," in *Proceedings of the First Conference on Fairness, Accountability and Transparency* (2018), http://proceedings.mlr.press/v81/.

3. The earliest recorded description of the camera obscura appears in a text by Mozi (470 BC–391 BC), a Chinese philosopher and founder of Mohism. Mohist ethics and epistemology are concerned with identifying objective standards to impartially and reliably guide judgment and action leading beneficial and morally correct outcomes. Mozi observed correctly that the image in a camera obscura is inverted because light travels in straight lines from its source. His disciples developed this observation into a theory of optics.

4. See Jonathan Crary, "The Camera Obscura and Its Subject," in *Techniques of the Observer: On Vision and Modernity in the Nineteenth Century* (Cambridge, MA: MIT Press, 1990).

5. See Crary, "Subjective Vision and the Separation of the Senses," in *Techniques of the Observer.*

6. William H. Whyte, *The Social Life of Small Urban Spaces* (Washington, DC: Conservation Foundation, 1980).

7. "Quantify the World with Placemeter," Placemeter, accessed August 14, 2016, https://www.placemeter.com

8. Rob Kitchin and Tracey Lauriault, "Small Data in the Era of Big Data," *GeoJournal* 80, no. 4 (1980): 463–475.

9. Rob Kitchin, "Big Data, New Epistemologies and Paradigm Shifts," *Big Data and Society* (April–June 2014): 1–12.

10. Abraham Maslow, *Toward a Psychology of Being* (New York: Van Nostrand, 1968).

11. Chris Anderson, "The End of Theory."

12. While Related Companies, the developer, initially planned for the entire project to be finished in 2024, it no longer offers an estimated completion date, reportedly due to the impact of the COVID-19 pandemic on the New York real estate market. See Matthew Haag and Dana Rubinstein, "How the Pandemic Left the $25 Billion Hudson Yards Eerily Deserted," *New York Times*, February 6, 2021, https://www.ny times.com/2021/02/06/nyregion/hudson-yards-nyc.html.

13. See, for example, Jessica Leber, "Beyond the Quantified Self: The World's Largest Quantified Community," *Fast Company*, April 22, 2014, https://www.fastcompany .com/3029255/beyond-the-quantified-self-the-worlds-largest-quantified-community.

14. Constantine Kontokosta, "The Quantified Community and Neighborhood Labs: A Framework for Computational Urban Science and Civic Technology Innovation," *Journal of Urban Technology* 23, no. 4 (2016): 67–84.

15. See the TED talk by Gary Wolf, "The Quantified Self," *TED@Cannes*, June 2010, https://www.ted.com/talks/gary_wolf_the_quantified_self.

16. Brian Libby, "Quantifying the Livable City," Bloomberg Citylab, October 21, 2014, http://www.citylab.com/tech/2014/10/quantifying-the-livable-city/381657/.

17. "NYU CUSP, Related Companies, and Oxford Properties Group Team Up to Create 'First Quantified Community' in the United States at Hudson Yards," NYU Center for Urban Science and Progress, press release, April 14, 2014, http://cusp.nyu .edu/press-release/nyu-cusp-related-companies-oxford-properties-group-team-create -first-quantified-community-united-states-hudson-yards/.

18. For more on the empiricist, behaviorist epistemology of the proposed quantified community at Hudson Yards, see William Davies, "The Chronic Social: Relations of Control within and without Neoliberalism," *New Formations* 84–85 (2015): 40– 57, and Shannon Mattern, "Instrumental City: The View from Hudson Yards, circa 2019," *Places Journal* (April 2016), https://placesjournal.org/article/instrumental-city -new-york-hudson-yards/.

19. See, for example, B. F. Skinner, *Beyond Freedom and Dignity* (New York: Knopf, 1971), and critiques by Noam Chomsky, "The Case against B. F. Skinner," *New York Review of Books*, December 30, 1971, and Arthur Koestler, *The Ghost in the Machine* (New York: Macmillan, 1968).

20. Shannon Mattern, *A City Is Not a Computer: Other Urban Intelligences* (Princeton: Princeton University Press, 2021).

21. Orit Halpern, Jesse LeCavalier, Nerea Calvillo and Wolfgang Pietsch, "Test-Bed Urbanism," *Public Culture* 25, no. 2 (2013): 272–306.

22. Hannah Arendt, *The Human Condition* (Chicago: University of Chicago Press, 1958), 322.

23. See Niel Brenner and Christian Schmid, "Towards a New Epistemology of the Urban?" *City* 19, no. 2–3 (2015): 151–182.

24. Emily Nonko, "Hudson Yards Promised a High-Tech Neighborhood—It Was a Greater Challenge Than Expected," *Metropolis*, February 5, 2019, https://www.metropolismag.com/cities/hudson-yards-technology-urbanism/.

25. For a discussion of these kinds of algorithmic neighborhoods and their intrinsic biases, see Wendy Hui Kyong Chun's work on homophily and segregation in *Discriminating Data: Correlation, Neighborhoods, and the New Politics of Recognition* (Cambridge, MA: MIT Press, 2021), and Laura Kurgan, Dare Brawley, Brian House, Jia Zhang, and Wendy Hui Kyong Chun, "Homophily: The Urban History of an Algorithm," *e-flux*, October 4, 2019, https://www.e-flux.com/architecture/are-friends-electric/289193/homophily-the-urban-history-of-an-algorithm/.

26. See Daniel Rosenberg, "Data before the Fact," in *"Raw Data" Is an Oxymoron*, ed. Lisa Gitelman (Cambridge, MA: MIT Press, 2013).

CHAPTER 7

1. In 1935, the Federal Home Loan Bank Board charged the Home Owners' Loan Corporation with creating "residential security maps" for 239 metropolitan areas to indicate the level of risk for mortgage lending. The areas considered desirable for lending (type A), typically affluent suburbs, were outlined in green. Areas outlined in blue (type B) were considered "Still Desirable." Older areas outlined in yellow (type C) were labeled "Declining." Areas outlined in red (type D) were typically inner-city neighborhoods with high populations of African Americans that were considered too risky for issuing mortgages.

2. See Ajjit Narayanan and Graham MacDonald, "Toward an Open Data Bias Assessment Tool: Measuring Bias in Open Spatial Data," Urban Institute, February 2019, https://www.urban.org/sites/default/files/publication/99844/toward_an_open_data_bias_assessment_tool_1.pdf.

3. Waterfront Toronto was established by the Government of Canada, the Province of Ontario, and the City of Toronto in 2001 to oversee and lead the renewal of the city's waterfront.

4. "Request for Proposals: Innovation and Funding Partner for the Quayside Development Opportunity," Waterfront Toronto, March 17, 2017, https://quaysideto.ca/wp-content/uploads/2019/04/Waterfront-Toronto-Request-for-Proposals-March-17-2017.pdf.

5. "Request for Proposals: Innovation and Funding Partner."

6. Jennifer Bonnell, "Don River Valley Historical Mapping Project," Maps.library.utoronto.ca (2009), accessed March 15, 2021, http://maps.library.utoronto.ca/dvhmp/ashbridges-bay.html.

7. See Gene Desfor, Lucian Vesalon, and Jennefer Laidley, *Reshaping Toronto's Waterfront* (Toronto: University of Toronto Press, 2011). The Toronto Harbour Commission was established by the Toronto Harbour Commissioners Act of 1911. This new body

represented a restructuring of the previously existing agency called the Commissioners of the Harbour of Toronto, or Harbor Trust, which had been created in 1850.

8. Jason McBride, "How the Sidewalk Labs Proposal Landed in Toronto: The Backstory," *Toronto Life*, September 4, 2019, https://torontolife.com/city/how-the-sidewalk -labs-proposal-landed-in-toronto-the-backstory/.

9. Waterfront Toronto notes on its website that one proponent was disqualified as not compliant with the requirements. It also notes that it had agreed to keep all proponents confidential. http://blog.waterfrontoronto.ca/nbe/portal/wt/home/blog -home/posts/Approach-to-Selecting-the-Quayside-Innovation-and-Funding-Partner -Backgrounder-on-the-Request-for-Proposal-Process.

10. Mark Harris, "Inside Alphabet's Money-Spinning, Terrorist-Foiling, Gigabit Wi-Fi Kiosks," *Vox: Recode*, July 1, 2016, https://www.vox.com/2016/7/1/12072122 /alphabet-sidewalk-labs-city-wifi-sidewalk-kiosks.

11. E. S. Levine and J. S. Tisch, "Analytics in Action at the New York City Police Department's Counterterrorism Bureau," *Military Operations Research* 19, no. 4 (2014): 5–14.

12. "Testimony Regarding Technology Oversight Hearing on LinkNYC," New York Civil Liberties Union, November 18, 2016, https://www.nyclu.org/en/publications /testimony-regarding-technology-oversight-hearing-linknyc.

13. "City Strengthens Public Wi-Fi Privacy Policy after NYCLU Raises Concerns," New York Civil Liberties Union, March 16, 2017, https://www.nyclu.org/en/press -releases/city-strengthens-public-wi-fi-privacy-policy-after-nyclu-raises-concerns.

14. Laura Bliss, "Meet the Jane Jacobs of the 21st Century," *CityLab*, December 21, 2018, https://www.citylab.com/life/2018/12/bianca-wylie-interview-toronto-quayside -protest-criticism/574477/.

15. Bianca Wylie, "Smart Communities Need Smart Governance," *Globe and Mail*, December 5, 2017, https://www.theglobeandmail.com/opinion/smart-communities -need-smart-governance/article37218398/.

16. Sidewalk Labs, "Master Innovation and Development Plan (MIDP)," *Sidewalk Toronto* (2019): 66–71, https://www.sidewalktoronto.ca/documents/. For a detailed account of Sidewalk Labs's approach to public engagement, see Shannon Mattern, "Post-It Note City," *Places Journal*, February 2020, https://placesjournal.org/article /post-it-note-city/.

17. Having attended the third and final public meeting on February 26, 2020, in Toronto, I can attest to a sustained public questioning of issues surrounding data harvesting and surveillance capitalism. Few of these questions received adequate responses. One outburst in particular, to the horror of the event's organizer, presented the politics of innovation versus social resistance as a function of body odor, referring to critics of the plan as "the stench in the room."

18. See Josh O'Kane, "Inside the Mysteries and Missteps of Toronto's Smart-City Dream," *Globe and Mail*, May 17, 2019, https://www.theglobeandmail.com/business /article-inside-the-mysteries-and-missteps-of-torontos-smart-city-dream/.

19. Alyssa Harvey Dawson, "An Update on Data Governance for Sidewalk Toronto," *Sidewalk Labs, Medium*, October 15, 2018, https://medium.com/sidewalk-talk/an-update-on-data-governance-for-sidewalk-toronto-d810245f10f7.

20. It should be noted that whether data can actually be de-identified effectively is questionable. For an example involving NYC taxi medallions, see Vijay Pandurangan, "On Taxis and Rainbows," *Medium*, June 21, 2014, https://tech.vijayp.ca/of-taxis-and-rainbows-f6bc289679a1. For an example involving health care data, see Luc Rocher, Julien M. Hendrickx, and Yves-Alexandre de Montjoye, "Estimating the Success of Re-Identifications in Incomplete Datasets Using Generative Models," *Nature Communications* 10, no. 3069 (2019), https://doi.org/10.1038/s41467-019-10933-3.

21. Leyland Cecco, "'Surveillance Capitalism': Critic Urges Toronto to Abandon Smart City Project," *Guardian*, June 6, 2019, https://www.theguardian.com/cities/2019/jun/06/toronto-smart-city-google-project-privacy-concerns.

22. Sidewalk Labs, "Master Innovation and Development Plan."

23. Figures are in Canadian dollars (CAD).

24. David Rider, "Google Firm Wins Competition to Build High-Tech Quayside in Toronto," *Toronto Star*, October 17, 2017, https://www.thestar.com/news/city_hall/2017/10/17/google-firm-wins-competition-to-build-high-tech-quayside-neighbourhood-in-toronto.html.

25. Sidewalk Labs, "Master Innovation and Development Plan," 398.

26. Sidewalk Labs, "Master Innovation and Development Plan," 424. Sidewalk Labs discusses the name change from Civic Data Trust to Urban Data Trust in a sidebar, claiming that the new name clarifies the roles and responsibilities of the organization. In response to questions from advisers and critics regarding who the trustee and the beneficiaries of this trust would be, Sidewalk Labs states that it intends the data trust not in the sense of a traditional legal trust but in the sense defined by the UK nonprofit organization Open Data institute as "a legal structure that provides for independent stewardship of data."

27. Sidewalk Labs, "Master Innovation and Development Plan," 420.

28. Sidewalk Labs, "Master Innovation and Development Plan," 416.

29. Sidewalk Labs, "Master Innovation and Development Plan," 426.

30. Sidewalk Labs, "Master Innovation and Development Plan," 426.

31. Sidewalk Labs, "Master Innovation and Development Plan," 418.

32. Sidewalk Labs, "Master Innovation and Development Plan," 418.

33. See, for example, David Harvey, "The Right to the City," *New Left Review* 2, no. 53 (2008): 23–40, or Niel Brenner, Peter Marcuse, and Margit Mayer, eds., *Cities for People, Not for Profit: Critical Urban Theory and the Right to the City* (New York: Routledge, 2011).

34. Lefebvre distinguishes between citizens and residents, arguing that those who live in or inhabit the city (*citadins*) can legitimately claim right to the city, more than those who are by birthright associated with the city (*citizens*).

35. Harvey, "The Right to the City."

36. Henri Lefebvre, *Writings on Cities* (New York: Blackwell, 1995), 66.

37. See Brenner, Marcuse, and Mayer, *Cities for People*. See also Cesare Di Felici-antonio, Paolo Cardullo, and Rob Kitchin, eds., *The Right to the Smart City* (Bingley: Emerald Publishing, 2019).

38. See Robert Hollands, "Will the Real Smart City Please Stand Up? Intelligent, Progressive or Entrepreneurial?" *City*, 12, no. 3 (2008): 303–320.

39. See Shoshana Zuboff, *The Age of Surveillance Capitalism: The Fight for a Human Future at the New Frontier of Power* (New York: Public Affairs, 2019).

40. "Organizational Plan as Programme," cybernetic diagram of the Fun Palace program by Gordon Pask, Cedric Price Archives, Canadian Centre for Architecture, Montréal.

41. Fun Palace Cybernetics Report (1964), Cedric Price Archives, cited in Molly Wright Steenson, *Architectural Intelligence* (Cambridge, MA: MIT Press, 2017), 132, who in turn cites Stanley Mathews, *From Agit-Prop to Free Space: The Architecture of Cedric Price* (London: Blackdog, 2007), 19.

42. Jay W. Forrester, *Urban Dynamics* (Cambridge, MA: MIT Press, 1969), 1.

43. Forrester, *Urban Dynamics*, 122.

44. For an overview of cybernetic urbanism and a critique of hegemonic forms of urban governance, see Maroš Krivý, "Towards a Critique of Cybernetic Urbanism: The Smart City and the Society of Control," *Planning Theory* 17, no. 1 (2018), 8–30.

45. See Michel Foucault, "Governmentality," in *The Foucault Effect: Studies in Govern-mentality*, ed. G. Burchell, C. Gordon, and P. Miller (Chicago: University of Chicago Press, 1991), 87–104. Much has been written on how smart city initiatives are in the process of reconfiguring traditional forms of urban governmentality. See, for example, Rob Kitchin, Claudio Coletta, and Gavin McArdle, "Urban Informatics, Governmental-ity and the Logics of Urban Control," SocArXiv, February 9, 2017, https://doi.org/10.31235/osf.io/27hz8; Jennifer Gabrys, *Program Earth: Environmental Sensing Technology and the Making of a Computational Planet* (Minneapolis: University of Minnesota Press, 2016); and Alberto Vanolo, "Smartmentality: The Smart City as Disciplinary Strategy," *Urban Studies* 51, no. 5 (2014): 883–898.

46. Shannon Mattern, "Instrumental City: The View from Hudson Yards, circa 2019," *Places Journal*, April 2016, https://placesjournal.org/article/instrumental-city-new-york -hudson-yards/.

47. Edith Ramirez, "The Privacy Challenges of Big Data: A View from the Lifeguard's Chair," keynote address, Technology Policy Institute Aspen Forum, Federal Trade Commission, August 19, 2013, https://www.ftc.gov/sites/default/files/documents /public_statements/privacy-challenges-big-data-view-lifeguard%E2%80%99s-chair /130819bigdataaspen.pdf.

48. Di Feliciantonio et al., *The Right to the Smart City*, 10.

49. See Danielle Ensign, Sorelle A. Friedler, Scott Neville, Carlos Scheidegger, and Suresh Venkatasubramanian, "Runaway Feedback Loops in Predictive Policing," in

Proceedings of the First Conference on Fairness, Accountability and Transparency (2018), http://proceedings.mlr.press/v81/.

50. See, for example, Batya Friedman and Helen Nissenbaum "Bias in Computer Systems," *ACM Transactions on Information Systems* 14, no. 3 (1996): 330–347, and Joy Buolamwini and Timnit Gebru, "Gender Shades: Intersectional Accuracy Disparities in Commercial Gender Classification" in *Proceedings of Machine Learning Research* (January 2018): 77–91.

51. Antoinette Rouvroy, "The End(s) of Critique: Data Behaviourism versus Due Process," In *Privacy Due Process and the Computational Turn: The Philosophy of Law Meets the Philosophy of Technology*, ed. Katja de Vries and Mireille Hildebrandt (London: Taylor & Francis, 2013).

52. See Gilles Deleuze, "Postscript on the Societies of Control," *October* 59 (1992); Kitchin et al., "Urban Informatics"; Vanolo, "Smartmentality"; and William Davies, "The Chronic Social: Relations of Control within and without Neoliberalism," *New Formations* 84/85, (2015): 40–57.

53. Daniel Doctoroff, "Why We're No Longer Pursuing the Quayside Project—and What's Next for Sidewalk Labs," *Sidewalk Labs, Medium*, May 7, 2020, https://medium.com/sidewalk-talk/why-were-no-longer-pursuing-the-quayside-project-and-what-s-next-for-sidewalk-labs-9a61de3fee3a.

54. Donovan Vincent, "Sidewalk Labs, Waterfront Toronto to Proceed with Quayside Project, But with Significant Changes," *Star*, October 31, 2019, https://www.thestar.com/news/gta/2019/10/31/sidewalk-labs-waterfront-toronto-reach-deal-to-go-forward-on-quayside-project.html.

CHAPTER 8

1. "Ruse, n.," *OED Online*, March 2021, Oxford University Press, https://www.oed.com/view/Entry/169021?rskey=k5mExO.

2. "Exploit, n.," *OED Online*, March 2021, Oxford University Press, https://www.oed.com/view/Entry/66646?rskey=gL6ThT&result=1.

3. Michel de Certeau, *The Practice of Everyday Life* (Berkeley: University of California Press, 1984), 37.

4. De Certeau, *The Practice of Everyday Life*, xix.

5. De Certeau, *The Practice of Everyday Life*, 36.

6. De Certeau, *The Practice of Everyday Life*, xix.

7. While Cambridge Analytica was directly involved with both the Ted Cruz and Donald Trump presidential campaigns, their precise role in the Brexit referendum is less clear. Arron Banks, the cofounder of Leave.EU, wrote in his book *The Bad Boys of Brexit* (London: Biteback Publishing, 2016) that in October 2015 his group had hired Cambridge Analytica, a company that uses "big data and advanced psychographics" to influence people. Leave.EU posted on its website in November 2015 that Cambridge Analytica "will be helping us map the British electorate and what they believe in, enabling us to better engage with voters." These statements have since

been retracted following government inquiries into the matter. However, reports did confirm that data analysis was indirectly provided to the Leave.Eu campaign by the United Kingdom Independence Party (UKIP), which had given data to Cambridge Analytica for analysis but reportedly had not paid for the services rendered. See Alex Hern, "Cambridge Analytica did work for Leave.EU, emails confirm," *Guardian*, July 30, 2019, https://www.theguardian.com/uk-news/2019/jul/30/cambridge-analytica -did-work-for-leave-eu-emails-confirm. However, the UK Information Commissioner's Office, which spent three years investigating the affair, found no evidence that Cambridge Analytica was directly involved, beyond an early proposal to work with UKIP. The Vote Leave campaign, Leave.EU's conservative counterpart that ultimately succeeded, did employ the services of AggregateIQ, a Canadian data targeting company which had historic links to Cambridge Analytica. See Jim Waterson, "Cambridge Analytica did not misuse data in EU referendum, says watchdog," *Guardian*, October 7, 2020, https://www.theguardian.com/uk-news/2020/oct/07/cambridge-analytica-did -not-misuse-data-in-eu-referendum-says-watchdog.

8. Carole Cadwalladr, "'I Made Steve Bannon's Psychological Warfare Tool': Meet the Data War Whistleblower," *Guardian*, March 17, 2018, https://www.theguardian .com/news/2018/mar/17/data-war-whistleblower-christopher-wylie-faceook-nix -bannon-trump.

9. See Kim Alexander and Keith Mills, "Voter Privacy in the Digital Age," California Voter Foundation (May 2014).

10. See David W. Nickerson and Todd Rogers, "Political Campaigns and Big Data," *Journal of Economic Perspectives* 28, no. 2 (2014): 51–74.

11. D. Rivers and B. Stults, "The Next Generation of Voter Data," Polimetrix (2005).

12. Nickerson and Rogers, "Political Campaigns and Big Data," 56.

13. Nickerson and Rogers, "Political Campaigns and Big Data," 54.

14. See Lewis R. Goldberg, "The Development of Markers for the Big-Five Factor Structure," *Psychological Assessment* 4, no. 1 (1992): 26–42, and Deborah R. Smith and William E. Snell Jr., "Goldberg's Bipolar Measure of the Big-Five Personality Dimensions: Reliability and Validity," *European Journal of Personality* 10 (1996): 283–299. The effectiveness of employing the Big-Five model for the targeting political advertising remains the subject of debate, however. See, for example, Elizabeth Gibney, "The Scant Science behind Cambridge Analytica's Controversial Marketing Techniques," *Nature*, March 29, 2018, https://www.nature.com/articles/d41586-018-03880-4.

15. Hannes Grassegger and Mikael Krogerus, "The Data That Turned the World Upside Down," *Vice*, January 28, 2017, https://www.vice.com/en_us/article/mg9vvn /how-our-likes-helped-trump-win.

16. Wu Youyou, Michal Kosinski, and David Stillwell, "Computer-Based Personality Judgments Are More Accurate Than Those Made by Humans," *Proceedings of the National Academy of Sciences* 112, no. 4 (2015): 1036–1040.

17. See, for example, Issie Lapowsky, "The Man Who Saw the Dangers of Cambridge Analytica Years Ago," *Wired*, June 19, 2018, https://www.wired.com/story/the-man

-who-saw-the-dangers-of-cambridge-analytica/, and Paul Lewis, Jamie Grierson, and Matthew Weaver, "Cambridge Analytica Academic's Work Upset University Colleagues," *Guardian*, March 24, 2018, https://www.theguardian.com/education/2018/mar/24/cambridge-analytica-academics-work-upset-university-colleagues.

18. Cadwalladr, "'I Made Steve Bannon's Psychological Warfare Tool.'"

19. Carol Cadwalladr, "Facebook Faces Fresh Questions over When It Knew of Data Harvesting," *Guardian*, March 16, 2019, https://www.theguardian.com/technology/2019/mar/16/facebook-fresh-questions-data-harvesting-cambridge-analytica.

20. Cecilia Kang, Matthew Rosenberg, and Sheera Frenkel, "Facebook Faces Broadened Federal Investigations over Data and Privacy," *New York Times*, July 2, 2018, https://www.nytimes.com/2018/07/02/technology/facebook-federal-investigations.html.

21. Nix would make this claim at the 2016 Concordia Annual Summit in New York in his presentation titled "Cambridge Analytica—The Power of Big Data and Psychographics," YouTube video, September 27, 2016, https://www.youtube.com/watch?v=n8Dd5aVXLCc. Many question the veracity of these claims and the degree to which the firm had an impact on either the US election or the Brexit referendum. In the wake of government investigations on both sides of the Atlantic, Cambridge Analytica executives walked back some of these claims, and little has been proven with regard to the effectiveness of the technology. See, for example, Nicholas Confessore and Danny Hakim, "Data Firm Says 'Secret Sauce' Aided Trump; Many Scoff," *New York Times*, March 6, 2017, https://www.nytimes.com/2017/03/06/us/politics/cambridge-analytica.html.

22. Cadwalladr, "'I Made Steve Bannon's Psychological Warfare Tool.'"

23. Solon Barocas, "The Price of Precision: Voter Microtargeting and Its Potential Harms to the Democratic Process," in *Proceedings of the First Edition Workshop on Politics, Elections and Data* (New York: Association for Computing Machinery, 2012).

24. See, for instance, Zeynep Tufekci, "Engineering the Public: Big Data, Surveillance and Computational Politics," *First Monday* 19, no. 7 (2014), https://firstmonday.org/article/view/4901/4097; Daniel Kreiss, "Yes We Can (Profile You): A Brief Primer on Campaigns and Political Data," *Stanford Law Review* 64 (February 2012): 70–74; Eli Pariser, *The Filter Bubble: What the Internet Is Hiding from You* (London: Penguin Press, 2011); and Cass Sunstein, *Republic.com 2.0* (Princeton: Princeton University Press, 2007).

25. D. Sunshine Hillygus and Todd G. Shields, *The Persuadable Voter: Wedge Issues in Presidential Campaigns* (Princeton: Princeton University Press, 2008).

26. Tufekci, "Engineering the Public."

27. Cadwalladr, "'I Made Steve Bannon's Psychological Warfare Tool.'"

28. As quoted in Barocas, "The Price of Precision." See Phillip Howard, *New Media Campaigns and the Managed Citizen* (Cambridge: Cambridge University Press, 2005).

29. Oscar H. Gandy, "Dividing Practices: Segmentation and Targeting in the Emerging Public Sphere," in *Mediated Politics: Communication in the Future of Democracy*, ed.

W. L. Bennett and R. M. Entman (Cambridge: Cambridge University Press, 2001), 141–159.

30. Barocas, "The Price of Precision."

31. Pariser, *The Filter Bubble*, 91.

32. Wendy Hui Kyong Chun, *Discriminating Data*, 34.

33. Hannah Arendt, *The Human Condition* (Chicago: University of Chicago Press, 1958), 50.

CHAPTER 9

1. Michel Foucault, *Discipline and Punish: The Birth of the Prison* (New York: Pantheon Books, 1977), 205.

2. Gilles Deleuze, "Postscript on the Societies of Control," *October* 59, no. 1 (1992): 3–7.

3. Michel Foucault, *Society Must Be Defended: Lectures at the Collège de France, 1975–1976* (New York: St. Martin's Press, 1997), 242.

4. Michel Foucault, *The History of Sexuality*, vol. 1 (New York: Pantheon Books, 1978), 138.

5. Steven Levy, "The Doctor Who Helped Defeat Smallpox Explains What's Coming," *Wired*, March 19, 2020, https://www.wired.com/story/coronavirus-interview-larry -brilliant-smallpox-epidemiologist/.

6. Giorgio Agamben, "The Invention of an Epidemic," *European Journal of Psycho- analysis*, February 20, 2020, https://www.journal-psychoanalysis.eu/coronavirus-and -philosophers/

7. See Ed Yong, "The U.K.'s Coronavirus 'Herd Immunity' Debacle," *Atlantic*, March 16, 2020, https://www.theatlantic.com/health/archive/2020/03/coronavirus-pandemic -herd-immunity-uk-boris-johnson/608065/, and "Swedish COVID-19 Response Chief Predicts Local Outbreaks, No Big Second Wave," Reuters, August 24, 2020, https:// www.reuters.com/article/us-health-coronavirus-sweden-secondwave/swedish-covid-19 -response-chief-predicts-local-outbreaks-no-big-second-wave-idUSKBN25K1B2.

8. COVID-19 dsashboard by the Center for Systems Science and Engineering at Johns Hopkins University (JHU), accessed January 19, 2022, https://coronavirus.jhu .edu/map.html.

9. Richard Luscombe, "Florida Scientist Says She Was Fired for Refusing to Change Covid-19 Data 'to Support Reopen Plan,'" *Guardian*, May 20, 2020, https://www .theguardian.com/us-news/2020/may/20/florida-scientist-dr-rebekah-jones-fired -refusing-change-covid-19-data-reopen-plan.

10. Dana Milbank, "By Order of Georgia Gov. Brian Kemp: The Day after Thursday Is Now Sunday," *Washington Post*, May 18, 2020, https://www.washingtonpost.com /opinions/2020/05/18/only-america-is-sunday-day-after-thursday/.

11. Bryan Pietsch, Jesse McKinley, and Ron DePasquale, "A Chaotic Vaccine Rollout and Allegations of a Cover-Up Threaten Cuomo's Perch," *New York Times*, February

16, 2021, https://www.nytimes.com/2021/02/16/world/a-chaotic-vaccine-rollout-and
-allegations-of-a-cover-up-threaten-cuomos-perch.html.

12. Dina Temple-Raston, "Irregularities In COVID Reporting Contract Award Process Raise New Questions," NPR, July 29, 2020, https://www.npr.org/2020/07/29
/896645314/irregularities-in-covid-reporting-contract-award-process-raises-new
-questions.

13. Charles Piller, "Federal System for Tracking Hospital Beds and COVID-19 Patients Provides Questionable Data," *Science*, November 29, 2020, https://www.sciencemag
.org/news/2020/11/federal-system-tracking-hospital-beds-and-covid-19-patients
-provides-questionable-data.

14. Charles Piller, "The Inside Story of How Trump's COVID-19 Coordinator Undermined the World's Top Health Agency," *Science*, October 14, 2020, https://www
.sciencemag.org/news/2020/10/inside-story-how-trumps-covid-19-coordinator
-undermined-cdc.

15. See, for example, Yannis Loukissas, *All Data Are Local* (Cambridge, MA: MIT Press, 2019), and Catharine D'Ignazio and Lauren Klein, *Data Feminism* (Cambridge, MA: MIT Press, 2020).

16. The COVID Racial Data Tracker, https://covidtracking.com/race.

17. UCLA Law Covid-19 Behind Bars Data Project, https://uclacovidbehindbars
.org/.

18. Institute for Health Metrics and Evaluation dashboard, https://covid19.healthdata
.org/.

19. This notion of the thermostat is a long-standing reference in cybernetics where balance is achieved through environmental feedback to a system. See Nicole Kogan et al., "An Early Warning Approach to Monitor COVID-19 Activity with Multiple Digital Traces in Near Real Time," https://arxiv.org/abs/2007.00756.

20. For background on this categorization of applications, see "Countries Are Using Apps and Data Networks to Keep Tabs on the Pandemic," *Economist*, March 26, 2020, https://www.economist.com/briefing/2020/03/26/countries-are-using-apps
-and-data-networks-to-keep-tabs-on-the-pandemic.

21. See American University student Milo Hsieh's firsthand report from Taiwan for the BBC: "Coronavirus: Under Surveillance and Confined at Home in Taiwan," *BBC News*, March 24, 2020, https://www.bbc.co.uk/news/technology-52017993.

22. "The Real Lessons from Sweden's Approach to Covid-19," *Economist*, October 10, 2020, https://www.economist.com/leaders/2020/10/10/the-real-lessons-from
-swedens-approach-to-covid-19.

23. "How Sweden Hopes to Prevent a Second Wave of Covid-19," *Economist*, October 10, 2020, https://www.economist.com/europe/2020/10/10/how-sweden-hopes
-to-prevent-a-second-wave-of-covid-19.

24. Dan Williams, "Israel to Halt Sweeping COVID-19 Cellphone Surveillance Next Month," Reuters, December 17, 2020, https://www.reuters.com/article/health
-coronavirus-israel-surveillance-idUKKBN28R1AH.

25. Richard Lloyd Parry, "How South Korea Stopped Coronavirus in Its Tracks," *Times*, Tuesday, March 24, 2020, https://www.thetimes.co.uk/article/how-south -korea-stopped-coronavirus-in-its-tracks-jxbnvxw9q.

26. Derek Thompson, "What's behind South Korea's COVID-19 Exceptionalism," *Atlantic*, May 6, 2020, https://www.theatlantic.com/ideas/archive/2020/05/whats -south-koreas-secret/611215/.

27. Andy Greenberg, "How Apple and Google Are Enabling Covid-19 Contact-Tracing," *Wired*, April 18, 2020, https://www.wired.com/story/apple-google-bluetooth -contact-tracing-covid-19/.

28. Jay Stanley and Jennifer Stisa Granick, "The Limits of Location Tracking in an Epidemic," ACLU report, April 8, 2020, https://www.aclu.org/sites/default/files /field_document/limits_of_location_tracking_in_an_epidemic.pdf.

29. Stanley and Granick, "The Limits of Location Tracking in an Epidemic,"

30. Ross Anderson, "Contact Tracing in the Real World," *Light Blue Touch Paper*, April 12, 2020, https://www.lightbluetouchpaper.org/2020/04/12/contact-tracing-in -the-real-world/.

31. This number has been disputed. See Patrick Howell O'Neill, "No, Coronavirus Apps Don't Need 60% Adoption to Be Effective," *MIT Technology Review*, June 5, 2020, https://www.technologyreview.com/2020/06/05/1002775/covid-apps-effective -at-less-than-60-percent-download/.

32. Katie Paul, Joseph Menn, and Paresh Dave, "In Coronavirus Fight, Oft-Criticized Facebook Data Aids U.S. Cities, States," Reuters, April 2, 2020, https://www.reuters .com/article/health-coronavirus-facebook-location/in-coronavirus-fight-oft-criticized -facebook-data-aids-u-s-cities-states-idUSKBN21K3BJ.

33. Paul et al., "In Coronavirus Fight."

34. See the project website: https://covid-mobility.stanford.edu/ and paper: Serina Chang, Emma Pierson, Pang Wei Koh, Jaline Gerardin, Beth Redbird, David Grusky, and Jure Leskovec, "Mobility Network Models of COVID-19 Explain Inequities and Inform Reopening," *Nature*, November 10, 2020, https://www.nature.com/articles /s41586-020-2923-3.epdf.

35. Richard Reeves and Jonathan Rothwell, "Class and COVID: How the Less Affluent Face Double Risks," Brookings Institute, March 2, 2020, https://www.brookings.edu /blog/up-front/2020/03/27/class-and-covid-how-the-less-affluent-face-double-risks/.

36. Shoshana Wodinsky, "Experian Is Tracking the People Most Likely to Get Screwed Over by Coronavirus," *Gizmodo*, April 15, 2020, https://gizmodo.com /experian-is-tracking-the-people-most-likely-to-get-scre-1842843363.

37. "Experian Offers New At-Risk Audience Segments, Free of Charge, to Essential Organizations to Help Identify Those Most Impacted by COVID-19," *Businesswire*, April 10, 2020, https://www.businesswire.com/news/home/20200410005011/en/Experian -Offers-New-At-Risk-Audience-Segments-Free.

38. Douglas MacMillan and Elizabeth Dwoskin, "The War inside Palantir: Data-Mining Firm's Ties to ICE under Attack by Employees," *Washington Post*, August 22,

2019, https://www.washingtonpost.com/business/2019/08/22/war-inside-palantir-data-mining-firms-ties-ice-under-attack-by-employees/.

39. Lisa Simunaci, "Tiberius Platform Aids COVID-19 Logistics, Delivery," US Department of Defense, December 16, 2020, https://www.defense.gov/Explore/News/Article/Article/2446061/tiberius-platform-aids-covid-19-logistics-delivery/.

40. Josh Holder, "Tracking Coronavirus Vaccinations around the World," *New York Times*, accessed March 22, 2021, https://www.nytimes.com/interactive/2021/world/covid-vaccinations-tracker.html.

41. Rob Kitchin, "Civil Liberties or Public Health, or Civil Liberties and Public Health? Using Surveillance Technologies to Tackle the Spread of COVID-19," *Space and Polity* 24, no. 3 (2020): 362–381.

42. See, for example, A. Narayanan and V. Shmatikov, "Privacy and Security: Myths and Fallacies of 'Personally Identifiable Information,'" *Communications of the ACM* 53, no. 6 (2010): 24–26; Y. A. de Montjoye, C. A. Hidalgo, M. Verleysen, and V. D. Blondel, "Unique in the Crowd: The Privacy Bounds of Human Mobility," *Nature*, Scientific Reports 3, art. 1376 (2013): 1–5; and P. Ducklin, "The Big Data Picture—Just How Anonymous Are 'Anonymous' Records?" *Naked Security*, February 12, 2015, http://nakedsecurity.sophos.com/2015/02/12/the-big-data-picture-just-how-anonymous-are-anonymous-records/.

43. Natasha Singer and Choe Sang-Hun, "As Coronavirus Surveillance Escalates, Personal Privacy Plummets," *New York Times*, March 23, 2020, https://www.nytimes.com/2020/03/23/technology/coronavirus-surveillance-tracking-privacy.html.

44. Martin Innes, "Control Creep" *Sociological Research Online* 6, no. 3 (2001), https://www.socresonline.org.uk/6/3/innes.html.

45. Kitchin, "Civil Liberties or Public Health?"

46. Panagiotis Sotiris, "Against Agamben: Is a Democratic Biopolitics Possible?" *Critical Legal Thinking*, March 14, 2020, https://criticallegalthinking.com/2020/03/14/against-agamben-is-a-democratic-biopolitics-possible/.

CODA

1. For examples of how COVID-19 altered the acoustic ecology of cities, see Quoctrung Bui and Emily Badger, "The Coronavirus Quieted City Noise. Listen to What's Left," *New York Times*, May 22, 2020, https://www.nytimes.com/interactive/2020/05/22/upshot/coronavirus-quiet-city-noise.html, and Linda Poon, "How the Pandemic Changed the Urban Soundscape," *CityLab*, October 22, 2020, https://www.bloomberg.com/news/articles/2020-10-22/the-changing-sounds-of-cities-during-covid-mapped.

2. Latour defines matters of concern as opposed to matters of fact, as gatherings of ideas, forces, players and arenas in which "things" and issues, not facts, come to be and to persist, because they are protected, cared for, and worried over. See Bruno Latour, "Why Has Critique Run Out of Steam? From Matters of Fact to Matters of Concern," *Critical Inquiry* 30, no. 2 (2004).

3. See Eric Kluitenberg, "The Zombie Public: Or, How to Revive 'the Public' and Public Space after the Pandemic," *Open! Platform for Art, Culture, and the Public Domain*, September 18, 2020, https://www.onlineopen.org/the-zombie-public.

4. Eric Kluitenberg, "Affect Space—Witnessing the Movement(s) of the Squares," *Open! Platform for Art, Culture, and the Public Domain*, March 10, 2015.

5. Nigel Thrift, "Intensities of Feeling: Towards a Spatial Politics of Affect," Geografiska Annaler: Series B, *Human Geography* 86 (2004): 57–78.

6. Kluitenberg, "The Zombie Public."

7. See Thrift, "Intensities of Feeling."

8. Brian Massumi, *Politics of Affect* (Malden, MA: Polity, 2015).

9. Apparently DeJoy had a direct interest in the failure of the public post, since he holds $30 million of stock in postal logistics provider XPO, which could take over for the Post Office. For reference, see this post by Brian Holmes to the nettime listserv: https://nettime.org/Lists-Archives/nettime-l-2009/msg00005.html.

10. See Timothy Snyder, "The American Abyss," *New York Times*, January 9, 2021, https://www.nytimes.com/2021/01/09/magazine/trump-coup.html.

11. The appearance of zip ties concerned people as they are typically used in these contexts as handcuffs to arrest protesters or abduct people. A plot to kidnap Michigan governor Gretchen Whitmer had recently been disrupted by the FBI. Whitmer had been targeted by Trump and Michigan Republicans for her positions on mitigating the spread of the coronavirus (by wearing masks, for instance).

12. Ronan Farrow, "An Air Force Combat Veteran Breached the Senate," *New Yorker*, January 8, 2021, https://www.newyorker.com/news/news-desk/an-air-force-combat-veteran-breached-the-senate.

13. Leland Nally, "The Hacker Who Archived Parler Explains How She Did It (and What Comes Next)," *Vice*, January 12, 2021, https://www.vice.com/en/article/n7vqew/the-hacker-who-archived-parler-explains-how-she-did-it-and-what-comes-next.

14. "GHIDRA," National Security Agency, accessed March 15, 2021, https://www.nsa.gov/resources/everyone/ghidra/.

15. Nally, "The Hacker Who Archived Parler."

16. To access the archive, see Lena V. Groeger, Jeff Kao, Al Shaw, Moiz Syed and Maya Eliahou, "What Parler Saw During the Attack on the Capitol," *ProPublica*, January 17, 2021, https://projects.propublica.org/parler-capitol-videos/.

17. Alec MacGillis, "Inside the Capitol Riot: What the Parler Videos Reveal," *ProPublica*, January 17, 2021, https://www.propublica.org/article/inside-the-capitol-riot-what-the-parler-videos-reveal.

18. Hannah Denham, "These Are the Platforms That Have Banned Trump and His Allies," *Washington Post*, January 11, 2021, https://www.washingtonpost.com/technology/2021/01/11/trump-banned-social-media/.

19. See Gillian Brockell, "Why March 4 Matters to QAnon Extremists, Leading to Fears of Another Capitol Attack," *Washington Post*, March 4, 2021, https://www .washingtonpost.com/history/2021/03/03/march-4-qanon-trump-inauguration/.

20. Drew Harwell, "Since Jan. 6, the pro-Trump Internet has descended into infighting over money and followers," *Washington Post*, January 3, 2022, https://www .washingtonpost.com/technology/2022/01/03/trump-qanon-online-money-war -jan6/.

21. See Chantal Mouffe, "Deliberative Democracy or Agonistic Pluralism?" *Social Research* 66, no. 3 (1999): 745–758.

BIBLIOGRAPHY

Agamben, Giorgio. "The Invention of an Epidemic." *European Journal of Psychoanalysis*, February 20, 2020. https://www.journal-psychoanalysis.eu/coronavirus-and -philosophers/.

Ahmed, Imran. *The Disinformation Dozen*. Center for Countering Digital Hate, March 24, 2021. https://www.counterhate.com/disinformationdozen.

Alexander, Kim, and Keith Mills. "Voter Privacy in the Digital Age." California Voter Foundation, May 2014.

Allen, Marshall. "Health Insurers Are Vacuuming Up Details about You—and It Could Raise Your Rates." *ProPublica*, July 17, 2018. https://www.propublica.org/article /health-insurers-are-vacuuming-up-details-about-you-and-it-could-raise-your-rates.

Amoore, Louise. *Cloud Ethics: Algorithms and the Attributes of Ourselves and Others*. Durham: Duke University Press, 2020.

Amoore, Louise. "Cloud Geographies: Computing, Data, Sovereignty." *Progress in Human Geography* 42, no. 1 (2018): 4–24.

Anderson, Chris. "The End of Theory: The Data Deluge Makes the Scientific Method Obsolete." *Wired*, June 23, 2008. https://www.wired.com/2008/06/pb-theory/.

Anderson, Ross. "Contact Tracing in the Real World." *Light Blue Touch Paper*, April 12, 2020. https://www.lightbluetouchpaper.org/2020/04/12/contact-tracing-in-the -real-world/.

Andrejevic, M. "The Work of Being Watched: Interactive Media and the Exploitation of Self Disclosure." *Critical Studies in Media Communication* 19, no. 2 (2002): 230–248.

Arendt, Hannah. *The Human Condition*. Chicago: University of Chicago Press, 1958.

Ariely, D. *Predictably Irrational: The Hidden Forces That Shape Our Decisions*. New York: HarperCollins, 2008.

Auslander, Philip. *Liveness: Performance in a Mediatized Culture*. London: Routledge, 1999.

Ballard, J. G. "Interview on October 30, 1982." In *Re/Search*, nos. 8–9, San Francisco: ReSearch Publications, 1984.

Banks, Arron. *The Bad Boys of Brexit*. London: Biteback Publishing, 2016.

Barocas, Solon. "The Price of Precision: Voter Microtargeting and Its Potential Harms to the Democratic Process." In *Proceedings of the First Edition Workshop on Politics, Elections and Data*. New York: Association for Computing Machinery, 2012.

Barocas, Solon, and Andrew D. Selbst. "Big Data's Disparate Impact." *California Law Review* 104, no. 3 (June 2016): 671–732.

Barthes, Roland. *Camera lucida: Reflections on Photography*. New York: Hill and Wang, 1981.

Baudrillard, Jean. *Selected Writings*. Stanford: Stanford University Press, 1988.

Benjamin, Ruha. *Race after Technology*. New York: Polity Press, 2019.

Benkler, Yochai. *The Wealth of Networks*. New Haven: Yale University Press, 2007.

Blanchette, Jean-François. "A Material History of Bits." *Journal of the American Society for Information Science and Technology* 62, no. 6 (2011): 1042–1057.

Bleecker, Julian, Nick Foster, Nicolas Nova, and Rhys Newman. "Convenience Newspaper." *Near Future Laboratory*, March 1, 2012. http://nearfuturelaboratory.com /2012/03/01/corner-convenience/.

Bliss, Laura. "Meet the Jane Jacobs of the 21st Century." *CityLab*, December 21, 2018. https://www.citylab.com/life/2018/12/bianca-wylie-interview-toronto-quayside -protest-criticism/574477/.

Böhlen, Marc, Varun Chandola, and Amol Salunkhe. "Server, Server in the Cloud. Who Is the Fairest in the Crowd?" Accessed September 27, 2021. https://arxiv.org /abs/1711.08801

Bonnell, Jennifer. "Don River Valley Historical Mapping Project." Maps.library .utoronto.ca, 2009. http://maps.library.utoronto.ca/dvhmp/ashbridges-bay.html.

Bosker, Bianca. "SIRI RISING: The Inside Story of Siri's Origins—and Why She Could Overshadow the iPhone." *Huffington Post*, December 6, 2017. https://www.huffpost .com/entry/siri-do-engine-apple-iphone_n_2499165.

Bowker, Geoffrey C. *Memory Practices in the Sciences*. Cambridge, MA: MIT Press, 2005.

Brecht, Bertolt. *Poems 1913–1956*. London: Methuen, 1976.

Brenner, Neil, Peter Marcuse, and Margit Mayer, eds. *Cities for People, Not for Profit: Critical Urban Theory and the Right to the City*. New York: Routledge, 2011.

Brenner, Neil, and Christian Schmid. "Towards a New Epistemology of the Urban?" *City* 19, no. 2–3 (2015): 151–182. Brockell, Gillian. "Why March 4 Matters to QAnon extremists, Leading to Fears of Another Capitol Attack." *Washington Post*, March 4, 2021. https://www.washingtonpost.com/history/2021/03/03/march-4-qanon-trump-inauguration/.

Brown, Joe. "The Amazon Echo Is More Than a Bluetooth Speaker—It's a Bedtime Buddy." *Vox*, February 9, 2015. https://www.vox.com/2015/2/9/11558754/the-amazon-echo-is-more-than-a-bluetooth-speaker-its-a-bedtime-buddy.

Bui, Quoctrung, and Emily Badger. "The Coronavirus Quieted City Noise. Listen to What's Left." *New York Times*, May 22, 2020. https://www.nytimes.com/interactive/2020/05/22/upshot/coronavirus-quiet-city-noise.html.

Bullinger, Jake. "Amazon's Checkout-Free Store Makes Shopping Feel Like Shoplifting." *Atlantic*, January 24, 2018. https://www.theatlantic.com/business/archive/2018/01/amazon-go-store-checkouts-seattle/551357/.

Buolamwini, Joy, and Timnit Gebru. "Gender Shades: Intersectional Accuracy Disparities in Commercial Gender Classification." *Proceedings of Machine Learning Research* (January 2018): 77–91.

Cadwalladr, Carole. "Daniel Dennett: 'I Begrudge Every Hour I Have to Spend Worrying about Politics.'" *Guardian*, February 12, 2017. https://www.theguardian.com/science/2017/feb/12/daniel-dennett-politics-bacteria-bach-back-dawkins-trump-interview.

Cadwalladr, Carole. "Facebook Faces Fresh Questions Over When It Knew of Data Harvesting." *Guardian*, March 16, 2019. https://www.theguardian.com/technology/2019/mar/16/facebook-fresh-questions-data-harvesting-cambridge-analytica.

Cadwalladr, Carole. "'I Made Steve Bannon's Psychological Warfare Tool': Meet the Data War Whistleblower." *Guardian*, March 17, 2018. https://www.theguardian.com/news/2018/mar/17/data-war-whistleblower-christopher-wylie-faceook-nix-bannon-trump.

Carr, Austin. "I Found Out My Secret Internal Tinder Rating and Now I Wish I Hadn't." *Fast Company*, January 11, 2016. https://www.fastcompany.com/3054871/whats-your-tinder-score-inside-the-apps-internal-ranking-system.

Cecco, Leyland. "'Surveillance Capitalism': Critic Urges Toronto to Abandon Smart City Project." *Guardian*, June 6, 2019. https://www.theguardian.com/cities/2019/jun/06/toronto-smart-city-google-project-privacy-concerns.

Chang, Serina, Emma Pierson, Pang Wei Koh, Jaline Gerardin, Beth Redbird, David Grusky, and Jure Leskovec. "Mobility Network Models of COVID-19 Explain

Inequities and Inform Reopening." *Nature*, November 10, 2020. https://www.nature .com/articles/s41586-020-2923-3.epdf.

Chomsky, Noam. "The Case against B. F. Skinner." *New York Review of Books*, December 30, 1971.

Chun, Wendy Hui Kyong. *Discriminating Data: Correlation, Neighborhoods, and the New Politics of Recognition*. Cambridge, MA: MIT Press, 2021.

Colbert Report. "The Word—Truthiness." *Comedy Central*. Video, 2:40. October 17, 2005. https://www.cc.com/video/63ite2/the-colbert-report-the-word-truthiness.

Cole, Samantha. "AI-Assisted Fake Porn Is Here and We're All Fucked." *Vice*, December 11, 2017. https://www.vice.com/en_us/article/gydydm/gal-gadot-fake-ai-porn.

Cole, Samantha. "Lawmakers Demand Intelligence Community Release a Report on Deepfakes." *Vice*, September 13, 2018. https://www.vice.com/en_us/article/zm5vw9 /deepfakes-letter-to-director-of-national-intelligence.

Confessore, Nicholas, and Danny Hakim. "Data Firm Says 'Secret Sauce' Aided Trump; Many Scoff." *New York Times*, March 6, 2017. https://www.nytimes.com /2017/03/06/us/politics/cambridge-analytica.html.

Connelly, Martin. "A Little Lesson in Knowledge, Courtesy of an Island That Disappeared (If It Ever Even Existed)." *Vice*, November 26, 2012. https://www.vice.com /en_us/article/d7747w/the-other-strange-sandy-an-island-that-totally-disappeared.

"Countries Are Using Apps and Data Networks to Keep Tabs on the Pandemic." *Economist*, March 26, 2020. https://www.economist.com/briefing/2020/03/26/countries-are -using-apps-and-data-networks-to-keep-tabs-on-the-pandemic.

Crampton, Jeremy W., and John Krygier. "An Introduction to Critical Cartography." *ACME: An International Journal for Critical Geographies* 4, no. 1 (2005): 11–33.

Crary, Jonathan. *Suspensions of Perception: Attention, Spectacle and Modern Culture*. Cambridge, MA: MIT Press, 1999.

Crary, Jonathan. *Techniques of the Observer: On Vision and Modernity in the Nineteenth Century*. Cambridge, MA: MIT Press, 1990.

Crawford, Kate. *Atlas of AI: Power, Politics, and the Planetary Costs of Artificial Intelligence*. New Haven: Yale University Press, 2021.

Crawford, Kate. "The Hidden Biases in Big Data." *Harvard Business Review*, April 1, 2013. https://hbr.org/2013/04/the-hidden-biases-in-big-data.

Crawford, Kate, and Trevor Paglen. "Excavating AI: The Politics of Images in Machine Learning Training Sets." Accessed September 27, 2021. https://excavating.ai/.

Crenshaw, Kimberle. "Demarginalizing the Intersection of Race and Sex: A Black Feminist Critique of Antidiscrimination Doctrine, Feminist Theory and Antiracist Politics." *University of Chicago Legal Forum* (1989): art. 8.

Davies, William. "The Chronic Social: Relations of Control within and without Neo-liberalism." *New Formations* 84/85 (2015): 40–57.

Dawson, Alyssa Harvey. "An Update on Data Governance for Sidewalk Toronto." *Sidewalk Labs, Medium*, October 15, 2018. https://medium.com/sidewalk-talk/an-update-on-data-governance-for-sidewalk-toronto-d810245f10f7.

Day, Matt, Giles Turner, and Natalia Drozdiak. "Amazon Workers Are Listening to What You Tell Alexa." Bloomberg, April 10, 2019. https://www.bloomberg.com/news/articles/2019-04-10/is-anyone-listening-to-you-on-alexa-a-global-team-reviews-audio.

de Certeau, Michel. *The Practice of Everyday Life*. Berkeley: University of California Press, 1984.

Deleuze, Gilles. "Postscript on Control Societies." *Negotiations: 1972–1990*. New York: Columbia University Press, 1995.

de Montjoye, Y. A., C. A. Hidalgo, M. Verleysen, and V. D. Blondel. "Unique in the Crowd: The Privacy Bounds of Human Mobility." *Scientific Reports* 3 (2013): art. 1376.

Denham, Hannah. "These Are the Platforms That Have Banned Trump and His Allies." *Washington Post*, January 11, 2011. https://www.washingtonpost.com/technology/2021/01/11/trump-banned-social-media/.

Desfor, Gene, Lucian Vesalon, and Jennefer Laidley. *Reshaping Toronto's Waterfront*. Toronto: University of Toronto Press, 2011.

di Feliciantonio, Cesare, Paolo Cardullo, and Rob Kitchin, eds. *The Right to the Smart City*. Bingley: Emerald Publishing, 2019.

D'Ignazio, Catherine, and Lauren Klein. *Data Feminism*. Cambridge, MA: MIT Press, 2020.

Doctoroff, Daniel. "Why We're No Longer Pursuing the Quayside Project—and What's Next for Sidewalk Labs." *Sidewalk Labs, Medium*, May 7, 2020. https://medium.com/sidewalk-talk/why-were-no-longer-pursuing-the-quayside-project-and-what-s-next-for-sidewalk-labs-9a61de3fee3a.

Dourish, Paul. *The Stuff of Bits: An Essay on the Materialities of Information*. Cambridge, MA: MIT Press, 2017.

Drucker, Johanna. "Humanities Approaches to Graphical Display." *Digital Humanities Quarterly* 5, no. 1 (2011). http://www.digitalhumanities.org/dhq/vol/5/1/000091/000091.html.

Ducklin, P. "The Big Data Picture—Just How Anonymous Are 'Anonymous' Records?" *Naked Security*, February 12, 2015. http://nakedsecurity.sophos.com/2015/02/12/the-big-data-picture-just-how-anonymous-are-anonymous-records/

Duhigg, Charles. "How Companies Know Your Secrets." *New York Times*, February 16, 2012. http://www.nytimes.com/2012/02/19/magazine/shopping-habits.html.

Duhigg, Charles. *The Power of Habit*. New York: Random House, 2012.

Ensign, Danielle, Sorelle A. Friedler, Scott Neville, Carlos Scheidegger, and Suresh Venkatasubramanian. "Runaway Feedback Loops in Predictive Policing." In *Proceedings of the First Conference on Fairness, Accountability and Transparency (PMLR)*, 2018. http://proceedings.mlr.press/v81/.

Environmental Protection Agency, Office of the Inspector General. "EPA's Response to the World Trade Center Collapse: Challenges, Successes, and Areas for Improvement." August 21, 2003. http://www.epa.gov/oig/reports/2003/WTC_report_20030821.pdf.

Fard, Ali. "Cloudy Landscapes: On the Extended Geography of Smart Urbanism." *Telematics and Informatics* 55 (2020). https://doi.org/10.1016/j.tele.2020.101450.

Farrow, Ronan. "An Air Force Combat Veteran Breached the Senate." *New Yorker*, January 8, 2021. https://www.newyorker.com/news/news-desk/an-air-force-combat -veteran-breached-the-senate.

Fertik, Michael, and David C. Thompson. *The Reputation Economy: How to Optimize Your Digital Footprint in a World Where Your Reputation Is Your Most Valuable Asset.* London: Piatkus, 2015.

Forrester, Jay W. *Urban Dynamics.* Cambridge, MA: MIT Press, 1969.

Forty, Richard. *Objects of Desire: Design and Society since 1750.* New York: Thames and Hudson, 2005.

Foucault, Michel. *The Birth of Biopolitics: Lectures at the Collège de France, 1978–1979.* New York: Palgrave MacMillan, 2008.

Foucault, Michel. *Discipline and Punish: The Birth of the Prison.* New York: Pantheon Books, 1977.

Foucault, Michel. *The History of Sexuality*, vol. 1. New York: Pantheon Books, 1978.

Foucault, Michel. *Society Must Be Defended: Lectures at the Collège de France, 1975– 1976.* New York: St. Martin's Press, 1997.

Foucault, Michel, Graham Burchell, Colin Gordon, and Peter Miller. *The Foucault Effect: Studies in Governmentality.* Chicago: University of Chicago Press, 1991.

Friedman, Batya, and Helen Nissenbaum. "Bias in Computer Systems." *ACM Transactions on Information Systems* 14, no. 3 (1996): 330–347.

Gabrys, Jennifer. *Program Earth: Environmental Sensing Technology and the Making of a Computational Planet.* Minneapolis: University of Minnesota Press, 2016.

Gandy, Oscar H. "Dividing Practices: Segmentation and Targeting in the Emerging Public Sphere." In *Mediated Politics: Communication in the Future of Democracy*, edited by W. L. Bennett and R. M. Entman. Cambridge: Cambridge University Press, 2001.

Gandy, Oscar H. "Toward a Political Economy of Personal Information." *Critical Studies in Media Communication* 10, no. 1 (1993): 70–97.

Garfinkel, Simson. *Architects of the Information Society: Thirty-Five Years of the Laboratory for Computer Science at MIT*. Edited by Hal Abelson. Cambridge, MA: MIT Press, 1999.

Gasparro, Annie, and Jaewon Kang. "Grocers Wrest Control of Shelf Space from Struggling Food Giants." *Wall Street Journal*, February 19, 2020. https://www.wsj.com/articles/grocers-wrest-control-of-shelf-space-from-struggling-food-giants-11582108202.

Georg, Simmel. "The Metropolis and Mental Life." *Simmel on Culture*. London: Sage, 1997.

Gibbs, Samuel. "Women Less Likely to Be Shown Ads for High-Paid Jobs on Google, Study Shows." *Guardian*, July 8, 2015. https://www.theguardian.com/technology/2015/jul/08/women-less-likely-ads-high-paid-jobs-google-study.

Gibney, Elizabeth. "The Scant Science behind Cambridge Analytica's Controversial Marketing Techniques." *Nature*, March 29, 2018. https://www.nature.com/articles/d41586-018-03880-4.

Gitelman, Lisa, ed. *"Raw Data" Is an Oxymoron*. Cambridge, MA: MIT Press, 2013.

Goldberg, Lewis R. "The Development of Markers for the Big-Five Factor Structure." *Psychological Assessment* 4, no. 1 (1992): 26–42.

Grassegger, Hannes, and Mikael Krogerus. "The Data That Turned the World Upside Down." *Vice*, January 28, 2017. https://www.vice.com/en_us/article/mg9vvn/how-our-likes-helped-trump-win.

Greenberg, Andy. "How Apple and Google Are Enabling Covid-19 Contact-Tracing." *Wired*, April 18, 2020. https://www.wired.com/story/apple-google-bluetooth-contact-tracing-covid-19/.

Gross, Ryan. "How the Amazon Go Store's AI Works." *Towards Data Science, Medium*, June 6, 2019. https://towardsdatascience.com/how-the-amazon-go-store-works-a-deep-dive-3fde9d9939e9.

Guattari, Félix. "Towards a Post-Media Era." *Metamute*, February 1, 2012. https://www.metamute.org/editorial/lab/towards-post-media-era.

Habermas, Jürgen. *The Structural Transformation of the Public Sphere: An Inquiry into a Category of Bourgeois Society*. Cambridge, MA: MIT Press, 1962.

Halpern, Orit. *Beautiful Data: A History of Vision and Reason since 1945*. Durham: Duke University Press, 2015.

Halpern, Orit, Jesse LeCavalier, Nerea Calvillo, and Wolfgang Pietsch. "Test-Bed Urbanism." *Public Culture* 25, no. 2 (2013): 272–306.

Hansen, W. G. "How Accessibility Shapes Land-Use." *Journal of the American Institute of Planners* 25 (1959): 73–76.

Haraway, Donna. *Simians, Cyborgs and Women: The Reinvention of Nature*. London: Routledge, 1991.

Harding, Luke. "The Pacific Island That Never Was." *Guardian*, November 22, 2012. https://www.theguardian.com/world/2012/nov/22/sandy-island-missing-google-earth.

Harley, J. B. "Can There Be a Cartographic Ethics?" *Cartographic Perspectives*, no. 10 (June 1991): 9–16.

Harris, Mark. "Inside Alphabet's Money-Spinning, Terrorist-Foiling, Gigabit Wi-Fi Kiosks." *Vox: Recode*, July 1, 2016. https://www.vox.com/2016/7/1/12072122/alphabet -sidewalk-labs-city-wifi-sidewalk-kiosks.

Harvey, David. *Rebel Cities: From the Right to the City to the Urban Revolution*. London: Verso, 2012.

Harvey, David. "The Right to the City." *New Left Review* 2, no. 53 (September– October 2008): 23–40.

Harwell, Drew. "Since Jan. 6, the Pro-Trump Internet Has Descended into infight- ing Over Money and Followers." *Washington Post*, January 3, 2022. https://www .washingtonpost.com/technology/2022/01/03/trump-qanon-online-money-war -jan6/.

Harwell, Drew, and Abha Bhattarai. "Inside Amazon Go: The Camera-Filled Conve- nience Store That Watches You Back." *Washington Post*, January 22, 2018. https:// www.washingtonpost.com/news/business/wp/2018/01/22/inside-amazon-go-the -camera-filled-convenience-store-that-watches-you-back/.

Hearn, Alison. "Structuring Feeling: Web 2.0, Online Ranking and Rating, and the Digital 'Reputation' Economy." *Ephemera*, 10, nos. 3–4 (2010): 421–438.

Heaven, Will Douglas. "Predictive Policing Algorithms Are Racist. They Need to Be Dismantled." *MIT Technology Review*, July 17, 2020. https://www.technologyreview .com/2020/07/17/1005396/predictive-policing-algorithms-racist-dismantled -machine-learning-bias-criminal-justice/.

Heidegger, Martin. *The Question Concerning Technology and Other Essays*. London: HarperCollins, 1977.

Heit, Helmut. "'There are no facts . . .': Nietzsche as Predecessor of Post-Truth?" *Studia Philosophica Estonica* 11 (2018): 44.

Hillier, Amy E. "Redlining and the Home Owners' Loan Corporation." *Journal of Urban History* 29, no. 4 (2003): 394–420.

Hillygus, D. Sunshine, and Todd G. Shields. *The Persuadable Voter: Wedge Issues in Presidential Campaigns*. Princeton: Princeton University Press, 2008.

Holder, Josh. "Tracking Coronavirus Vaccinations around the World." *New York Times*. Accessed March 22, 2021. https://www.nytimes.com/interactive/2021/world /covid-vaccinations-tracker.html.

Hollands, Robert. "Will the Real Smart City Please Stand Up? Intelligent, Progressive or Entrepreneurial?" *City* 12, no. 3 (2008): 303–320.

Houser, Kimberly and Debra Sanders. "The Use of Big Data Analytics by the IRS: Efficient Solutions or the End of Privacy as We Know It?" *Vanderbilt Journal of Entertainment and Technology Law* 817 (2017).

Howard, Phillip. *New Media Campaigns and the Managed Citizen.* Cambridge: Cambridge University Press, 2005.

Huang, Haomiao. "How Amazon Go (Probably) Makes 'Just Walk Out' Groceries a Reality." *Ars Technica*, April 10, 2017. https://arstechnica.com/information-technology/2017/04/how-amazon-go-probably-makes-just-walk-out-groceries-a-reality/.

Hunt, Elle. "Trump's Inauguration Crowd: Sean Spicer's Claims versus the Evidence." *Guardian*, January 22, 2017. https://www.theguardian.com/us-news/2017/jan/22/trump-inauguration-crowd-sean-spicers-claims-versus-the-evidence.

Hvistendahl, Mara. "Questions Mount about Controversial Hunter Biden–China Dossier." *Intercept*, November 11, 2020/ https://theintercept.com/2020/11/11/hunter-biden-china-dossier/.

Ingram, Matthew. "Facebook's Fact-Checking Program Falls Short." *Columbia Journalism Review*, August 2, 2019. http://www.cjr.org/the_media_today/facebook-fact-checking.php.

Innes, Martin. "Control Creep" *Sociological Research Online* 6, no. 3 (2001). https://www.socresonline.org.uk/6/3/innes.html

Jaeger, Paul T., Jimmy Lin, Justin M. Grimes, and Shannon N. Simmons. "Where Is the Cloud? Geography, Economics, Environment, and Jurisdiction in Cloud Computing." *First Monday* 14, no. 5 (2009). https://doi.org/10.5210/fm.v14i5.2456.

Jameson, Fredric. *Postmodernism, or, The Cultural Logic of Late Capitalism.* Durham: Duke University Press, 1991.

Kang, Cecilia, Matthew Rosenberg, and Sheera Frenkel. "Facebook Faces Broadened Federal Investigations over Data and Privacy." *New York Times*, July 2, 2018. https://www.nytimes.com/2018/07/02/technology/facebook-federal-investigations.html.

Kelling, Steve, Wesley M. Hochachka, Daniel Fink, Mirek Riedewald, Rich Caruana, Grant Ballard, and Giles Gooker. "Data-Intensive Science: A New Paradigm for Biodiversity Studies." *BioScience* 59, no. 7 (2009): 613–620.

Kessler, Glenn. "Trump Made 30,573 False or Misleading Claims as President. Nearly Half Came in His Final Year." *Washington Post*, January 23, 2021. https://www.washingtonpost.com/politics/how-fact-checker-tracked-trump-claims/2021/01/23/ad04b69a-5c1d-11eb-a976-bad6431e03e2_story.html.

Kitchin, Rob. "Big Data, New Epistemologies and Paradigm Shifts," *Big Data and Society* (April–June 2014): 1–12.

Kitchin, Rob. "Civil Liberties or Public Health, or Civil Liberties and Public Health? Using Surveillance Technologies to Tackle the Spread of COVID-19." *Space and Polity* 24, no. 3 (2020): 362–381.

Kitchin, Rob. *The Data Revolution: Big Data, Open Data, Data Infrastructures and Their Consequences*. London: Sage, 2014.

Kitchin, Rob, Claudio Coletta, and Gavin McArdle. "Urban Informatics, Governmentality and the Logics of Urban Control." SocArXiv, February 9, 2017. http://doi.org/10.31235/osf.io/27hz8.

Kitchin, Rob, and Martin Dodge. *Code/Space: Software and Everyday Life*. Cambridge, MA: MIT Press, 2011.

Kitchin, Rob, and Scott Freundschuh. *Cognitive Mapping: Past, Present, and Future*. London: Routledge, 2000.

Kitchin, Rob, and Tracey Lauriault. "Small Data in the Era of Big Data." *GeoJournal* 80, no. 4 (1980): 463–475.

Kleber, Sophie. "As AI Meets the Reputation Economy, We're All Being Silently Judged." *Harvard Business Review*, January 29, 2018. https://hbr.org/2018/01/as-ai-meets-the-reputation-economy-were-all-being-silently-judged.

Kluitenberg, Eric. "Affect Space—Witnessing the Movement(s) of the Squares." *Open! Platform for Art, Culture, and the Public Domain*, March 10, 2015.

Kluitenberg, Eric. "The Zombie Public: Or, How to Revive 'the Public' and Public Space after the Pandemic." *Open! Platform for Art, Culture, and the Public Domain*, September 18, 2020. https://www.onlineopen.org/the-zombie-public.

Kobie, Nicole. "The Complicated Truth about China's Social Credit System." *Wired UK*, June 7, 2019. https://www.wired.co.uk/article/china-social-credit-system-explained.

Koestler, Arthur. *The Ghost in the Machine*. New York: Macmillan, 1968.

Kofman, Ava. "Bruno Latour, the Post-Truth Philosopher, Mounts a Defense of Science." *New York Times*, October 25, 2018. www.nytimes.com/2018/10/25/magazine/bruno-latour-post-truth-philosopher-science.html.

Kogan, Nicole, Leonardo Clemente, Parker Liautaud, Justin Kaashoek, Nicholas B. Link, André T. Nguyen, Fred S. Lu, et al. "An Early Warning Approach to Monitor COVID-19 Activity with Multiple Digital Traces in Near Real-Time." https://arxiv.org/abs/2007.00756.

Kontokosta, Constantine. "The Quantified Community and Neighborhood Labs: A Framework for Computational Urban Science and Civic Technology Innovation." *Journal of Urban Technology* 23, no. 4 (2016): 67–84.

Kościński, Krzysztof. "Facial Attractiveness: Variation, Adaptiveness and Consequences of Facial Preferences." *Anthropological Review* 71 (2008): 77–108.

Kraus, Rosalind. "Notes on the Index: Seventies Art in America." *October* 3 (1977): 68–81.

Kreiss, Daniel. "Yes We Can (Profile You): A Brief Primer on Campaigns and Political Data." *Stanford Law Review* 64 (2012): 70–74.

Krivý, Maroš. "Towards a Critique of Cybernetic Urbanism: The Smart City and the Society of Control." *Planning Theory* 17, no. 1 (2018): 8–30.

Krulwich, Robert. "An Imaginary Town Becomes Real, Then Not. True Story." NPR, March 18, 2014. https://www.npr.org/sections/krulwich/2014/03/18/290236647/an-imaginary-town-becomes-real-then-not-true-story.

Krygier, John, and Denis Wood. *Making Maps: A Visual Guide to Map Design for GIS.* New York: Guilford Press, 2016.

Kurgan, Laura. *Close Up at a Distance: Mapping, Technology, and Politics.* New York: Zone Books, 2013.

Kurgan, Laura, Dare Brawley, Brian House, Jia Zhang, and Wendy Hui Kyong Chun. "Homophily: The Urban History of an Algorithm." *e-flux*, October 4, 2019. https://www.e-flux.com/architecture/are-friends-electric/289193/homophily-the-urban-history-of-an-algorithm/.

Kyrk, Hazel. *Economic Problems of the Family.* London: Harper, 1933.

Lapowsky, Issie. "The Man Who Saw the Dangers of Cambridge Analytica Years Ago." *Wired*, June 19, 2018. https://www.wired.com/story/the-man-who-saw-the-dangers-of-cambridge-analytica/.

Latour, Bruno. *Down to Earth: Politics in the New Climatic Regime.* Cambridge: Polity Press, 2018.

Latour, Bruno. "Why Has Critique Run Out of Steam? From Matters of Fact to Matters of Concern." *Critical Inquiry* 30, no. 2 (2004).

Latour, Bruno, and Steve Woolgar. *Laboratory Life: the Construction of Scientific Facts.* Princeton: Princeton University Press, 2006.

Leber, Jessica. "Beyond the Quantified Self: The World's Largest Quantified Community." *Fast Company*, April 22, 2014. https://www.fastcompany.com/3029255/beyond-the-quantified-self-the-worlds-largest-quantified-community.

LeCun, Y., B. Boser, J. S. Denker, D. Henderson, R. E. Howard, W. Hubbard, and L. D. Jackel. "Backpropagation Applied to Handwritten Zip Code Recognition." *Neural Computing* 1, no. 4 (1989): 541–551.

LeCun, Y., L. Bottou, Y. Bengio, and P. Haffner. "Gradient-Based Learning Applied to Document Recognition." *Proceedings of the IEEE* 86, no. 11 (1998): 2278–2324.

Lefebvre, Henri. *The Production of Space.* Oxford: Blackwell, 1991.

Lefebvre, Henri. *Writings on Cities.* Oxford: Blackwell, 1996.

Lemke, Thomas. "Foucault, Governmentality, and Critique." *Rethinking Marxism* 14, no. 3 (2002): 49–64.

Lenhart, Amanda. "How Teens Hang Out and Stay in Touch with Their Closest Friends." *Teens Technology and Friendships*. Pew Research Center, August 6, 2015.

http://www.pewinternet.org/2015/08/06/chapter-2-how-teens-hang-out-and-stay-in
-touch-with-their-closest-friends.

Levine, E. S., and J. S. Tisch. "Analytics in Action at the New York City Police
Department's Counterterrorism Bureau." *Military Operations Research* 19, no. 4 (2014):
5–14.

Levy, Steven. "The Doctor Who Helped Defeat Smallpox Explains What's Coming."
Wired, March 19, 2020. https://www.wired.com/story/coronavirus-interview-larry
-brilliant-smallpox-epidemiologist/.

Lewis, Paul, Jamie Grierson, and Matthew Weaver. "Cambridge Analytica Academic's Work Upset University Colleagues." *Guardian*, March 24, 2018. https://www
.theguardian.com/education/2018/mar/24/cambridge-analytica-academics-work
-upset-university-colleagues.

Libby, Brian. "Quantifying the Livable City." *Bloomberg Citylab*, October 21, 2014.
http://www.citylab.com/tech/2014/10/quantifying-the-livable-city/381657/.

Lichfield, John. "Boris Johnson's £350m Claim Is Devious and Bogus. Here's Why."
Guardian, September 18, 2017. https://www.theguardian.com/commentisfree/2017
/sep/18/boris-johnson-350-million-claim-bogus-foreign-secretary.

Loukissas, Yanni Alexander. *All Data Are Local: Thinking Critically in a Data-Driven
Society*. Cambridge, MA: MIT Press, 2005.

Lovelace, A. A. "Notes by A. A. L. [August Ada Lovelace]." In *Taylor's Scientific Memoirs*, 666–731. London, 1843.

Low, Setha, and Niel Smith. *The Politics of Public Space*. London: Routledge, 2006.

Lowerre, B. T. "The Harpy Speech Recognition System." PhD diss., Carnegie Mellon
University, 1976.

Luscombe, Richard. "Florida Scientist Says She Was Fired for Refusing to Change
Covid-19 Data 'to Support Reopen Plan.'" *Guardian*, May 20, 2020. https://www
.theguardian.com/us-news/2020/may/20/florida-scientist-dr-rebekah-jones-fired
-refusing-change-covid-19-data-reopen-plan.

Lynch, Kevin. *The Image of the City*. Cambridge, MA: MIT Press, 1960.

Lyotard, Jean-François. *The Postmodern Condition: A Report on Knowledge*. Minneapolis: University of Minnesota Press, 1984.

MacGillis, Alec. "Inside the Capitol Riot: What the Parler Videos Reveal." *ProPublica*,
January 17, 2021. https://www.propublica.org/article/inside-the-capitol-riot-what
-the-parler-videos-reveal.

MacMillan, Douglas, and Elizabeth Dwoskin. "The War inside Palantir: Data-Mining
Firm's Ties to ICE under Attack by Employees." *Washington Post*, August 22, 2019.
https://www.washingtonpost.com/business/2019/08/22/war-inside-palantir-data
-mining-firms-ties-ice-under-attack-by-employees/.

Manthorpe, Rowland. "Beauty.AI's 'Robot Beauty Contest' Is Back—and This Time It Promises Not to Be Racist." *Wired UK*, March 2, 2017. https://www.wired.co.uk /article/robot-beauty-contest-beauty-ai

Manyika, James, Michael Chui, Brad Brown, Jacques Bughin, Richard Dobbs, Charles Roxburgh, and Angela Hung Byers. *Big Data: The Next Frontier for Innovation, Competition, and Productivity*. McKinsey Global Institute, 2011.

Marres, Noortje. "Why We Can't Have Our Facts Back." *Engaging Science, Technology, and Society* 4 (2018): 423.

Maslow, Abraham. *Toward a Psychology of Being*. New York: Van Nostrand, 1968.

Massumi, Brian. *Politics of Affect*. Malden, MA: Polity, 2015.

Mathews, Stanley. *From Agit-Prop to Free Space: The Architecture of Cedric Price*. London: Blackdog, 2007.

Matsakis, Louise. "How the West Got China's Social Credit Score Wrong." *Wired*, July 19, 2019. https://www.wired.com/story/china-social-credit-score-system/.

Mattern, Shannon. *A City Is Not a Computer: Other Urban Intelligences*. Princeton: Princeton University Press, 2021.

Mattern, Shannon. *Code + Clay, Data and Dirt: Five Thousand Years of Urban Media*. Minneapolis: University of Minnesota Press, 2017.

Mattern, Shannon. "Instrumental City: The View from Hudson Yards, circa 2019." *Places Journal*, April 2016. https://placesjournal.org/article/instrumental-city-new -york-hudson-yards/.

Mattern, Shannon. "Post-It Note City." *Places Journal*, February 2020. https:// placesjournal.org/article/post-it-note-city/.

McBride, Jason. "How the Sidewalk Labs Proposal Landed in Toronto: The Backstory." *Toronto Life*, September 4, 2019. https://torontolife.com/city/how-the-sidewalk-labs -proposal-landed-in-toronto-the-backstory/.

McCarthy, Lauren. "Feeling at Home: Between Human and AI." *Immerse*, January 8, 2018. https://immerse.news/feeling-at-home-between-human-and-ai-6047561e7f04.

McCulloch, Warren, and Walter Pitts. "A Logical Calculus of Ideas Immanent in Nervous Activity." *Bulletin of Mathematical Biophysics* 5 (1943): 115–133.

McCullough, Malcolm. *Ambient Commons: Attention in the Age of Embodied Information*. Cambridge, MA: MIT Press, 2013.

McCullough, Malcolm. *Digital Ground Architecture, Pervasive Computing, and Environmental Knowing*. Cambridge, MA: MIT Press, 2004.

Metz, Cade. "Meet GPT-3. It Has Learned to Code (and Blog and Argue)." *New York Times*, November 24, 2020. https://www.nytimes.com/2020/11/24/science/artificial -intelligence-ai-gpt3.html.

Milbank, Dana. "By Order of Georgia Gov. Brian Kemp: The Day after Thursday Is Now Sunday." *Washington Post*, May 18, 2020. https://www.washingtonpost.com /opinions/2020/05/18/only-america-is-sunday-day-after-thursday/.

Minsky, Marvin, and Seymour Papert. *Perceptrons; An Introduction to Computational Geometry*. Cambridge, MA: MIT Press, 1969.

Mogel, Lize, and Alexis Bhagat, *An Atlas of Radical Cartography*. Los Angeles: Journal of Aesthetics and Protest Press, 2007.

Morrison, P., and E. Morrison. *Charles Babbage and His Calculating Engines: Selected Writings by Charles Babbage and Others*. New York: Dover, 1961.

Mouffe, Chantal. "Deliberative Democracy or Agonistic Pluralism?" *Social Research* 66, no. 3 (1999): 745–758.

Nadler, Anthony, and Lee McGuigan. "An Impulse to Exploit: The Behavioral Turn in Data-Driven Marketing." *Critical Studies in Media Communication* 35, no. 2 (2018): 151–165.

Nagel, Thomas. *The View from Nowhere*. Oxford: Oxford University Press, 1986.

Nally, Leland. "The Hacker Who Archived Parler Explains How She Did It (and What Comes Next)." *Vice*, January 12, 2021. https://www.vice.com/en/article/n7vqew/the -hacker-who-archived-parler-explains-how-she-did-it-and-what-comes-next.

Narayanan, Ajjit, and Graham MacDonald. "Toward an Open Data Bias Assessment Tool: Measuring Bias in Open Spatial Data." Urban Institute, February 2019. https:// www.urban.org/sites/default/files/publication/99844/toward_an_open_data_bias_ assessment_tool_1.pdf.

Narayanan, Ajjit, and V. Shmatikov. "Privacy and Security: Myths and Fallacies of 'Personally Identifiable Information.'" *Communications of the ACM* 53, no. 6 (2010): 24–26.

National Security Agency. "GHIDRA." Accessed March 15, 2021. https://www.nsa .gov/resources/everyone/ghidra/.

New York Civil Liberties Union. "City Strengthens Public Wi-Fi Privacy Policy after NYCLU Raises Concerns," March 16, 2017. https://www.nyclu.org/en/press-releases /city-strengthens-public-wi-fi-privacy-policy-after-nyclu-raises-concerns.

New York Civil Liberties Union. "Testimony Regarding Technology Oversight Hearing on LinkNYC," November 18, 2016. https://www.nyclu.org/en/publications /testimony-regarding-technology-oversight-hearing-linknyc.

Nickerson, David W., and Todd Rogers. "Political Campaigns and Big Data." *Journal of Economic Perspectives* 28, no. 2 (2014): 51–74.

Nietzsche, Friedrich Wilhelm. *The Portable Nietzsche*. New York: Viking Press, 1954.

Nonko, Emily. "Hudson Yards Promised a High-Tech Neighborhood—It Was a Greater Challenge Than Expected." *Metropolis*, February 5, 2019. https://www.metropolismag .com/cities/hudson-yards-technology-urbanism/.

Nuckols, Ben. "Inaugural Crowds Sure to Be Huge—But How Huge?" Associated Press, January 19, 2017. https://www.apnews.com/7afad98b7d78423cbb5140fe810e3480.

O'Kane, Josh. "Inside the Mysteries and Missteps of Toronto's Smart-City Dream." *Globe and Mail*, May 17, 2019. https://www.theglobeandmail.com/business/article -inside-the-mysteries-and-missteps-of-torontos-smart-city-dream/.

O'Neil, Cathy. "How Algorithms Rule Our Working Lives." *Guardian*, September 1, 2016. https://www.theguardian.com/science/2016/sep/01/how-algorithms-rule-our -working-lives.

O'Neill, Patrick Howell. "No, Coronavirus Apps Don't Need 60% Adoption to Be Effective." *MIT Technology Review*, June 5, 2020. https://www.technologyreview.com /2020/06/05/1002775/covid-apps-effective-at-less-than-60-percent-download/.

Ovadya, Aviv. "Deepfake Myths: Common Misconceptions about Synthetic Media." Alliance for Securing Democracy, June 14, 2019. https://securingdemocracy.gmfus .org/deepfake-myths-common-misconceptions-about-synthetic-media/.

Oxford Dictionaries. "Word of the Year 2016 Is . . ." Oxford University Press. Accessed October 1, 2021. https://languages.oup.com/word-of-the-year/word-of-the -year-2016.

Pandurangan, Vijay. "On Taxis and Rainbows." *Medium*. June 21, 2014. https://tech .vijayp.ca/of-taxis-and-rainbows-f6bc289679a1

Pariser, Eli. *The Filter Bubble: What the Internet Is Hiding from You*. London: Penguin Press, 2011.

Parry, Richard Lloyd. "How South Korea Stopped Coronavirus in Its Tracks." *Times*, March 24, 2020. https://www.thetimes.co.uk/article/how-south-korea-stopped -coronavirus-in-its-tracks-jxbnvxw9q.

Paul, Katie, Joseph Menn, and Paresh Dave. "In Coronavirus Fight, Oft-Criticized Facebook Data Aids U.S. Cities, States." Reuters, April 2, 2020, https://www.reuters .com/article/health-coronavirus-facebook-location/in-coronavirus-fight-oft-criticized -facebook-data-aids-u-s-cities-states-idUSKBN21K3BJ.

Peluso, Nancy. "Whose Woods Are These? Counter-Mapping Forest Territories In Kalimantan, Indonesia." *Antipode* 27 (1995): 383–406.

Piaget, Jean. *The Construction of Reality in the Child*. New York: Basic Books, 1959.

Pietsch, Bryan, Jesse McKinley, and Ron DePasquale. "A Chaotic Vaccine Rollout and Allegations of a Cover-Up Threaten Cuomo's Perch." *New York Times*, February 16, 2021. https://www.nytimes.com/2021/02/16/world/a-chaotic-vaccine-rollout-and -allegations-of-a-cover-up-threaten-cuomos-perch.html.

Piller, Charles. "Federal System for Tracking Hospital Beds and COVID-19 Patients Provides Questionable Data." *Science*, November 29, 2020. https://www.sciencemag .org/news/2020/11/federal-system-tracking-hospital-beds-and-covid-19-patients -provides-questionable-data.

Piller, Charles. "The Inside Story of How Trump's COVID-19 Coordinator Undermined the World's Top Health Agency." *Science*, October 14, 2020. https://www.sciencemag.org/news/2020/10/inside-story-how-trumps-covid-19-coordinator-undermined-cdc.

Poon, Linda. "How the Pandemic Changed the Urban Soundscape." *CityLab*, October 22, 2020. https://www.bloomberg.com/news/articles/2020-10-22/the-changing-sounds-of-cities-during-covid-mapped.

Ramirez, Edith. "The Privacy Challenges of Big Data: A View from the Lifeguard's Chair." Keynote address at the Technology Policy Institute Aspen Forum, Federal Trade Commission, August 19, 2013. https://www.ftc.gov/sites/default/files/documents/public_statements/privacy-challenges-big-data-view-lifeguard%E2%80%99s-chair/130819bigdataaspen.pdf.

"Real Lessons from Sweden's Approach to Covid-19, The." *Economist*, October 10, 2020. https://www.economist.com/leaders/2020/10/10/the-real-lessons-from-swedens-approach-to-covid-19.

Reeves, Richard, and Jonathan Rothwell. "Class and COVID: How the Less Affluent Face Double Risks." Brookings Institute, March 2, 2020. https://www.brookings.edu/blog/up-front/2020/03/27/class-and-covid-how-the-less-affluent-face-double-risks/.

Rider, David. "Google Firm Wins Competition to Build High-Tech Quayside Neighbourhood in Toronto." *Toronto Star*, October 17, 2017. https://www.thestar.com/news/city_hall/2017/10/17/google-firm-wins-competition-to-build-high-tech-quayside-neighbourhood-in-toronto.html.

Robertson, Lori, and Robert Farley. "The Facts on Crowd Size." FactCheck.org, January 23, 2017. https://www.factcheck.org/2017/01/the-facts-on-crowd-size/.

Rocher, Luc, Julien M. Hendrickx, and Yves-Alexandre de Montjoye. "Estimating the Success of Re-identifications in Incomplete Datasets Using Generative Models." *Nature Communications* 10, no. 3069 (2019). https://doi.org/10.1038/s41467-019-10933-3

Roose, Kevin. "What Is QAnon, the Viral Pro-Trump Conspiracy Theory?" *New York Times*, March 4, 2021. https://www.nytimes.com/article/what-is-qanon.html.

Rosen, R. J. "Is This the Grossest Advertising Strategy of All Time?" *Atlantic*, October 3, 2013. https://www.theatlantic.com/technology/archive/2013/10/is-this-the-grossestadvertising-strategy-of-all-time/280242/.

Rothschild, Mike. *The Storm Is Upon Us: How QAnon Became a Movement, Cult, and Conspiracy Theory of Everything*. London: Melville House, 2021.

Rouvroy, Antoinette. "The End(s) of Critique: Data Behaviourism versus Due Process." In *Privacy Due Process and the Computational Turn: The Philosophy of Law Meets the Philosophy of Technology*, edited by Katja de Vries and Mireille Hildebrandt. London: Taylor & Francis, 2013.

Rowley, Jennifer. "The Wisdom Hierarchy: Representations of the DIKW Hierarchy." *Journal of Information Science* 33, no. 2 (2007): 163–180.

Rumelhart, D. E., G. E. Hinton, and R. J. Williams. "Learning Representations by Back-Propagating Errors." In *Neurocomputing: Foundations of Research*, edited by James A. Anderson and Edward Rosenfeld. Cambridge, MA: MIT Press, 1988.

Ryle, Gilbert. *The Concept of Mind*. Chicago: University of Chicago Press, 1949.

Sartre, Jean-Paul. *The Imaginary: A Phenomenological Psychology of the Imagination*. London: Routledge, 2004.

Satariano, Adam. "How the Internet Travels across Oceans." *New York Times*, March 10, 2019. https://www.nytimes.com/interactive/2019/03/10/technology/internet-cables-oceans.html.

Schemmel, Matthias. "Towards a Historical Epistemology of Space: An Introduction." In *Spatial Thinking and External Representation*, edited by Matthias Schemmel. Berlin: Max Planck Institute for the History of Science, 2016.

Schwartz, Oscar. "In the 17th Century, Leibniz Dreamed of a Machine That Could Calculate Ideas." *IEEE Spectrum*, November 4, 2019. https://spectrum.ieee.org/tech-talk/artificial-intelligence/machine-learning/in-the-17th-century-leibniz-dreamed-of-a-machine-that-could-calculate-ideas.

Sennett, Richard. *The Fall of Public Man*. New York: Knopf, 1977.

Seton, Maria, Simon Williams, and Sabin Zahirovic. "Obituary: Sandy Island (1876–2012)." *Eos, Transactions, American Geophysical Union* 94, no. 15 (2013): 141–148.

Shafir, E. *The Behavioral Foundations of Public Policy*. Princeton: Princeton University Press, 2013.

Sidewalk Labs. "Master Innovation and Development Plan (MIDP)." *Sidewalk Toronto*, 2019. https://www.sidewalktoronto.ca/documents/.

Silver, Nate. *The Signal and the Noise: Why So Many Predictions Fail-But Some Don't*. East Rutherford: Penguin Books, 2012.

Simunaci, Lisa. "Tiberius Platform Aids COVID-19 Logistics, Delivery." US Department of Defense, December 16, 2020. https://www.defense.gov/Explore/News/Article/Article/2446061/tiberius-platform-aids-covid-19-logistics-delivery/.

Singer, Natasha, and Choe Sang-Hun. "As Coronavirus Surveillance Escalates, Personal Privacy Plummets." *New York Times*, March 23, 2020. https://www.nytimes.com/2020/03/23/technology/coronavirus-surveillance-tracking-privacy.html.

Skinner, B. F. *Beyond Freedom and Dignity*. New York: Knopf, 1971.

Smith, Deborah R., and William E. Snell, Jr. "Goldberg's Bipolar Measure of the Big-Five Personality Dimensions: Reliability and Validity." *European Journal of Personality* 10 (1996): 283–299.

Snyder, Timothy. "The American Abyss." *New York Times*, January 9, 2021. https://www.nytimes.com/2021/01/09/magazine/trump-coup.html.

Sontag, Susan. *On Photography*. New York: Farrar, Straus and Giroux, 1977.

Soper, Spencer. "Amazon Will Consider Opening Up to 3,000 Cashierless Stores by 2021." Bloomberg, September 19, 2018. www.bloomberg.com/news/articles/2018 -09-19/amazon-is-said-to-plan-up-to-3-000-cashierless-stores-by-2021.

Sotiris, Panagiotis. "Against Agamben: Is a Democratic Biopolitics Possible?" *Critical Legal Thinking*, March 14, 2020. https://criticallegalthinking.com/2020/03/14 /against-agamben-is-a-democratic-biopolitics-possible/.

Spärck Jones, Karen. "Natural Language Processing: A Historical Review." In *Current Issues in Computational Linguistics: In Honour of Don Walker*, edited by Antonio Zampolli, Nicoletta Calzolari, and Martha Palmer. Dordrecht: Springer Netherlands, 1994.

Stanley, Jay, and Jennifer Stisa Granick. "The Limits of Location Tracking in an Epidemic." ACLU report, April 8, 2020. https://www.aclu.org/sites/default/files/field_doc ument/limits_of_location_tracking_in_an_epidemic.pdf.

Steenson, Molly Wright. *Architectural Intelligence: How Designers and Architects Created the Digital Landscape*. Cambridge, MA: MIT Press, 2017.

Suwajanakorn, Supasorn, Steven M. Seitz, and Ira Kemelmacher-Shlizerman. "Synthesizing Obama: Learning Lip Sync from Audio." *ACM Transactions on Graphics* 36, no. 4 (2017): art. 95.

Swain, John. "Trump Inauguration Crowd Photos Were Edited after He Intervened." *Guardian*, September 6, 2018. https://www.theguardian.com/world/2018/sep/06 /donald-trump-inauguration-crowd-size-photos-edited.

Temple-Raston, Dina. "Irregularities In COVID Reporting Contract Award Process Raise New Questions." NPR, July 29, 2020. https://www.npr.org/2020/07/29/896645314 /irregularities-in-covid-reporting-contract-award-process-raises-new-questions.

Tesich, Steve. "A Government of Lies." *Nation* (January 6/13, 1992): 12–14.

Thaler, R. H., and C. R. Sunstein. *Nudge: Improving Decisions about Health, Wealth, and Happiness*. New York: Penguin, 2009.

Thompson, Clive. "QAnon Is Like a Game—a Most Dangerous Game." *Wired*, September 22, 2020. https://www.wired.com/story/qanon-most-dangerous-multiplatform -game/.

Thompson, Derek. "What's behind South Korea's COVID-19 Exceptionalism." *Atlantic*, May 6, 2020. https://www.theatlantic.com/ideas/archive/2020/05/whats-south -koreas-secret/611215/.

Thrift, Nigel. "Intensities of Feeling: Towards a Spatial Politics of Affect." *Geografiska Annaler: Series B, Human Geography* 86 (2004): 57–78.

Tufekci, Zeynep. "Engineering the Public: Big Data, Surveillance and Computational Politics." *First Monday* 19, no. 7 (2014), https://firstmonday.org/article/view/4901/4097.

Turing, Alan "Computing Machinery and Intelligence." *Mind* 49, no. 236 (1950): 433–460.

Turner, Stephen P. *Liberal Democracy 3.0: Civil Society in an Age of Experts*. London: Sage, 2003.

Turow, J. *The Daily You: How the New Advertising Industry Is Defining Your Identity and Your Worth*. New Haven, CT: Yale University Press, 2011.

Vale, V. "Interview with J. G. Ballard (30 October 1982)." *Re/Search*, nos. 8–9 (1984).

Vanolo, Alberto. "Smartmentality: The Smart City as Disciplinary Strategy." *Urban Studies* 51, no. 5 (2014): 883–898.

Varnelis, Kazys. "Eyes That Do Not See: Tracking the Self in the Age of the Data Center." *Harvard Design Magazine*, no. 38 (2014). http://www.harvarddesignmagazine .org/issues/38/eyes-that-do-not-see-tracking-the-self-in-the-age-of-the-data-center.

Vincent, Donovan. "Sidewalk Labs, Waterfront Toronto to Proceed with Quayside Project, but with Significant Changes." *Star*, October 31, 2019. https://www.thestar .com/news/gta/2019/10/31/sidewalk-labs-waterfront-toronto-reach-deal-to-go -forward-on-quayside-project.html.

Vosoughi, Soroush, Deb Roy, and Sinan Aral. "The Spread of True and False News Online." *Science* 359, no. 6380 (2018): 1146–1151.

Waterfront Toronto. "Request for Proposals: Innovation and Funding Partner for the Quayside Development Opportunity." March 17, 2017. https://quaysideto.ca /wp-content/uploads/2019/04/Waterfront-Toronto-Request-for-Proposals-March-17 -2017.pdf.

Waterson, Jim. "Cambridge Analytica Did Not Misuse Data in EU Referendum, Says Watchdog." *Guardian*, October 7, 2020. https://www.theguardian.com/uk-news/2020 /oct/07/cambridge-analytica-did-not-misuse-data-in-eu-referendum-says-watchdog.

Weizenbaum, Joseph. *Computer Power and Human Reason: From Judgment to Calculation*. London: W. H. Freeman, 1976.

Whyte, William H. *The Social Life of Small Urban Spaces*. Washington, DC: Conservation Foundation, 1980.

Williams, Dan. "Israel to Halt Sweeping COVID-19 Cellphone Surveillance Next Month." Reuters, December 17, 2020. https://www.reuters.com/article/health-coro navirus-israel-surveillance-idUKKBN28R1AH.

Williams, Sarah, Wenfei Xu, Shin Bin Ton, Michael J. Foster, and Changping Chen. "Ghost Cities of China: Identifying Urban Vacancy through Social Media Data." *Cities* 94 (2008): 275–285.

Wingfield, Nick. "Inside Amazon Go, a Store of the Future." *New York Times*, January 21, 2018. https://www.nytimes.com/2018/01/21/technology/inside-amazon-go-a -store-of-the-future.html.

Wodinsky, Shoshana. "Experian Is Tracking the People Most Likely to Get Screwed Over by Coronavirus." *Gizmodo*, April 15, 2020. https://gizmodo.com/experian-is -tracking-the-people-most-likely-to-get-scre-1842843363.

Wong, Edward. "Trump Has Called Climate Change a Chinese Hoax. Beijing Says It Is Anything But." *New York Times*, November 18, 2916. https://www.nytimes.com /2016/11/19/world/asia/china-trump-climate-change.html.

Woods, Heather Suzanne. "Asking More of Siri and Alexa: Feminine Persona in Service of Surveillance Capitalism." *Critical Studies in Media Communication* 35, no. 4 (2018): 334–349.

"World's Most Valuable Resource Is No Longer Oil, But Data, The." *Economist*, May 6, 2017. www.economist.com/leaders/2017/05/06/the-worlds-most-valuable-resource-is -no-longer-oil-but-data.

Wylie, Bianca. "Smart Communities Need Smart Governance." *Globe and Mail*, December 5, 2017. https://www.theglobeandmail.com/opinion/smart-communities -need-smart-governance/article37218398/.

Wyner, G. "Behavioral Economics: A Marketing Capability." *Marketing News* 50, no. 10 (2016), 34–36.

Yankelovich, Daniel, and David Meer. "Rediscovering Market Segmentation." *Harvard Business Review* 84 (January 2006): 122–131.

Yong, Ed. "The U.K.'s Coronavirus 'Herd Immunity' Debacle." *Atlantic*, March 16, 2020. https://www.theatlantic.com/health/archive/2020/03/coronavirus-pandemic -herd-immunity-uk-boris-johnson/608065/.

Youyou, Wu, Michal Kosinski, and David Stillwell. "Computer-Based Personality Judgments Are More Accurate Than Those Made by Humans," *Proceedings of the National Academy of Sciences* 112, no. 4 (2015): 1036–1040.

Zhang, Chenchen. "Governing (through) Trustworthiness: Technologies of Power and Subjectification in China's Social Credit System." *Critical Asian Studies* 52, no. 4 (2020): 565–588.

Zuboff, Shoshana. *The Age of Surveillance Capitalism*. New York: Public Affairs, 2019.

INDEX

Page numbers in italics indicate figures.